COMPARATIVE CONSTITUTIONAL TRADITIONS

TEACHING TEXTS IN LAW AND POLITICS

David A. Schultz
General Editor

Vol. 27

PETER LANG
New York • Washington, D.C./Baltimore • Bern
Frankfurt am Main • Berlin • Brussels • Vienna • Oxford

JAMES T. McHUGH

COMPARATIVE
CONSTITUTIONAL
TRADITIONS

PETER LANG
New York • Washington, D.C./Baltimore • Bern
Frankfurt am Main • Berlin • Brussels • Vienna • Oxford

Library of Congress Cataloging-in-Publication Data
McHugh, James T.
Comparative constitutional traditions / James T. McHugh.
p. cm. — (Teaching texts in law and politics; vol. 27)
Includes bibliographical references and index.
1. Constitutional law. 2. Comparative law. 3. Law
and politics. I. Title. II. Series.
K3165 .M39   342—dc21   2001050633
ISBN 0-8204-5800-7
ISSN 1083-3447

Die Deutsche Bibliothek-CIP-Einheitsaufnahme
McHugh, James T.:
Comparative constitutional traditions / James T. McHugh.
–New York; Washington, D.C./Baltimore; Bern;
Frankfurt am Main; Berlin; Brussels; Vienna; Oxford: Lang.
(Teaching texts in law and politics; Vol. 27)
ISBN 0-8204-5800-7

Cover design by Dutton & Sherman Design

© 2002 Peter Lang Publishing, Inc., New York

All rights reserved.
Reprint or reproduction, even partially, in all forms such as microfilm,
xerography, microfiche, microcard, and offset strictly prohibited.

Table of Contents

Acknowledgments vii

1 Fundamental Components of Constitutional Law
   and Development 1
2 American Constitutional Tradition 33
3 British Constitutional Tradition 47
4 Chinese Constitutional Tradition 65
5 Canadian Constitutional Tradition 83
6 Indian Constitutional Tradition 101
7 Japanese Constitutional Tradition 117
8 Nigerian Constitutional Tradition 133
9 French Constitutional Tradition 147
10 German Constitutional Tradition 159
11 Mexican Constitutional Tradition 175
12 Saudi Arabian Constitutional Tradition 193
13 Constitutionalism, Sovereignty,
   and Human Freedom 213

Bibliography 219
Index 225

Acknowledgments

I would like to thank Dr. David Schultz, the series editor, for his advice and encouragement. I also would like to thank Bernadette Alfaro, Phyllis Korper, and everyone at Peter Lang who provided me with assistance and encouragement in preparing this manuscript for publication. I further want to thank Michelle Parker and Kimberly Kunio of Roosevelt University for their valuable technical assistance. I remain, as always, grateful for the support and encouragement of my family toward this process and all my endeavors.

CHAPTER 1

Fundamental Components of Constitutional Law and Development

Constitutions can be found at the apex of the legal system. All other expressions of law, within a given community, emanate from a constitution. Any law, from a conventional perspective, that fails to conform to the standards of a constitution cannot, in fact, continue to function *as* a law. But constitutions are more than legal categories. They serve as the ultimate expression of the entire political system; in fact, they actually define the polity. Constitutions perform this function in two ways. First, constitutions establish the guiding principles that the political system will express and enforce. Second, constitutions provide limits and constraints upon the political system. Thus, constitutions can inhibit people, but they also can liberate them. The ultimate role a constitution plays depends upon the sovereign source of the fundamental values upon which it is based and, indeed, the very identity (more importantly, the *self*-identity) of each source of sovereign authority.

This chapter will introduce some of the most fundamental legal ideas that form the basis for all constitutional traditions. It engages in a study of contrasts, beginning with very broad categorizations and narrowing toward more parochial, yet fundamental, legal concepts. It attempts to address constitutional development in its multitudinous facets, in order to provide a comprehensive appreciation. Thus it will provide a foundation for the rest of the book. Each chapter devoted to a particular constitutional tradition will make reference to sources, concepts, ideas, and historical events that have shaped and define that functioning constitutional system. These references may not be fully developed within the respective chapter but will require the introductory explanations that this chapter provides. Each chapter devoted to a particular constitutional tradition will rely upon certain assumptions regarding the terms that it uses. *This* chapter will serve as a guide that should make reasonable those expectations of a rudimentary basis for a preliminary knowledge that supports the subjects of the subsequent chapters.[1]

---

1   Each of these themes are addressed in greater detail in James T. McHugh, *The Essential Concept of Law* (New York: Peter Lang, 2002), and the reader is encouraged to refer to it as a source for gaining a broader explanation of concepts introduced within this chapter.

Constitutions serve as the actual expression of sovereignty. The definition of sovereignty is, arguably, the most important concept in law and politics. Sovereignty refers to a condition of power, in which authority is exercised over the community, while *no* formal power is exercised over the sovereign, itself. "Sovereignty" is to "states" as "autonomy" is to "people"; without it, a community cannot qualify as a "state" within the international community. One way to demonstrate sovereign status is through a legitimate, enforceable constitution. Once established, the constitution produces government institutions, laws, and social conditions that constitute the modern polity.

Therefore, constitutions rose simultaneously with the concept of the modern state. Certainly, a concept of a constitution predates the modern period of history; Aristotle devoted an important treatise to a comparative study of the constitutions of the ancient Greek city-states, with his study of the Athenian Constitution remaining an important example of modern political and legal analysis. But in the sense that the world has come to understand a constitution, this institution is associated with the rise of the nation-state, modern ideologies, the concept of a society, and, more gradually, the notion of sovereign authority being vested within a people. This last development has made the study of constitutions particularly important for practitioners, scholars, and the public, but it also has made that study more complex, particularly in terms of determining fundamental values.

Purposes of the Law and Constitutions

Law can be perceived in terms of neutral rules that guide human interaction. It also can be perceived as a source of control that a sovereign employs as a tool over members of a state. However, it also can be lauded as a source of human liberation, especially against the potential abuse of sovereign authority. The idea of law as "mere rules" underscores a commitment to a general concept of legal neutrality. It envisions a legal system as though it were a sporting match, in which judges play the part of referees, lawyers play the part of coaches, legal scholars play the part of sports analysts, and subject people (particularly plaintiffs and defendants) are the competitors. The "playing field" ideally is designed to deny an advantage to one side or another, the object of the contest is to win, and the outcome is determined by the evenly matched struggle that will reveal the side that is most worthy of victory—not through moral deserts, but through superior abilities, resources, and an understanding and use of the rules of the contest.

Again, this image (and the implied criticism of it) may seem extreme, yet the rhetoric that surrounds this perception of law frequently evokes this sentiment. But more thoughtful commentary and perceptions have evoked an impression of law as a source of order and control and a device for expressing and enforcing the will of the sovereign. That sovereign can be a monarch, an oligarchy, or a democratic populace, but the ultimate purpose of law remains the same. Law, within this context, is a device that ensures safety and protection, particularly against the less noble features of human nature. It presupposes an inclination of the members of a community toward deceit, violence, and evil, with a need to check these impulses for the community and its sovereign to survive and, hopefully, thrive. The experience of many people often confirms this impression, for the law routinely is perceived by casual observers in a punitive way, visibly vigilant, guarding against crime, and punishing transgressors of the legal system.

But modern observers have detected an evolving idea of law that seeks to empower people, generally. Two purposes are achieved, according to this interpretation. First, law defines government and its powers and, by achieving this purpose, establishes implicit limits upon its authority over the community. Second, law provides tools that people can use for expanding their own ability to achieve personal and collective goals. It furnishes a source of predictability in political and social relationships, protects interests, establishes common terms of reference and a means of political communication, and it can be used to develop and implement broad social, economic, and political policies that enhance the autonomy of people and groups. This concept of "autonomy" refers to the human capacity to make choices, be decisive, and control one's own destiny. It is, in that sense, the individual equivalent of the condition of sovereignty and, like this definition of a state, it defines a particular connotation of power. Therefore, under this perception, law does not merely control—it liberates.

Constitutions and the Fundamental Concepts of Law

Constitutions are a classification of public law, and public law is a category of a very broad and overarching concept of law. The specific characteristics of a constitutional tradition are determined by its relationship to other legal, political, and philosophical ideals and experiences. Law is *not* objective, despite the insistence of many practitioners. It also is not the exclusive domain of the well-trained practitioner or, even, the expert commentator or well-educated scholar. In fact, the categorical apex of law, in which constitutional traditions are found, is labeled "*public* law" because it emanates from the human experience, in all its variety. Constitutions can be meaningfully understood only by appreciating, and exploring, that overriding characteristic.

Unfortunately, many modern observers often tend to associate all law, including constitutional law, primarily with a series of technical rules. These rules may be related to certain abstract principles and methods of organization, but they are not expected to conform to a unifying theme or ideal. That impression is based upon a tragic misconception. A more genuine concept of constitutional law can be expanded into large, yet interrelated, variations upon broader theses and premises. In fact, an appreciation of those themes and premises makes it possible to discern constitutional traditions in ways that are predictable, consistent, and tied to larger ideas, values, and aspects of the human experience. A constitution *is* an extrapolation of political, philosophical, sociological, economic, and other ideas and, furthermore, a manifestation of a higher purpose. It is the product of a general evolution of law; unless that evolution is understood and examined, critically, any constitutional evaluation is doomed to superficiality and illusion.

Western Legal Tradition

All law can be divided, roughly, into two overarching culturally and geographically identifiable categories. Scholars of cultural anthropology, comparative religion, social psychology, and other areas have identified certain broad features that distinguish Eastern and Western patterns of thought and perception. Two particularly conspicuous areas of distinction concern the concepts of time and power. Western cultures tend to express these concepts in *linear* terms. Time, for example, is conceived of having a beginning and, potentially, an end. People exist at a particular point upon a horizontally conceived time line known as "history." Power normally is expressed in vertical terms; people exercise power "over" other people and things, or power is delegated "down" to other sources.

Eastern perceptions can be described, in contrast, as being *cyclical* in nature. Both time and power can be conceived as relative relationships that are shared, recurring, and not subject to the neatness and simplicity of a linear model. An Eastern concept of time tends to emphasize a condition from which people seek, ultimately, to escape, rather than a line upon which people travel. Likewise, power is a shared phenomenon of a community, even though certain forces within that community appear to wield, at least superficially, superior authority and prestige. This perspective contrasts markedly with the Western hierarchical approach.

Western law can be divided into "natural law" and "positive law" traditions. Natural law rests upon universal (applying to all people, places, and cultures), transhistorical (remaining as true, today and tomorrow, as it has been in the past), *ontological* (derived from a theory of "being," since it is grounded upon an essential definitional focus, such as nature or the human condition), and *deontological* (derived from a theory of moral duty, since it imposes requisite behavior upon its subjects, rather than merely setting limits *upon* that behavior) criteria. It has evolved, historically, from the ancient Greek attempt to emulate the lessons of the natural world to the medieval desire to adhere to the plan of God's universe and, finally, to a modern humanist perspective.

Laws of human communities that do not conform to its precepts are regarded as lacking the moral authority to qualify as laws, at all, and are merely reduced to an exercise in force. Although natural law has been widely displaced as an overarching model of legal legitimacy, it remains relevant to current features and explanations of international law and human rights as demonstrated by Nuremberg Trials. The Nazi laws that sought to legitimize the persecution and extermination of certain peoples were held to be untenable and void, and the defendants were condemned, in part, for failing in a universal moral duty to oppose these directives. That conclusion of the International War Crimes Tribunal demonstrated the continuing influence of the natural law tradition, even if only as a "higher law" that can serve as a model of critical evaluation for other legal systems.

Positive law, or "legal positivism," emerged as a condition of the rise of the modern nation-state (beginning, most notably, during the sixteenth and seventeenth centuries) and the desire for a "scientific," or "objective" approach to law that would be responsive to the subjective perspective of society. Political, social, and economic goals were recognized as being unique to each political and legal system and not subject to a supposed universal norm. Furthermore, the fascination with modern scientific discovery and innovation inspired similar attempts to adhere to empirically satisfying methods for constructing other institutions and practices of modern society.

Legal positivism rests upon the "command theory" of law, which identifies law as the will of the sovereign. The legitimacy of law is determined by the ability to articulate and enforce it, rather than upon any overarching criteria of its substance, especially in terms of its moral quality. The success of legal positivism relies upon the consistency of legal processes and applications (often expressed in terms of the principle of the "rule of law"), success in achieving the practical recognition of laws, and an inner logic of implementation as measures of the pragmatic effectiveness of laws, rather than their righteousness. Positive law stresses the authority of sovereignty as a source of political power that is, itself, not subject to any other authority, and it has become the dominant model for all Western legal systems. It is, therefore, an essential approach to the interaction of sovereign states that serves as a foundation of international law, in addition to being a means of providing order and stability within the modern state. Lofty rules and principles can be developed as supplemental means of making laws more efficient and effective or of legitimizing the sovereign's political objectives through the legal process. However, actual legal authority is grounded upon its successful legal enforcement, making it politically separate from any larger understanding of the "higher" nature of law.

Eastern Legal Tradition

Eastern law is manifested through various cultural experiences, all stressing the holistic nature of human activity and the interconnected qualities of all legal, political, social, economic, family, and other phenomena. An especially important source for an Eastern expression of law can be found within the East Asian philosophy of Confucianism. This tradition (developed during the fifth century, B.C.E., by the teacher and mandarin, Kung Fu-tse, whose name was transposed by the Jesuit scholars who first translated his teachings as Confucius) has inspired a concept of law that is influenced by the central principles of *jen* and *giri*, stressing, respectively, a concept of "righteous behavior" and the performance of "reciprocal duties" among members of a community, especially through mutually supportive legal relationships.

Each member of the community owes duties to every other member of the community. The performance of these duties is not regarded as optional, even for a political ruler. A subject has a duty to support the ruler, but the ruler has a very real *reciprocal* duty to provide for the needs of the subject and to respect the prerogatives of the subject, especially within those areas that are not relevant to the subject's reciprocal duties toward the ruler. Subjects who refuse to obey and support their rulers contribute to instability and chaos, ultimately undermining the conditions they need for security and prosperity. Likewise, rulers who exploit their subjects will weaken them to the extent that they are unable to generate the overall productivity that provides the basis for the rulers' own resources, as well as an unwillingness of these subjects to support their rulers in time of crisis. *Giri* is a central premise of *li*, or the Confucian conceptualization of truly "lawful" behavior.

Li reflects a concept of correct legal conduct that is based upon the guidance of *giri*. It is a guiding principle, rather than a set of rules or specific commands. *Li*, in fact, underscores a perception of law that rejects the abstract rules, structures, and institutions that characterize Western legal systems. The ruler and subject who conform to the expectations of *jen* perceive this distinction and behave accordingly. They understand the duties expected of them and conduct their respective lives and activities in ways that reflect this guidance. Rulers who are influenced by this philosophical approach tend to abstain from the imposition of specific legal procedures, edicts, and prohibitions, relying, instead, upon shared measurements of the true, holistic purpose of legal relationships and their proper conduct as a guide for all members of the community, often as reinforced through the symbolic and practical performance of ritual.

"Legalism" is a contrasting philosophical source of Eastern law. It emphasizes a corrupted concept of obedience to authority and paternalistic assumptions. The most prominent advocate of this interpretation was Han Fei-tzû. His doctrine, developed during the second century, B.C.E., emphasized the formulation of positive laws that would dictate the duties of all subjects. They would be required to obey these laws, without challenge, and they would provide strict guidance for all subjects of the government.

The ruler would be the sole authority for interpreting the law. This emphasis rests upon a sense of imposed order. The Confucian concept of *li*, which refers to behavior that is "lawful" in the sense that it conforms to the harmony promoted by *giri*, is displaced, under Legalist doctrine, with a concept of *fa*. This term also roughly translates as "law," but its more precise meaning conveys a sense of "force," rather than a guiding principle. Legalism was developed for the benefit of powerful elites as a means of rationalizing their autocratic rule. It has not enjoyed general success as an alternative interpretation of the sort of beliefs and values articulated by Confucianism, especially as received through the school of thought established by Mencius. Yet its precepts often are cited, especially as a justification for dictatorial regimes imposed upon certain Eastern cultures.

Taoism is another source of influence upon Eastern expressions of law. It emphasizes the harmony among seemingly contrasting legal relationships. The word *tao* refers to the idea of a "path," and it is the desire to conform to the guidance provide by this path, rather than a resistance to it in search of separate goals, that can lead to human happiness. The fifth century B.C.E. spiritual leader and political counselor, Lao Tzu, is credited, by tradition, with the establishment of a comprehensive explanation of Taoist principles.

The central symbol of Taoism depicts the different forces of *yin* and *yang* that create a visual representation of a circle through their interaction. This symbolism stresses the belief that seemingly opposite forces are not really in opposition to each other, since one force relies upon the other for its very existence. The true path is to appreciate this complementary relationship of all things and use it as a model for one's own life and the principles that govern a community. Politically and legally, for example, the ability to reconcile divergent policies, rules, and goals that permit all parties to achieve their true purpose is the result of finding and pursuing the *tao*.

Since the *tao* is a guide, and not a definitive set of ideals or beliefs, it is receptive to the influence of other systems of thought and perception. In this way, it is possible for Taoist principles to find effective expression within more conventional areas of public life, including laws and methods of legal interpretation. The legal relationship of the "benefactor," the motivating concept of "shame" (especially in contrast to the Western concept of "sin"), and the desire to resolve legal disputes in a manner that is most beneficial to the whole community, are aspects of this influence. The role of government within the business sector of certain Eastern communities often reflects the influence of this model, with government officials seeking to reconcile the broader, often different interests of labor and industry by creating a holistic response to the relationship and guiding these interests toward a concordance benefiting society, according to the overall vision of the government.

Hinduism offers a religious and philosophical source for understanding the legal values of Eastern cultures, especially within India. It stresses a sense of overwhelming detachment, guided by law, through a performance of *dharma*, or duty. It explains the sense of order that guides social relationships, which the law preserves. Hinduism describes humanity as an abstraction, seeking union with a greater cosmos. Humans achieve harmony only by being released from the limits of the physical world and achieving oneness with the universal *ohm*, which is the essence of all things. Hinduism offers knowledge of human limitation and a means for achieving dispassionate detachment from the things of this world that will make this spiritual fulfillment attainable.

The central Hindu concept for understanding law is the principle of *dharma*. Its rough translation from Hindi is "duty," but it also can be interpreted as "lawfulness." It encompasses the customs and practices that all people are expected to observe, especially in terms of their relationships with each other. It identifies behavior that is based upon a person's fundamental status. This identity is expressed in terms of social and economic groupings known as "castes," organized upon four principal divisions of people into the fundamental categories of "spiritual and intellectual authorities (*brahmin*)," "political and military leaders and guardians (*kshattriya*)," "merchants and other producers of wealth (*vaisyas*)," and "servants and workers (*sudras*)," with those people lacking formal caste being relegated to the status of "outcaste," or "untouchable." Caste status was established by religious tradition and is determined by birth, rather than through individual or, even, collective preferences. The goals of "detachment" and "harmony" can be achieved only through a dispassionate pursuit of the duties ascribed to a person in accordance with their caste status. *Dharma* provides guidance for attaining this purpose. It serves as "law" that provides a *deontological* imperative. The interpretation of the requirements of *dharma* can be modified, according to the needs or conditions of the community and its people, but the lack of personal motive must remain paramount.

Legal authorities are bound by the laws that are promulgated for their community, but they may apply the principles of *dharma* for their application to various circumstances. People who have committed crimes, for example, should be convicted and punished, but Hindu precepts may determine that mitigating circumstances exist for someone whose reason for committing the crime can be explained in terms of the attempt to conform to *dharma* as it applies to that person's caste. Law serves as a guide for the interpretation of specific rules and policies, offering an overall moral authority to legal and political behavior, based upon a sense of detachment.

Eastern civilizations are as diverse as their Western counterparts, yet they exhibit similar patterns of expression that prompt similar responses to the concept of law. The non-hierarchical comprehension of political and legal power, the lack of distinction among various fields of human life and activity, the interrelationship of personal and social existence, provide dynamic responses to this idea of law, even though Western observers might find them frustratingly subtle. Specific philosophical expressions offer variations upon this theme, but the holistic approach to human existence and the political and legal community is a relatively consistent theme that has distinguished the Eastern tradition of law from the more systematic expressions developed throughout the course of Western history.

Ideology and Law

Modern Western law is motivated by philosophical beliefs derived from the equally modern concept of ideology. The value system of an ideology offers a conceptual justification of that economic reality through the promotion of supportive principles, norms, and the institutions that emanate from the emergence of these forces. Philosophers and political theorists articulate the beliefs and values that explain and justify these institutions within an abstract, comprehensive, theoretical framework that (within the modern Western tradition, in particular) is called "ideology," since it represents an applied "study" of higher "ideas." The relationship between ideology and law is pivotal for achieving a meaningful comprehension of constitutional law.

Western ideological development emerged from the transitional medieval period of European history. It was the product of fundamental economic changes and political responses to them. Therefore, beliefs and values were a reaction to politics and law, rather than a motivation for, or cause of, these changes. The ultimate emergence of the modern society as an association of diverse people, united by mutual economic activity, prompted the equally modern emergence of ideologies as an explanation of, and justification for, these changes and the laws created to provide order and expression of these societies. Before this ideological phenomenon can be addressed, its philosophical antecedents, rooted within a broadly defined economic and political order, need to be understood.

The collapse of the Roman Empire in the West produced an economic order that was labor intensive, precarious, and dependent upon the control of land and the extraction of its resources. Tribal legal traditions and local customs (introduced by the invading tribal peoples originally migrating from the East) were a response to the emergence of the resulting labor intensive economic system, prompting the formation of a rigidly hierarchical political order, reinforced by an equally hierarchical, institutionalized Christian presence, throughout Europe, that justified its organizational principles through a theological construct of an equally hierarchical, ordered, and static universe. But effective control could not be maintained so centrally, so more local sources of political authority, in the form of the lower nobility, constituted the true source of effective power and control throughout the medieval period.

The feudal system of vassal relationships, in which an overlord granted a vassal exclusive use of a portion of land (but not, technically, outright ownership) in exchange for personal loyalty, economic and military support, and a pledge to maintain this system, expressed this fundamental perspective. Its values included (in addition to an image of hierarchical authority and a *deontological* requirement to obey that authority in all things) personal and collective identities that were inextricably tied to hierarchical rank, strict stratification of the community, and the constraint of accepting one's station, determined by birth, and fulfilling its expectations and obligations as part of a broader, mechanistic system. Legal expression of this perspective described the feudal order.

Increased prosperity gradually occurred through technical advances in agriculture, which became increasingly apparent by the fifteenth century. These improvements created surplus wealth that the beneficiaries of this growing affluence sought to use for their own advantage. Towns grew in size and importance as displaced peasants sought an alternative means of support. The result of these changes was an economic shift toward a mercantile economy, grounded upon the process of buying and selling, that gradually supplanted the feudal system. Simultaneously, a middle class emerged to challenge this former value system and replace it with increasingly attractive beliefs that reflected this emerging economic and social reality, especially during the sixteenth and seventeenth centuries.

This mercantile sector began to achieve economic domination. Its members resented the continuation of feudal norms and institutions. Centralized governments, which had been relatively ineffectual, became beneficiaries of this trend. This process prompted the development of a new set of widely held beliefs and values which reflected, and promoted, this transformation. The most basic of these values was an abstract conceptualization of "property" that referred not only to commodities that people could physically own, but to anything that people could exchange for any other sort of "property," including their labor.

Feudal constraints, including the belief that everything ultimately belonged to feudal overlords, needed to be eliminated as a means of securing this principle. It became the core of an emerging philosophical system, based upon theoretical premises that could be applied, practically, which is a characteristic of the modern concept of ideology, itself. A demand for freedom from constraint (especially within the marketplace) became included among its prevailing values, so liberty became a core principle of this ideological system. This liberty to dispense with one's own property on an individual basis would be useless, however, without the means to make *meaningful* decisions. The negative emphasis of the value of liberty is balanced, therefore, by the positive emphasis of autonomy, which imposes certain obligations upon society and its government to maintain the means to operate effectively throughout this environment.

The actions of the marketplace are not based upon predetermined status or rank, so they are not collectively driven. All people participating within it are evaluated upon the basis of their own merits. This emerging ideological system, therefore, needed to embrace a concept of individualism as an essential premise for political and social, as well as economic, purposes. These four key principles of "property," "liberty," "individualism," and "autonomy" would become the core of an ideological tradition that would derive its name from that defining principle of freedom and become known, therefore, as "liberalism." Eventually, prompted by the consequences of a merit-based system and an evolved comprehension of individualism, it would be augmented by the related principle of equality. This ideology and its fundamental values would become so prevalent among Western societies, generally, that its members often would fail to recognize them as part of a distinct and subjective system and would simply accept that ideological perspective as being conventional.

Democratic notions eventually were a consequence of the evolution of a liberal society, although this development was not an automatic result of that process. Provided that a government is constrained by liberal ideological values, its benefits theoretically should be enjoyed by all members of society. The notion that the very choice of a government and its policies should be determined by the sum of those persons who constitute the political society is a later development that occurred relatively gradually, and with some resistance. Nonetheless, Western societies eventually were dominated not only by liberal ideology, but by that evolved variant of its premises that would become the ideology of "liberal democracy."

The fact that law serves as the means for indicating the distinction between public and private realms of society is a conspicuous contribution of liberal ideology. The fact that so much of the law is dedicated to the protection and regulation of "property" and the marketplace (especially in terms of contract law) is a profound testament to this relationship. The evolution of constitutional government was an even more prominent example, with constitutions, themselves, serving as the guarantors that the laws of a society would, indeed, conform to the expectations of a liberal democratic society, especially in terms of the premise of the "social contract" between individual people and their governments (imposing strict limits and responsibilities upon those governments) that liberal and liberal democratic theorists would articulate.

The core principles of liberal democracy are fairly rudimentary, so a good deal of variation among different expressions of liberal democratic thought is possible. Diverse interpretations of this malleable ideological tradition are addressed within those chapters (such as chapters two, three and five, among others) devoted to constitutional traditions that embrace some version of liberal democracy, including "libertarian," "republican," and "communitarian" variants. But that ideological influence is so pervasive that an essential comprehension and appreciation of liberal democracy is needed, first, before these constitutional traditions can be approached.

The fact that liberalism and liberal democracy are so dominant does not mean that they impose exclusive ideological influences upon constitutional traditions around the world. Other constitutionally significant ideological traditions also exist. Arguably, the most conspicuous of these ideological challenges has been Marxism. Its constitutional influence continues to be considerable, even following the late-twentieth century demise of the Soviet Union.

The economic and political turmoil of Europe, during the late-eighteenth through the mid-nineteenth centuries, inspired an ideological response, based upon previous ideas, that was articulated with particular effectiveness by Karl Marx. He adapted a method called the "dialectic" (first developed by his former professor, Georg Wilhelm Friedrich Hegel) to his own study of economic history. The result was Marx's theory of "dialectical materialism," in which he determined that all human history is the saga of economic dominance and exploitation. The segment of a population that controls the source of economic wealth also imposes a value system (called the "thesis") that rationalizes this dominance and the principles that bolster it. However, an alternative economic process (called the "antithesis") becomes offered as an alternative, especially from that segment which does not enjoy the dominance of the current source of economic control. The conflict between these economic alternatives results in the emergence of a new economic order (called the "synthesis"), dominated, again, by a particular segment that finds itself, again, struggling to maintain that dominance (which becomes the new "thesis") against a rising alternative.

The current "thesis" is, according to Marx, rooted in the control of capital and industry. Capitalism, as an economic system and foundation of a liberal democratic society, is dominated so completely by an extremely small class of investors and industrialists (called the *bourgeoisie*) that the rest of the population of workers (called the *proletariat*) have no choice but to accept the economic conditions imposed upon them. These workers further have their "property," in the form of labor, stolen from them, since their wages do not truly represent the profit that ultimately is generated. Capitalists and industrialists need to "steal" this "labor-property," since it is the basis of their profits. Marx argued that his illogical arrangement eventually must collapse, resulting in a revolutionary elimination of all institutions and norms that support it. The cycle of dialectical materialism then will be ended and replaced by a system of communal ownership.

Marxists argue that the capitalist system is upheld by a "false consciousness" that is augmented by various political institutions, including liberal democratic laws that promote the illusion of popular sovereignty and the primacy of individual "property." A Marxist concept of law seeks to replace private ownership and exploitation by the *bourgeoisie* with a system of no private property. All members of the political community will share, according to their needs, and contribute, according to their abilities. Laws ultimately will guide this process, especially during an intermediate phase of socialism, in which a government (according to modifications of Marxist theory as advanced by Lenin), led by a party dedicated to leading this revolutionary process, controls the means of production on behalf of the *proletariat* until that class is ready to assume control for itself—at which point, the state and its institutions (including laws and the legal system) will "wither away." These laws are geared, according to this Marxist-Leninist argument, toward a sense of "class consciousness," replacing individual comprehensions of law with a collective understanding of society.

A Marxist concept of justice asserts that liberal democratic legal institutions are designed to protect exclusive property interests. Therefore, again, it seeks to eliminate the capitalist concept of private property, although a contingency for people to possess certain goods, based upon their immediate needs, is accepted and mediated. Goods and services are derived from all members of society according to their specific talents and ability to provide them; they are distributed according to each person's needs, rather than capabilities. A Marxist judicial system upholds this principle, advancing the ultimate elimination of an individualistic society grounded upon "false" and destructive individualistic tendencies which, Marxists contend, denies *true* freedom and autonomy.

The terms "liberal" and "conservative" generally are misapplied. Less accurate references to these terms do not refer to ideologies but to varying interpretations and applications of broader ideological traditions, especially liberal democracy. But a meaningful, "classic" conservative ideological tradition does exist. It emerged within Europe, during the sixteenth and seventeenth centuries, in response to the decline of feudal ideals and institutions and reaction against the growing popularity of liberal principles and practices.

Conservatives are not necessarily opposed to liberal democratic values, but they are concerned about the consequences of an uncritical and unrestrained imposition of them that could lead to a society lacking control, order, stability, security, and general conditions that are conducive to peace and prosperity. *Classic* conservatives explain the relationship between a sovereign and its subjects in terms of a relationship between a father and his children, upon whom he imposes benevolent limits. The father grants his children a measure of freedom so they can mature, but within the constraints ordained by paternal care. Their very ability to enjoy these benefits and this freedom depends upon the stable environment that the father provides. Therefore, children owe their father unquestioned obedience.

Otherwise, their lack of judgment and maturity would lead them to make decisions and engage in conduct that could be harmful to themselves and other people, resulting in a chaotic environment in which growth, development, and safety are impossible.

Thus classic conservatives emphasize this need for restraint, especially in terms of "prudent" responses toward threats and opportunities. Law provides these limits, so it becomes the expression of unrestrained sovereignty. Traditional social, political, and religious institutions reinforce this relationship. A constitution should not limit the government; instead, it should reinforce its dominant role to provide support for its responsibilities. Individual rights and privileges may be invoked and upheld, but the sovereign (potentially including a democratic majority), and not individual people, is the final authority for interpreting and enforcing them.

The ideological challenge of gender has not offered a comprehensive alternative to any prevailing constitutional tradition. This approach is based upon the perception that gender, in fact, matters in terms of reevaluating other ideological assumptions. The "liberal feminist" challenge to liberal democracy has been a prominent ideological approach. This challenge does not seek to displace liberal democratic ideological norms but, instead, confronts liberal democratic societies with the premise of making them and their values inclusive of all persons, both female and male.

Other feminist theorists have rejected all conventional ideologies, including liberal democracy, as being inescapably male dominated. These feminist theorists advocate a conceptual departure from customary ideological assumptions in favor of the advancement of feminism *as* an ideological approach. They often are identified as "radical" feminists, for they have broken entirely with conventional, gender-neutral methods of philosophical analysis.

Feminists contend that characteristics of this male legal perspective include a tendency to express legal concepts in abstract terms, requiring a conformity of circumstances to rules that must be applicable in all circumstances. A female perspective arguably is more contextual, allowing for variances in circumstance, environment, and relationship. Many feminist legal scholars seek to temper that sterile method, with its competitive overtones, in favor of a more cooperative understanding of law as a tool for mediation and reconciliation of disputes and difficulties.

The constitutional implications of a feminist approach to law and ideology are considerable. Ongoing debates about the meaning of gender equality reveal the significance of this ideological challenge. Neither liberal feminist or radical feminist responses generally have been offered as an ideological basis for a comprehensive constitutional system, but they do offer an important challenge to prevailing ideological foundations of the constitutions of modern countries.

Other ideological traditions also could be included within this appraisal, such as "anarchism," which challenges the very idea of law and any need for coercive political (including legal) institutions. Indeed, a myriad of sources of legal beliefs, values, and principles must be undertaken for the purpose of useful comparative constitutional analysis, from throughout the world. But Western ideologies, usually emerging from the modern European experience, are especially notable, because of their influence upon constitutional systems throughout the rest of the world. Therefore, without an appreciation of modern ideologies, an accurate and meaningful evaluation of modern constitutional traditions would be futile.

Common Law Systems

The two most prevalent institutional expressions of law throughout the modern world are the common law and civil law systems. Most comparative law texts emphasize, almost exclusively, these two systems, although a third system of "socialist law" (reflecting many of the same institutional features as a civil law system, but with different socio-political emphasis) has been addressed by some of these authors. This structural approach often ignores more substantive legal themes, but its central importance to an overall study of law should not be underestimated.

Common law systems first emerged in medieval England. Countries that have adopted this structural model generally were once part of the British Empire, including the United States. This system evolved from the diverse examples of customary law that existed throughout England. Attempts to increase centralized political control (especially under King Henry II) resulted in judicial officials who, while trying cases and considering appeals of local legal decisions throughout the country, began to formulate legal rules and principles that were "common" to all parts of the realm. They would rely upon a record of previous judicial decisions, especially in terms of broadly similar conclusions shared by different localities. This reliance evolved into an overarching principle of *stare decisis* (meaning "let the [prior] decision stand"), also known as "precedent." Legal rules and principles would be based upon these precedents, which would be learned largely through the experience of judges and the gradual emergence of other legal practitioners.

The English also developed a unified judicial system, with courts handling a diverse category of cases and a system of geographically based appeals courts, culminating in a final court of appeal for the entire country, which, in England, was centered upon the king and the judicial role of the House of Lords. Responsibility for making judicial determinations was divided: a judge would interpret and apply matters of "law," including an explanation of the relevant statutes, rules of judicial conduct, definitions of relevant legal terms and concepts, imposition of appropriate punishments, and other, general legal principles; a jury of legal lay persons, considered to be equals, or "peers," of the person being judged, would interpret and apply specific facts to the guidance and expectations of the law, as imposed upon them by the judge. Appeals of these decisions could be based only upon alleged mistakes in the interpretation and application of the law, and not upon the facts of a case. Therefore, only judges would participate in judicial appeals.

Legal practitioners would achieve their status through practical experience, rather than formal education. The rise of the medieval English Inns of Court provided a venue for aspiring students of law to engage in a process of apprenticeship, followed by an examination that would determine their ultimate suitability to become a member of the profession and practice law—an examination that would enable them, once passed, to "approach the bar" of the court, which led to the term "bar exam." A member of the legal profession could be elevated to the role of judge through an appointment that also was based upon wide experience and the respect earned from fellow practitioners, especially given the important role that judges play within the system. Elevation to an appellate court also was based largely on experience.

Modern innovations within countries that have adopted the common law system have included the introduction of law schools that have become largely mandatory, although a separate examination remains a general requirement for practicing law. Furthermore, judges sometimes may be elected to their positions, although candidates usually are required to have a certain degree of previous experience before being eligible for that post. Law, itself, remains largely based upon the guidelines established by precedent, the statutes created by the political system, some guidance from legal scholars, and the broad training of the jurists, themselves. Courts typically have geographically determined jurisdictions (although some specialized courts, especially administrative ones, often exist, too), and the system tends to be governed by an appellate structure that is dominated, ultimately, by a single final court of appeal, imposing uniformity upon the interpretation and application of law within that particular common law system.

Civil Law Systems

Most of the judicial systems in the world have adopted a variation of the civil law structure. Its basic rules and structures can be found, in some form, throughout the world, even within socialist legal systems. Despite its ancient origins and Eurocentric features, the civil law system has proven to be highly adaptable to the legal requirements of a diverse modern world.

This system emerged from the model provided by ancient Rome. Law became an effective instrument for uniting the Roman people. Roman law provided a summation of legal principles. The *jus civile*, or "law of the city," was intended to be peculiar to the Romans, their experiences, their history, and their culture. The interpretation of these laws required a level of scholarly expertise on the part of jurists who received an intellectual training that combined a broadly theoretical appreciation of Roman law and its link to its cultural heritage with the edicts, codes, declarations, and other expressions of the sovereign will.

The combination of these features reached their ultimate expression under the Byzantine Emperor Justinian the Great. The *Corpus Juris Civile* that he commissioned organized the scattered and diverse components of Roman law within a single source. It was divided into four parts: the *Institutes*, providing an accessible introduction to the basic principles of Roman law; the *Digests*, providing a detailed summary of Roman legal ideas and scholarship; the *Codes*, which was a collection of all previous Roman edicts, legislation, and other laws; the *Novels*, which was a section that would include all future codes. Each of these parts were mutually reinforcing, especially in terms of providing a source of detailed legal interpretation and consistency of legal application.

The collapse of Roman authority resulted in the absence of centralized legal institutions. The rise of the modern European nation-state spurred a renewed interest in the development of a consistent and unified legal system in support of this political emergence. The fascination with antiquity that inspired much of the Renaissance was extended to the area of law. The University of Bologna was a leading center for the study of Roman law, and scholars throughout Europe adapted its lessons to the creation of their own country's legal systems. This trend resulted in the rise of the modern civil law system, dedicated to the creation of law as a "civil" instrument of sovereign expression and authority.

Two different models of a civil law system eventually emerged. The *Code Napoléon*, commissioned by the French emperor, sought to promote equality before the law through standardization and consistency. A commission of political and legal scholars created detailed codes, organized according to purpose and function (and placed within separate books, corresponding to the different broad areas of criminal, civil, procedural, and penal law), that could be cross-referenced and applied by jurists to legal enforcement and disputes. Legal interpretation was provided within the codes, based upon theoretically abstract principles of law as inspired by the Roman model of "universal" law.

A second model was developed during the latter part of the nineteenth century, most notably by German scholars who desired to promote and define German national identity in the wake of a history of formerly decentralized German political entities. The civil law structure offered a good framework, but the French model of "universal" principles seemed insufficient for achieving a German law for a German people. The result was the formulation of the *pandectist* system of civil law, which sought to create codes and principles derived from German legal and cultural history (especially within the first book of the codes, known as the "General Part") that would be directly relevant to the politics, society, and culture of a distinctly German people. Legal antecedents, such as the Prussian Land Law of the eighteenth century, contributed to this adaptation of the "historical" school of German legal thought. This *pandectist* approach to the civil law subsequently served as a model that could be adapted to other societies and their own, particular historical practices and cultural norms.

Despite different approaches, cultural influences, and even institutional expressions, civil law systems tend to share certain fundamental characteristics. Legal practitioners achieve their status through formal education. A university degree in the law traditionally qualifies a person to be a member of the profession, although some subsequent examinations also might be included. Furthermore, this education tends to be specialized, with students becoming qualified to pursue careers within relatively parochial areas of legal service, including as advocates, counselors, litigators, scholars, and administrators.

A further area of specialization is reserved for judges. Students who want to pursue a career as a judge within a civil law system typically choose a program of university study for that purpose and begin that specific career upon graduation. They advance within that specific profession through a process that often resembles the career of a civil servant. Judges within civil law systems do not generally enjoy the same prestige as their counterparts within common law systems. Formal training, rather than experience, generally is the key to all legal practice within civil law systems. Furthermore, specialization often is extended to the precise area of adjudication, for the judicial structure of civil law systems also tends to be specialized.

Different areas of law have their own system of trial and appellate courts. Jurisdiction is not dependent upon geography, in that sense, but upon the type of legal issue that is being examined, including criminal courts, civil courts, family courts, commercial courts, and administrative courts. Furthermore, civil law systems do not generally make use of juries; panels of judges usually assume responsibility for evaluating matters of both fact and law at both the trial and appellate levels. Indeed, the trial phase is preceded, within most civil law systems, by a lengthy pre-trial phase that involves the active participation of judges, government officials, prosecutors, representatives of accused persons, and law enforcement officials. Only when a preponderance of evidence is determined at this stage will an accused person be brought to trial, creating the erroneous impression among some observers from common law countries that a person within a civil law judicial proceeding is considered "guilty until proven innocent."

Since legal ideas, rules, and principles are codified, civil law judges have little opportunity to exercise interpretive discretion, contributing to the lesser status they tend to have in comparison with common law judges. The codes (or, occasionally, other institutionalized but unentrenched legal doctrines) and other sources of law (including statutes) are regarded as being complete, so previous versions or decisions are not treated as relevant sources of legal interpretation and application within civil law systems. These codes are amended or replaced, periodically, especially under the supervision of legal scholars, rather than legal practitioners.

This process promotes a consistency that also affects the appellate process, in which evaluations of the facts of a dispute often are more relevant than challenges to the interpretation of law and legal principles, since discretion within that area is so relatively rare. Each specialized court system has its own appellate system, including a separate final court of appeal. A single, unified final court of appeal for the entire judicial system is not the norm for a civil law system and, in instances in which they do occur, they tend to be divided into distinct sections, each one dedicated to a particular subject-based jurisdiction. Again, judges tend to administer, rather than interpret, the law within a civil law system.

Variations exist regarding these characteristics of the civil law system, especially within societies that have a "mixed" system of both common law and civil law institutions. But these basic features have been fairly consistent attributes of this institutional legacy that has influenced legal development, throughout the world. The structural features of the civil law have made it particularly useful for political systems seeking to create their own law and jurisprudence, whether using the *Code Napoléon, pandectist*, or other models. The underlying principles and institutional assumptions of the civil law system, as initially inherited from the Roman law, remain recognizable, despite this variety, making it the most dominant institutional influence upon the law, globally.

Western Religion and Its Law

Western religions tend to be distinguished from other areas of society, including politics, economics, ideology, and law, in contrast to the holistic experience of Eastern cultures. Nonetheless, many of the theological beliefs and values of the major Western religions parallel developments in other areas and institutions. Often, major Western religions have actually played a significant role in shaping other aspects of Western life, including legal development.

The canon law of the Roman Catholic tradition (also found within Orthodox and Anglican Christianity) offered a model that retained characteristics of Roman law during a period when that influence had been, otherwise, lost. Certain themes of this legal heritage are particularly notable, the most prominent being the advancement of unity, the promotion of central authority, the imposition of moral duties, and the elucidating role of a *teleological* method (derived from Aristotle's approach to evaluating phenomena according their perceived ultimate "ends," or *telos*) for revealing and fulfilling this law. These themes are consistent with the broader Western tradition of natural law. But they also are consistent with many of the structural characteristics and purposes of civil law systems, especially in terms of the nature and organization of legal codification.

The expression of religious belief through the promulgation, interpretation, and implementation of the law is a foundational feature of Judaism, which also corresponds to certain developments of a general Western legal heritage. The central expression of this law is found within the *Talmud*. It supplements the commandments of God found within sacred scripture, especially the *Torah* (the first five books of the Hebrew Bible), and it includes the decisions of recognized scholarly authorities, particularly *rabbis*. Current authorities refer to these earlier decisions, prior to offering further legal interpretation or modification. This cumulative record, therefore, roughly resembles the underlying premise of *stare decisis* found within the common law system. The laws are organized in a manner that allows for immediate cross-reference to the comments that interpret, and expand upon, them. The *Talmud* provides both restrictions and guidance for revealing ideas and techniques that have become part of the development of secular Western legal practices, especially within the techniques of legal analysis.

The most prominent theme of Islamic law, or *Shari'a*, arguably is the concept of "consensus." This theme has additional significance through the added requirement that, once a consensus of legal analysis is achieved, future variations of interpretation are not permitted. Therefore, the law is intended to promote the unity of the community. The most important source of *Shari'a* is the *Qur'an* revealed to Mohammed by God. However, since the *Qur'an* does not address every area that the law affects, it is supplemented, for Sunni Moslems, by the *Sunna*, providing accounts of the collected traditions of the actions and statements of Mohammed, known as the *hadith*. The science of Islamic law, known as the *fiqh*, is directed toward a revelation of legal truths, rather than their development. The consensus of the community is established and applied by Islamic judges, or *kādī*, achieved through a result called *ijmā*, resulting from a process called *ijtihad*, which proceeds from one technique to another, until a unity of opinion can be agreed among recognized judges and scholars. Superficially, *Shari'a* appears to share, with the common law system, a deference for the legal opinions of previous jurists, while it seems to rely upon the authoritative writings of scholars in a manner that is reminiscent of the civil law system. The process of analogy, and the need to reconcile the law with the needs and practices of the community, offers an interesting comparison with a secular Western legal heritage.

Tribal Law

"Tribe" is a political, economic, and legal term, and it applies only to people who exist, currently, within a very particular category of active community. This term is most applicable to the various indigenous peoples who continue to exist in traditional communities and relationships. The diverse tribal communities of the world generally have not been influenced by, or necessarily even aware of, each other, so they have not developed a strictly uniform system of law. However, a discernable concept of tribal law does exist. It includes an holistic approach, especially in relation to an often precarious environmental balance. Physical necessities are attained directly, through the coordinated efforts of the whole community. Prosperity also is dependent upon a marshaling and maintenance of this symbiotic relationship.

One of the most conspicuous features of tribal "legal" arrangements is a division of responsibilities, largely grounded upon family, and other kinship, ties. People who dominate a family, kinship group, or the tribe may appear to wield exclusive authority. However, the role of the leader usually rests upon a foundation of consensus. Members of a tribe, including leaders, do not *own* property, in the liberal sense. However, they do *control* it for the purpose of meeting the needs of their family, group, or tribe. Leaders control greater quantities of property, because their responsibilities are, correspondingly, greater. This responsibility does, indeed, include greater privileges, but they exist for distributive purposes. Shared tribal resources are controlled in a similar manner, especially under the hereditary purview of a particular family or kinship group.

Legal disputes may be submitted to leading members of the tribe who often retain a memory of the customs that have guided the community for several generations. Customary law often is bolstered by a respect for ancestors who continue to be regarded as a part of the living community. Tribes traditionally render their choices through consensus. Therefore, the tribe often is divided into groups that reflect the broad positions and responsibilities of members, according to their capacities, experiences, and talents, and each group renders a collective decision upon matters of importance to the whole community. Tribal legal norms of the promotion of a holistic community, the distributive control of property, kinship ties, collective identities within the community, and the consensual approach to decision making offer a useful contrast to other, more conventional (especially modern Western) legal systems and their respective norms.

Unitary, Federal, and Confederal Systems

Political and legal systems can be categorized according to their institutional expression of sovereign authority. That ultimate sovereignty is not necessarily vested within a single source. Shared sovereign arrangements (such as provided by federal and confederal systems) provide for an exclusive and enduring division of political and legal control that *remains* a permanent prerogative of these separate sources of authority, while a single sovereign source (such as provided by a unitary system) may merely delegate administrative authority that can be withdrawn by the single, central sovereign. That unified sovereign authority of a unitary system offers a direct expression of authority, political legitimacy, and national identity, especially in suppressing challenges and ensuring unity and consistency through the state. Ultimate discretion, within a unitary system, remains at the center, even while political and legal authority is delegated to other levels.

A federal system (which has become increasingly popular in the modern world) is the result of separate, fully sovereign, or potentially sovereign, political states uniting for the purpose of promoting their common benefit, stemming from a recognition, among these states, of a mutual advantage or necessity. National identity generally does not prompt the creation of a federal system, but a successful federal system often can provide the basis for the emergence of a sense of nationalism. Federal systems conventionally are formed when several sovereign states agree to surrender a portion of their sovereignty and delegate it to a central government. The precise degree of sovereign authority that is delegated and retained often is a subject of ongoing political competition and jurisdictional disputes, with some federal systems becoming relatively centralized and other systems becoming more decentralized.

Confederal systems are relatively rare within the modern world, but certain trends in international relations have made this sort of sovereign arrangement increasingly relevant. These systems are not merely highly decentralized federal systems, nor a mere synonym for federalism, although some commentators often appear to regard these systems in this way. They also experience shared sovereignty, but they differ from federal systems because, while the component states of a federal system permanently surrender a portion of their sovereignty, units that comprise a confederal system retain the option of reclaiming their full sovereign authority and formally withdrawing from the union. Although true confederal states have become a rarity, certain international organizations, such as the European Union, could be described as confederal systems, adding to the overall evolution of the fundamental concept of legal and political sovereignty.

Crime, Injury, Punishment, and the State

Sovereign authority has come to express itself, within the modern world, through a principle called the "rule of law," which, ironically, binds the sovereign as much as its subjects. The rule of law refers to the ideal that no person, institution, or source of authority within society is "above the law." Its underlying premise is advanced further by the ideological assumptions of liberal democracy, especially in terms of the priority of limited government. Thus the sovereign establishes, through the institutions of the state, legal prescriptions and, then, commits itself to follow them. The state, as the source of practical political power within a political system (or even as a synonym for "government"), is, essentially, a legal concept, particularly, but not exclusively, in relation to this role as the legitimate defender of society, its interests, and its members. That conception is particularly pertinent to a liberal democratic definition of the state related to most of the world's legal systems.

The state can be conceived as an unlimited patriarch, a restrained agent of the sovereign will (especially from a liberal perspective), or as a neutral social, economic, and political mediator. But the liberal democratic image of the limited state that serves the will of a popular sovereign increasingly has become, at least theoretically, the most persuasive description. The most basic legal and political division established through this image of the state is the distinction between "public" and "private" law. The difference between these two categories is based upon the relationship that they impose between the state and its legal subjects. The public realm includes those matters that are, properly, the responsibility of the state (especially in terms of its responsibility for protecting society), while all matters beyond its concern are properly relegated to the private realm. "Commercial law," for example, is the public law of economics. Concepts of commercial fairness, honesty, standards of quality, and principles guiding transactions are included within its scope. Thus the economic imperative of modern legal systems makes commercial law a crucial component of the public realm.

Most observers might identify "criminal law" as the ultimate expression of the public role of the state, since it fulfills those central political requirements of compelling obedience to the state and protects society from harm. Any action or condition can be "criminalized," provided that the state can offer a justification for perceiving it as harmful. This role of government often is perceived as the most appropriate purpose of the state and is labeled as its proper "police powers." Private law is more conventionally labeled "civil law." That term is descriptive of the role it plays in mediating relationships among citizens and civil society. Its most essential purpose is the prevention of disruptive private quarrels by establishing norms of behavior that guide personal behavior and reconciling personal disputes.

The enforcement of the law requires, in the last resort, recourse to "penal law." The justification for the state's authority to punish is, essentially, the same as its general legal legitimacy. Furthermore, most ideological defenses of the role of the state, including liberal democracy, contend that the state, by its political nature, not only may employ constrained violence in support of its responsibilities, but has a monopoly over that sanctioned violence. "Penology," as a scholarly basis for establishing penal policy, offers rationales for the different punishment options, including the immediate protection of society, deterrence from future harmful activity, rehabilitation, and converted recompense for the damage caused by harmful acts. Punishment also can be motivated by a desire for revenge, although that purpose often remains unacknowledged or, even, disavowed. Yet the state's legitimacy and, indeed, necessity in providing punishment remains, generally, upheld.

All ideas, including legal ones, require some sort of medium to be conveyed to humanity. These ideas can be conveyed as abstractions, but they can be usefully applied only through some tangible source. The state is a theoretical abstraction, but its institutions provide it a medium of legal expression. Those institutions include the various categories of public and private law and the devices of sovereign authority that create, enforce, and interpret them.

Property and Contract

Contracts have been, arguably, the most basic of all legal institutions. Liberal ideology has refined the modern understanding of contracts through its theoretical expression of "property." Two categories of property exist for expressing this theoretical ideal: "real property" is associated with generally immovable commodities, traditionally tied to land, including houses and other examples of "real estate"; "personal property" encompasses all other property, including possessions, intangible examples such as labor and intellectual property, and media of exchange. Both categories of property can be "converted" into another form, such as labor that is compensated with a wages, or a house that is sold for money.

An agreement between two parties resulting in some sort of permanent exchange traditionally constitutes a "contract." While the area of contract law can be extremely complex, conventional contracts, even outside liberal societies, largely can be reduced to four fundamental elements. All contracts are based upon an "agreement," consisting of an "offer" and an "acceptance." Contracts also are dependent upon "consideration," consisting of a "promise" to deliver some form of property and a "performance" of that promise. Contracts further include the element of "capacity," including matters related to "standing" (the legal status necessary to engage in a legitimate contract), "competence" to engage in a contract and understand its consequences, and "relevance" to the property and ownership involved in the transaction. Finally, contracts must fulfill the requirement of "legality," both in terms of avoiding criminal sanction and conforming to the interests of public policy.

A contract that conforms to the standards indicated through these basic elements is regarded as "valid." It is the primary means for exchanging property in all of its forms. A system for ensuring valid contracts facilitates the general success of the legal system—especially, but not exclusively, within liberal societies. But even within non-liberal systems, the concepts of property and contract remain the most fundamental expressions of law and legal relationships, especially as a "building block" for constructing other legal expressions.

Rights and Liberties

The most dynamic legal concept of the twentieth and twenty-first centuries has been the idea of rights. It has become part of both the legal lexicon and conventional life. It is a politically charged term, subject to grave misunderstanding and potential misuse. It is one of the most prominent considerations of contemporary global politics and an indispensable feature of all modern constitutional traditions and international law, especially in the aftermath of the Second World War and the Cold War period that followed it.

The terms "rights" and "liberties" typically are invoked interchangeably, though they refer to two slightly different concepts, for people have a right *to* something, while they have a liberty *from* something. A liberty (which is synonymous with "freedom") from something, demands a response of constraint by government or other people. A right, though, demands a positive response from external parties (usually the government) toward the party seeking to exercise the right. Generally, guarantees of rights require an institutional response. Most assurances of due process, for example, require the establishment of a legal system that can meet those criteria. The same conditions are necessary for responding to a claim for voting rights. Therefore, this definition of rights occasionally is labeled as a "positive right," in contrast to liberties, which are occasionally called "negative rights," because they require the *absence* of response (such as the freedom of speech, which requires the absence of any obstruction of someone's ability to express themselves) from external forces.

The word "right" has been subject to different meanings: privileges that a person receives as a result of rank or office; obligations imposed by a broader social, legal, and political order; the French concept of *droit* that traditionally refers to "law," in general; a personal sense of entitlement, such as "I have a right to that job," "I have a right to that piece of pie," or "I have a right to drive on a two-way street in either direction." Frequently, this sort of language represents an inaccurate and "inflationary" trend in the language of rights. But the true identification of any right or liberty depends upon its association with a fundamental condition or feature that is absolutely essential for achieving and identifying it. Rights and liberties, properly understood, are based upon a claim to something that, if absent, would diminish the very identity of the party making this claim.

Rights and liberties can be identified under two broad categories: civil and human. *Civil* rights and liberties are grounded upon those fundamental qualities that a citizen needs to function, truly, *as* a citizen. They are not simply the rights of citizens, but rights *for* citizens; without them, persons could not function *as* citizens within their polity. *Ontologically*, therefore, they are the rights and liberties of property-bearing citizens (or legal "persons"), as conceived within liberal theory, although this standing can be achieved by certain classes of non-citizens, such as registered corporations and other organizations. Civil rights and liberties often are identified in terms of their perceived origins. Inalienable rights are retained by individual persons, even after they become members of society, so they are not acquired from any outside source. Consensual rights are determined through a broad consensus of the community as being essential and, thus, determined through a process that transcends, for example, the mere majority or plurality necessary for directing the policy of a sovereign populace.

Human rights and liberties, as the term implies, are grounded upon an *ontological* analysis of the human condition. Achieving a consistent definition of humanity can prove difficult, though. However, its most distinctive quality relates to human intellectual self-awareness and an unavoidable capacity for making choices, being decisive, and controlling one's own destiny. That quality is the principle of "autonomy," and it also is an essential component of liberal democratic thought, although it transcends any particular philosophical tradition or human culture. This autonomous capacity confers both self-identity and dignity upon human beings, for the more humans can impose control over their own destinies, the more "human" they feel. A right to education is a good example; it is a *human* right, because education provides humans with the essential intellectual tools they need to think critically, make decisions, and shape their future. Shelter, work, companionship, and the political benefits associated with civil rights and liberties also can be included within its scope.

It is a tribute to the power of rights and liberties, as a concept and political practice, that it is susceptible to an inflation of the language and expectations associated with it. International covenants designed to protect and promote human rights and liberties have been particularly impressive, in this respect, even when they fail to achieve their goal. It has become practically inconceivable for contemporary states to create a constitutional order that does not include some official reference to rights and liberties, even among non-liberal and authoritarian political systems. The overriding importance and enduring legacy of this ideal of both civil and human rights and liberties remain firmly established, throughout the world, even though it is honored very inconsistently and imperfectly.

Constitutional Diversity

The constitutional traditions chosen for this book strive to represent a variety of regions, socio-economic conditions, and cultural approaches to law and politics. These constitutions bear a distinct relationship with their respective political and legal systems. They also reflect, inextricably, the sovereign power that expresses itself through them and the people who are subject to, and served by, that authority. This book is as much about political systems, ideals and cultures as it is about a parochial, formal-legal appraisal of constitutional law.

But all legal institutions are part of a broad tradition of law. The essential concepts of law that are present within constitutions are not, necessarily, apparent, but that presence remains, nonetheless, real. Therefore, it is crucial to be aware of this presence and the influence these concepts have upon constitutional development and interpretation. This chapter has been preparatory to that analytical process, and that relationship needs to be stressed, even when these concepts are not expressly represented or explained within these diverse constitutional expositions. Subsequent chapters will provide more critically satisfying and relevant explorations of this ultimate idea of public law.

References

Charles Auerbach, *The Talmud: A Gateway to the Common Law*. Cleveland, Western Reserve University Press, 1952.
John Austin, *Lectures on Jurisprudence*, Robert Campbell, ed. London, John Murray, 1885.
John Hamilton Baker, *The Common Law Tradition: Lawyers, Books, and the Law*. London, Hambledon, 2000.
Jeremy Bentham, *The Works of Jeremy Bentham*, John Bowring, ed. Edinburgh, William Tait, 1843.
Sir Isaiah Berlin, *Four Essays on Liberty*. Oxford, Oxford University Press, 1986.
John Eaton Calthorpe Blofeld, *Taoism: The Road to Immortality*. Boston, Shambhala, 2000.
Sir George Bowyer, *Introduction to the Study and Use of the Civil Law*. London, Stevens, 1874.
James A. Coriden, *An Introduction to Canon Law*. New York, Paulist, 2000.
Rodolphe A. J. De Seife, *The Shari'a: An Introduction to the Law of Islam*. San Francisco, Austin and Winfield, 1994.
Jack Donnelly, *The Concept of Human Rights*. London, Routledge, 1989.
Jerry Dupont, *The Common Law Abroad: Constitutional and Legal Legacy of the British Empire*. Littleton, CO, Fred B. Rothman, 2001.
Ronald Dworkin, *Taking Rights Seriously*. Cambridge, MA, Harvard University Press, 1978.
Daniel J. Elazar, *Exploring Federalism*. London, University of Alabama Press, 1987.
Daniel Engster, *Divine Sovereignty: The Origins of Modern State Power*. DeKalb, IL, Northern Illinois University Press, 2001.
John Finnis, *Natural Law and Natural Rights*. Oxford, Clarendon, 1980.
George P. Fletcher, *Rethinking Criminal Law*. Oxford, Oxford University Press, 2000.
Max Gluckman, *Politics, Law, and Ritual in Tribal Society*. Oxford, Blackwell, 1965.
H. L. A. Hart, *Punishment and Responsibility: Essays in the Philosophy of Law*. Oxford, Clarendon Press, 1995.
Robert A. Hillman, *The Richness of Contract Law: An Analysis and Critique of Contemporary Theories of Contract Law*. Dordrecht, The Netherlands, Kluwer Academic, 1998.
Paul Q. Hirst, *On Law and Ideology*. Atlantic Highlands, NJ, Humanities Press, 1979.
Hsin-chung Yao, *An Introduction to Confucianism*. Cambridge, Cambridge University Press, 2000.
Frederick K. Lister, *The European Union, the United Nations, and the Revival of Confederal Governance*. Westport, CT, Greenwood, 1996.
Denis Lloyd [Lord Lloyd of Hampstead], *The Idea of Law*. London, Penguin, 1987.
C. B. Macpherson, *The Life and Times of Liberal Democracy*. Oxford, Oxford University Press, 1989.
Susan Marks, *The Riddle of All Constitutions: International Law, Democracy, and the Critique of Ideology*. Oxford, Oxford University Press, 2000.
Brian E. McKnight, ed., *Law and the State in Traditional East Asian Law*. Honolulu, University of Hawaii Press, 1987.
Susan Millns and Noel Whitty, eds., *Feminist Perspectives on Public Law*. London, Cavendish, 1999.

Bradford W. Morse, ed., *Aboriginal Peoples and the Law*. Ottawa, Carleton University Press, 1989.
Stephen R. Munzer, *A Theory of Property*. New York, Cambridge University Press, 1990.
John K. Nelson, *Enduring Identities: The Guise of Shinto in Contemporary Japan*. Honolulu, University of Hawaii Press, 2000.
Evgenii Bronislavovich Pashukanis, *Law and Marxism: A General Theory*, Barbara Einhorn, trans., Chris Arthur, ed. London, Pluto, 1989.
John Rawls, *A Theory of Justice*. Cambridge, MA, Belknap, 1971.
Heinrich Rommen, *The Natural Law: A Study in Legal and Social History and Philosophy*, Thomas R. Hanley, trans. St. Louis, Herder, 1959.
Marshall S. Shapo, *Basic Principles of Tort Law*. St. Paul, West, 1999.
Peter Stein, *Roman Law in European History*. Cambridge, Cambridge University Press, 1999.
Max Weber, *The Religion of India: The Sociology of Hinduism and Buddhism*, Hans H. Gerth and Don Martindale, trans. and ed. New Delhi, Munshiram Manoharlal, 1992.
Lloyd L. Weinreb, *Natural Law and Justice*. Cambridge, MA, Harvard University Press, 1987.
Konrad Zweigert and Hein Kötz, *An Introduction to Comparative Law*, Toney Weir, trans. Amsterdam, North Holland, 1977.

CHAPTER 2

American Constitutional Tradition

The constitutional tradition of the United States of America has become the most readily recognized example of an entrenched constitutional tradition. Arguably, it also has become a model for all modern constitutional development, especially since it predates almost all of the world's constitutional systems. Therefore, it may be convenient to begin this second part of the text by focusing upon the United States Constitution, its principles, its structure, and its important example for comparative legal, and constitutional, analysis.

The United States Constitution generally is cited as a "written" constitution. However, a more accurate and meaningful designation would be to refer to it as an "entrenched" constitution. This distinction may seem semantic, but it is a legally and politically powerful distinction. In fact, the United States Constitution often is regarded as the leading example of an entrenched constitution, globally. Therefore, this concept bears separate consideration, before proceeding with further analysis of the American constitutional tradition.

Entrenched Constitutions

The concept of "entrenchment" refers not to the presence of a written document but to the manner in which it is created and maintained. Constitutions, by their nature, should not be subject to the degree of change possible through the normal legislative process. An entrenched document is created in a manner that imposes certain obstacles, even upon a general expression of the sovereign will, and its amendment or replacement is made equally difficult. Generally, an indication of some form of broad consensus is required to create or alter an entrenched constitutional document, thus raising its status above all other law within a society.

Entrenched constitutions are placed at the apex of public law and receive their political legitimacy through this process of institutional recognition. Although entrenched constitutions are represented in terms of written documents, they are most properly identified through the institutional restraints imposed upon their modification. The United States Constitution, for example, can be altered only through an amending process (which will be mentioned, again, within this chapter), mandated within that same document, that imposes a far more rigorous indication of sovereign approval than normal statutes require.

One of the most important consequences of entrenched constitutions is the tendency to interpret them closely in terms of the construction of the written document. Arguably, this inclination can inspire a stronger interpretive bias in favor of the "letter" of the law, rather than its "spirit." This proclivity can be prompted by the fact that, since the process of entrenchment often necessitates a delicate political compromise in order to achieve the necessary consensus for approval, the language of this entrenched document often has been crafted with meticulous care. However, such an interpretation also can undermine a meaningful appreciation of the broad underlying values that this source of all public law provides to its society. Therefore, the fact of entrenchment is not concerned simply with legal and political mechanics; it is a defining feature of the constitutional tradition that should be remembered as part of the process of its analysis.

Formal Constitutional Structure

The United States Constitution is, in addition to being the oldest, still-functioning, entrenched constitutional tradition, also one of the shortest written constitutions. It was drafted in 1787 and ratified by the following year. It was the product of a constitutional convention that had been specially arranged to amend the previous, confederal constitutional arrangement. The constitution known as the Articles of Confederation was abandoned as providing an insufficiently strong political union of the various states that constituted the new United States. The result of this convention was a political compromise, encompassed within the United States Constitution.

This document is organized into an extremely brief preamble and seven substantive articles. A previous document, the Declaration of Independence, espousing the essential ideological principles and grievances that inspired the American Revolution against British imperial rule, sometimes is treated by scholars, informally, as a sort of *de facto* constitutional preamble. This constitution is augmented by several amendments (twenty-seven of them, by the early twenty-first century) of varying subjects and significance.

The first three articles describe, respectively, the legislative, executive, and judicial branches of government. The remaining articles are devoted to the federal arrangement, the national debt, and the entrenchment process. The first ten amendments, as a block, were added quickly to the recently ratified document and address essential civil rights and liberties, as do some of the other, subsequent amendments, especially the Fourteenth Amendment that defines national citizenship, ensures equal protection, and further promotes due process under the law. Its brevity and its often legalistic and ambiguous language provide enormous potential for interpretive discretion.

Principal Constitutional Themes

The United States Constitution defines a federal polity of liberal democratic principles. These considerations are largely responsible for other principal themes that permeate this document and guide all American public law. The structure of American government, the arrangement of relations among the states, and attention to civil rights and liberties are particularly indicative of these influences.

These themes are derived from the dominant ideological influences of American political culture. Certain institutions of constitutional government are especially prominent in this respect. The practical workings of the American legal system, the prominence of the constitutional Bill of Rights, and the structure of government are all indicative of this constitutional foundation. The theme of federalism proves to be particularly definitional, but the structure of American government mandated by this constitutional arrangement also merits attention.

Separation of Powers

The liberal emphasis upon limited government is revealed, within this constitution, through promotion of a "separation of powers." This theme is articulated through the first three articles. Popular sovereignty over policy (particularly as a function of law making) is delegated specifically to the legislature, called Congress, consisting of a bicameral body that includes an upper house, styled the Senate, with two elected officials for each state, and a lower house, styled the House of Representatives, consisting of members elected from districts drawn upon the basis of a principle of representation by population. The executive branch, centered upon the president and vice-president, is made responsible for enforcing the legislative results of policy and other laws. The role of the judiciary as a "branch" of government with primary responsibility for interpreting all public law, including constitutional law, was not as clearly asserted within this document, but it became an established principle, once the United States Supreme Court laid claim to it.

This separation of powers provides an indication of the concern that the constitutional delegates had concerning the potential power of this new government. It also underscores the desire of the various, sovereign states that formed this union over the potentially overwhelming presence of its central government. Interestingly, it seems that the legislative branch was expected to be the more dominant of the branches, especially in terms of shaping policy. However, the executive branch has taken advantage of its ability to initiate political action within certain key areas of policy (especially foreign policy) and the greater ease of decisiveness and initiative that a branch centered upon a primary office-holder has, to emerge as the more practically effective political force.

The result of this arrangement has been a system of "non-responsible" government. This expression refers to the fact that the political executive serves a fixed term of office and is not dependent, for that purpose, upon the direct support of the legislative branch. The policy process tends to be more inefficient, since the governmental operation is not dependent upon any discernable measurement of policy success. Therefore, since the practical operation of government can proceed without guaranteed legislative sanction, political impasses arising from conflict among the branches of government are common.

The judicial branch also can frustrate the policy process by establishing constitutional limits upon governmental activity, especially in support of federal powers and civil rights and liberties. It completes the philosophical conception of American government inspired by liberal political theorists such as John Locke and, especially, the Baron de Montesquieu. Each branch of government is intended to reflect a different component of the policy process: the legislature creates the law, the executive enforces the law, the judiciary interprets and applies the law. A divided government is prevented, through this device, from accumulating sufficient power for wresting ultimate political authority from the democratic sovereign. Therefore, this constitutional theme prompts a particular need for all components of American government to operate according to a political strategy of political compromise and conciliation, which still achieves policy results, but in a slower and more diffuse way. Another, even more significant, variation upon this theme is revealed through the American federal scheme.

Federal Government

Particular attention is devoted by scholars of American constitutional law to the omnipresent theme of federalism. It has been a cause and focus of the most constructive, destructive, and defining events of American history. The thirteen states that originally had rebelled against British authority united into a loose alliance of mutual support and security, under a confederal document called the Articles of Confederation. The decision of these states to surrender, permanently, part of their sovereignty and delegate it to a central government provides a classic example of the theory of a "social compact." The United States Constitution reveals both the feelings of promise and anxiety attendant upon the forming of this federal union.

This constitution's primary purpose was the definition of federal authority, and it established seemingly strict limits upon the scope of the powers of the central government. The theme of a separation of powers was, in fact, provided primarily as a safeguard against the centralization of authority at the expense of the various state governments, more than a means of protecting the sovereign American people as a whole. This intention is demonstrated by the brevity of the document and its greater emphasis upon describing central governmental (especially legislative) powers over matters of policy and protection. It was reaffirmed by the inclusion of the Tenth Amendment, which provided an explicit declaration that powers not specifically delegated to the federal government were retained as part of the sovereign authority of the state governments.

These explicitly written, or "express" powers, initially promoted a concept of decentralized federalism. Gradually, though, American federalism has become increasingly centralized in character. The federal government has been able to extend its authority through an appeal to the "implied" powers that have been deemed to be (through the constitutional interpretation of the courts) "necessary and proper" (as stated in article one, section eight of the United States Constitution) for exercising express sovereign powers. Tensions prompted by perceptions of gradual expansions of central authority and conflicts over fundamental economic policy, including the debate concerning slavery, eventually erupted into armed conflict. The American Civil War, fought between the industrialized northern states and the more agrarian, seceding southern states (who adopted their own, confederal constitutional system for a country they called the Confederate States of America), was fought, primarily, over this federal controversy (the southern states, for example, claimed a sovereign "right" to secede, consistent with the principles of confederal constitutionalism), with issues such as slavery providing an emotional moral context.

The northern victory resulted in a further extension of the authority of the central government, especially through the adoption of three amendments (Thirteenth, Fourteenth, and Fifteenth) that clarified the scope of federal authority over matters such as civil rights and liberties protections, general due process guarantees, slavery and other forms of forced servitude, voting, and the establishment of a uniform designation of citizenship for the entire country. Additionally, the federal government developed more effective means of raising revenues, aided by constitutional provisions such as the Sixteenth Amendment, which confirmed the authority of the federal government to enact an income tax. The result of these developments has been a federal system in which the central government can impose a strong control over the policy agenda, even within areas that fall clearly outside its express, and even its implied, constitutional authority. State governments still must enact laws within these areas, but the federal government can extort or bribe these state governments with promises of additional funding or threats to withhold sources of funding that the central government voluntarily has provided to these states.

An example of this practical federal relationship occurs within the area of speed-limit enforcement on roads and highways. The United States Constitution does not delegate, in any way, authority over road and highway regulation and enforcement within state boundaries; therefore, this sovereign authority is retained by the state governments. However, in an attempt to impose a uniform speed limit for the entire country, the federal Congress enacted a directive which authorized federal executive authorities to withdraw federal highway funds, shared with the state governments, from any state that did not impose a speed limit consistent with federal recommendations. State governments, whether or not they complied with this directive, still needed to pass the necessary legislation for establishing these speed limits. However, the practical need for these funds compelled these state governments to submit to this indirect expansion of federal authority over a policy area that continues to belong, formally, to their sphere of sovereign constitutional authority.

Express constitutional authority provided to the federal government, such as the power to regulate interstate commerce (described in article one of the United States Constitution), also has become a source of this centralizing trend. It has become increasingly futile, given the intricacies and pervasiveness of contemporary industrial and post-industrial markets, to distinguish economic activity that is conducted purely within a state from similar activity that has an affect upon more than one state. Again, the practical application of these powers, rather than their constitutional delegation, has been the most effective force behind the centralizing trend of the American federal system, despite conscious attempts, during the late twentieth and early twenty-first centuries, to reverse that trend, especially on the part of federal authorities within all three branches of American government. It is crucial, therefore, to recognize this fact and the larger constitutional reality that a formal-legal constitutional evaluation cannot adequately describe and explain.

The nature of this "social compact" arrangement restricts the attention of the United States Constitution to a description of the sovereign authority of the federal government, alone, with the exception of article four, which establishes a vague, general requirement that state governments be "republican" in character. Therefore, constitutional descriptions of state governments cannot be found within the federal document. Each state has its own constitutional tradition. Generally, these state constitutions provide a political and legal system that imitates their federal counterpart. Variations do exist, especially in terms of specific institutional features and the promotion of unique traditions of political culture that have emerged within many of these state societies.

However, for the purpose of American constitutional analysis from this comparative perspective, it is sufficient to assert that the fifty state constitutions offer a general institutional parallel to their federal counterpart. They are part of this general theme of federalism that is so crucial to the American constitutional tradition and which has dominated both its legal development and the political history of this country. It is a development that remains highly centralized, thus further influencing the general political and legal system.

Political Culture

The United States Constitution clearly describes the values of a democratic society. Sovereignty is identified as being vested in a democratic polity of all citizens, especially within the preamble and within those sections that describe the process for choosing government officials. The formal constitutional source of this democratic principle includes the electoral provisions of articles one and two, the institutional reforms of the Twelfth Amendment, and the voting rights guaranteed by the Fifteenth (for all male citizens, including former slaves), Twentieth (for women), and Twenty-Second (for citizens who are at least eighteen years old) Amendments. Article four also indirectly ensures that state governments also will reflect this principle of democratic sovereignty by compelling state constitutions to provide a "republican form of government" that includes, by implication, an electoral system open to all citizens, especially as described, now, by federal constitutional standards.

The United States Constitution also clearly describes the values of a liberal society. The explicit attention given to civil rights and liberties, especially within the Bill of Rights (advancing broad property, due process, speech, privacy and other guarantees), is the most dramatic indication of this influence. However, the limited structure of the government also is a reflection of the sort of "social contract" premise, as advanced by classic liberal theorists such as John Locke, that underscores this liberal constitutional foundation.

Libertarian Influences

The precise ideological expression of this liberal democratic heritage found within the American constitutional tradition has been a subject of both scholarly and practical political debate. Traditionally, a libertarian interpretation of American liberal democracy seemed to prevail. Copious references to the influence of John Locke and a "classic" interpretation of liberalism (including the expression of Lockean principles within the Declaration of Independence) bolstered this conclusion. It also has been reflected through general impressions of American political culture, including observations of the fierce individualism popularly associated with Americans, especially in terms of their frontier heritage.

This libertarian heritage also has been related to a very strong American affinity for rights and liberties throughout their history. These trends find constitutional expression, especially through the Bill of Rights, the ideal of limited government promoted by the separation of powers, and judicial interpretations of the scope and nature of these rights, including the "discovery" of a fundamental "right to privacy," despite the lack of its formal constitutional inclusion. It has remained a prominent basis for the philosophical interpretation and application of the American constitutional tradition, especially in terms of judicial tendencies to impose strict limits upon governmental powers (at both the federal and state levels) in terms of claims to individual protection of citizens through recourse to those civil rights and liberties described within the Bill of Rights and elsewhere within the United States Constitution and various state constitutional traditions.

Republican Influences

More recent scholarship, and constitutional rulings from some prominent American jurists, have challenged that libertarian assumption. Instead, they have insisted that American liberal democracy actually reflects a revolutionary sentiment that was more strongly influenced by the values and principles of modern republicanism.

The influence of republican political theorists has been linked to the activists and leaders of the American Revolution, and that influence also has been demonstrated in relation to the emerging, and continuing, American constitutional tradition.

The separation of powers can be attributed to this ideological influence, rather than the more libertarian emphasis upon this separation as a device for advancing the cause of limited government. Each branch can be linked, in this sense, to a different "class" of society, providing the institutional inclusion that was a feature of ancient republican government and had been extolled by modern republican theorists. The executive branch provides the "chief magistrate" who offers strong and decisive leadership, especially in times of emergency, as indicated by the president's constitutional authority as "commander-in-chief" during wartime. It also serves the role of "tribune" to the people, with the power to prevent, or *veto*, legislative actions deemed to be harmful to popular interests. The Senate represents the federal principle, especially in terms of the original conception of a legislative body whose experienced members (who must be older than their counterparts in the lower house) were selected by the state governments (specifically, the state legislatures) and, thus, delegates of that collective body, until the Seventeenth Amendment changed that process to direct election during the early twentieth century. The House of Representatives is the forum of the *vox populi*, much like the ancient assembly of the plebs.

According to this republican interpretation, the Supreme Court could be regarded as the unelected representative of the well-educated, professional elite, who keep the aspirations of the more populous institutions of government from constitutionally rash or self-destructive acts. Furthermore, the relatively recent trend of providing another feature of republican inclusion, called "virtual representation," on the high court by making certain that the most significant groups in American society (including women, African-Americans, Latino people, and Jewish people) are present within that body. This argument offers an interesting ideological challenge to traditional conceptions of the unique constitutional structure of American government.

Indeed, the theory of "checks and balances" advanced by Montesquieu, which framers and supporters of the United States Constitution advanced as a primary reason for a government based upon a separation of powers, reflects republican traditions and ideals (as also advanced among British political reformers of the eighteenth century) that this French *philosophe* admired and advocated. Certain constitutional rulings by the judicial branch also have advanced this perspective, at times. Restrictions upon free expression (as protected by the First Amendment) in the areas of obscenity and profanity often reflect a desire to promote "civic virtue," even at the expense of the sort of absolute liberty embraced by libertarians. Seminal rulings by the United States Supreme Court occasionally have interpreted the scope of the constitutional powers of the state and the practical application of civil rights protections provided by the Bill of Rights in a manner consistent with this republican interpretation, especially in terms of arguments that extend the breadth of a "compelling state interest" to include the protection from moral, in addition to physical, harm, including policy areas such as education.

The debate concerning the "correct" ideological perspective of the liberal democratic tradition within American society has been an underlying source of conflict among constitutional jurists and scholars, alike. This conflict is particularly apparent within the process of judicially imposing constitutional limits and protections upon governments and citizens, especially when the jurists are divided in their opinions. This process of judicial decision making is, itself, a central feature of American constitutional law which must be appreciated for the purpose of understanding the significance of this theme and American public law, in general.

Constitutional Adjudication

The institutional process for interpreting the United States Constitution follows the structural guidelines of the common law system. Judges at the trial court level impose constitutional standards upon proceedings and instruct juries regarding relevant constitutional matters that may affect their decisions. Appellate court judges review the decisions of trial courts solely upon the basis of "law," which frequently (perhaps, overwhelmingly) involves alleged violations of constitutional standards, either within the trial (in terms of violations of due process guarantees) or in relation to the offense, especially in terms of statutes that are deemed to violate constitutional standards of federalism, civil rights and liberties, or other standards. These decisions constitute "precedents," and future jurists are expected to refer to them as part of their own constitutional adjudication.

This role, however, was not always accepted as proper for American courts. Initially, it was unclear whether article three of the United States Constitution established a judicial "branch" of government or merely an independent judiciary, confined to applying the law as Congress and the citizens constitutionally would choose. The idea of three branches of government was advocated by Montesquieu, while Locke emphasized only two branches. This controversy was settled by the United States Supreme Court, under Chief Justice John Marshall, when it claimed, and managed to uphold, its authority to be the proper institution of American government for interpreting the scope and meaning of American constitutional law, within the 1804 case of *Marbury vs. Madison*. Since that time, American appellate courts have assumed that role, which has been highly consequential.

Jurists often are divided by different interpretive approaches and ideological perspectives they apply to the process of ascertaining American constitutional legal norms. "Judicial activists" tend to be aggressive in adapting these constitutional standards to changing social, political, and economic beliefs and practices, or in correcting (in their opinion) faulty constitutional precedents. Advocates of "judicial restraint" tend to believe that aggressive constitutional adjudication can undermine the democratic basis of constitutional sovereignty, so they tend to defer to the interpretations of elected representatives who create laws under this system and to indications of an "original understanding" of the United States Constitution on the part of its framers and the members of the society of that time.

Certain decisions by the United States Supreme Court impose such a momentous interpretation upon a given area of American constitutional law that they constitute "seminal" precedents that are instrumental for guiding all future interpretations by jurists, politicians, and society, alike. These seminal precedents have been particularly important in terms of imposing limitations upon government "police powers" in favor of those civil rights and liberties protected by the Bill of Rights. The authority of the federal courts has been expanded, in this respect, over laws and rulings at the state level, especially through reference to the "equal protection" clause of the Fourteenth Amendment, which establishes a uniform standard for all American citizens in matters of due process and basic civil guarantees. Rulings concerning the scope and application of First Amendment guarantees of religious liberty, "separation of church and state," free speech, and free association have been particularly important, as have the warrant requirement of the Fourth Amendment, guarantees against self-incrimination found within the Fifth Amendment, prohibitions against "cruel and unusual punishment" provided by the Eighth Amendment, and privacy rights derived, in part, from a determination that they are included as one of the unspecified "rights retained by the people" declared within the Ninth Amendment.

Court System

The American judicial system follows the practice of the common law system of uniting all courts under a single final court of appeal. These courts also tend to be the setting for all types of legal cases, including both criminal and civil matters.

These courts are geographically allocated, with the country divided into 90 districts, providing jurisdiction for federal trial courts. These districts are grouped into 11 circuits, each one providing an immediate appellate court for the districts that fall under its jurisdiction. Finally, circuit courts fall under the appellate jurisdiction of the United States Supreme Court, which serves as the final court of appeal for the entire federal system. Both circuit courts and the Supreme Court can serve as courts of original jurisdiction under certain special and specified circumstances.

State court systems tend to parallel the organizational model of the federal system. States frequently are divided into districts that serve as jurisdictions for state trial courts. Often, additional local courts and justices of the peace exist for handling "petty" criminal and "small claims" civil matters. Mid-level appellate courts also are distributed throughout the state, with some version of a state-level supreme court serving as a court of final appeal for the entire state. Decisions rendered by the state high court may be appealed to the United States Supreme Court if they address, in addition to matters of law that fall under state constitutional authority, controversies arising under the United States Constitution.

Administrative law controversies frequently are addressed by separate tribunals within both the state and federal spheres of authority. Tax courts and regulatory agencies provide this sort of jurisdictional setting. These bodies must conform to the same standards of due process and constitutional principles that are imposed upon conventional courts, and their rulings and decisions are equally subject to the jurisdiction of the appellate courts and, ultimately, the United States Supreme Court or, if appropriate, the respective state's highest court of appeal.

The United States Constitution also provides separate military courts, with jurisdiction over members of the armed forces, especially during time of war. A separate body of law, the Uniform Code of Military Justice, is a separate source for criminal, and some civil, law for the armed forces, including offenses, relating to morale and discipline, that are not found among civilian statutes. The rulings and decisions of these military courts also are subject, ultimately, to the appellate jurisdiction of the United States Supreme Court, which unites the entire federal judicial system (consistent with the practice of the common law system, generally) under a single interpretation of American legal standards and constitutional law.

The Future of American Constitutionalism

The judicial branch of American government is noted for its prominent role within the American political system. Many political observers have charged that

American society is particularly litigious, with citizens who are highly aware of those constitutional standards that are relevant to their lives, especially within the area of civil rights and liberties. The frequent recourse to the courts regarding challenges to the constitutionality of public policy is cited as having a profound effect upon the development of, and arguably undermining, the policy process.

The American constitutional tradition remains a strong feature of the American polity. It serves as a source of national unity and identity, promoting many of the best values of this liberal democratic society. Its stability has been maintained throughout many crises of American history (especially the American Civil War, the Great Depression, and the Watergate scandal that eventually forced President Richard M. Nixon to resign from office), and it serves as a model of constitutional government for other countries, even though most other political systems choose a parliamentary alternative to the institutional structure that American government provides, especially under its constitutional theme of the "separation of powers." Ultimately, the successful future of the American constitutional tradition appears to be extremely secure.

References

Bernard Bailyn, *The Ideological Origins of the American Revolution*. Cambridge, MA, Belknap, 1967.
Daniel J. Elazar, *The American Constitutional Tradition*. Lincoln, University of Nebraska Press, 1988.
Donald S. Lutz, *The Origins of American Constitutionalism*. Baton Rouge, Louisiana State University Press, 1988.
James McClellan, *Liberty, Order, and Justice: An Introduction to the Constitutional Principles of American Government*. Indianapolis, Liberty Fund, 2000.
David M. O'Brien, *Constitutional Law and Politics*. New York, Norton, 2000.
Charles H. Sheldon, *Essentials of the American Constitution: The Supreme Court and Fundamental Law*. Boulder, CO, Westview, 2001.
G. Alan Tarr, *Constitutional Politics in the States*. Westport, CT, Greenwood, 1996.
Laurence Tribe, *American Constitutional Law*. Mineola, NY, Foundation, 2000.
Gordon Wood, *Creation of the American Republic*. Chapel Hill, University of North Carolina Press, 1969.

CHAPTER 3

British Constitutional Tradition

The legal and political development of the British Isles has a very old and rich history. Prior to the union of England, Wales, and Scotland (and the still-controversial union with Ireland, now restricted to Northern Ireland), a constitutional tradition was emerging which would politically merge the island of Great Britain and provide a model of constitutional government that would be widely imitated by other countries throughout the world, especially countries that once had been part of Britain's formerly extensive global empire. The most dominant of the national entities that ultimately joined to form the United Kingdom of Great Britain and Northern Ireland has been, especially for legal and political purposes, England, so the constitutional history of that country is a particularly important source for understanding the current British constitutional tradition.

Unentrenched Constitutions

Many observers commonly refer to the British constitutional tradition as the prime example of an "unwritten constitution." However, that term is inaccurate. First, the British constitutional tradition can be identified in terms of numerous written documents, statutes, and other, positive sources that can be read and analyzed. Second, it is not truly distinctive because of the absence of a single, identifiable constitutional document, *per se*, but because of the institutional means of identifying constitutional provisions and norms and the methods that have been recognized for establishing, modifying, and altering it.

The British constitutional tradition is more accurately identified as an "unentrenched" constitution. Its interpretation and application depend upon an ability to recognize its presence without the need for a formal document that defines it, succinctly. Furthermore, it is grounded upon expectations that are, while informal in appearance, just as powerful and binding as any formally entrenched constitutional legacy. It relies upon an appreciation of the "spirit" of the law for constitutional enforcement and guidance, and this feature often seems perplexing to observers and critics whose perspectives are affected by their own entrenched constitutional systems, which adhere more strongly to the "letter" of the law.

One colloquial expression that may be found among some members of modern British society may be a reference to something that is, in practical terms, prohibited, simply because it is considered to be "not the done thing." If forced to choose between the strict construction of a rule or the general tenor and intent of that rule, a typical member of British society might be much more inclined to adhere to the latter interpretation. Certainly, prominent political and legal elites of modern British society often have exhibited, through words and actions, that preference. An unentrenched constitutional tradition absolutely depends upon that sort of attitude in order for it to function with any semblance of feasibility.

Part of the success of an unentrenched constitutional tradition is based upon the fact that, without this arrangement, the legal and political structure of that tradition would prove to be practically unworkable. Violators of its fundamental tenets conceivably might gain a temporary political success, but their actions would undermine the entire system so catastrophically that it would become unsustainable. This reliance is so widely espoused that any constitutional violations which might occur normally can be attempted only under circumstances that would be perceived as acceptably extenuating exceptions to the conventional constitutional practices of *any* system. An unentrenched system will succeed *only* within a society that is culturally attuned to this ideal.

Constitutional Structure

An unentrenched constitution does not have a formal structure. Its norms and principles are located in a diversity of sources that are well known to constitutional scholars, legal practitioners, and political elites. Most other members of society may be only vaguely aware of its components or, even, of its very presence. However, this problem is not unknown to members of societies that are governed through entrenched constitutional traditions. Furthermore, within democratic societies, the fact that the constitutional tradition is an articulation of sovereign will should be reflected by popular beliefs and attitudes, even though sovereign responsibility for maintaining, applying, and interpreting constitutional government has been delegated to those political and legal elites who occupy its formal offices.

The British constitutional tradition often is associated with key statutes that are maintained as part of the public record. Its informal structure also is identified within scholarly texts written for that purpose and the practical guidance of jurists. These texts are important, for much of this constitutional tradition is based upon beliefs and practices that are not contained within any particular, positive source of authority. It is useless to describe the British constitutional tradition in terms of any sort of formal structure. But it is very useful and, indeed, essential to describe it in terms of a consistent, and functionally applicable, theoretical structure.

However, one political structure that is central to the constitutional process ought to be described, especially for the purpose of clarifying the British governmental process to uninitiated observers and scholars. The parliamentary system of government, as it has evolved to the present, was initiated in medieval England. Its influence has become so widespread that its central institutions (the House of Lords and the House of Commons), housed in the Royal Palace of Westminster, are still known as the "mother of all parliaments." Its operation is crucial to British constitutional government, and an ability to distinguish between its formal-legal, *de jure* procedures and the *de facto* exercise of political power, using parliament as its "stage," needs to be understood and appreciated for any meaningful analysis of the British constitutional tradition to be possible.

Parliament

Originally, parliament evolved from the medieval English assemblies (initially restricted to members of the nobility) that gathered, at the command of the monarch, to offer support and advice. It was expanded to include representatives of other, non-noble classes of subjects, who eventually held their proceedings in another chamber and deliberated, separately. Scotland and Wales developed similar institutions. Parliament was not a permanent body, but different parliaments, representative of the "nation," were summoned by the monarch, at various times, usually for the purpose of raising funds and mobilizing political support in relation to some great need or crisis, including warfare. Eventually, two chambers emerged that deliberated upon these matters, separately: an assembly of the landed aristocracy, eventually known as the House of Lords; an assembly of non-aristocratic representatives, eventually evolving into the House of Commons.

Gradually, because the monarch came to depend upon these parliaments for raising revenue, they became increasingly powerful. The rise of a mercantile economy enhanced the authority of representatives of the merchants, tradesmen, and businessmen of the House of Commons, owing to their superior ability to raise the revenues necessary for promoting the sovereign will. Eventually, the monarch could not govern without the active support of parliament, especially its House of Commons. Therefore, by the seventeenth century, the monarch's ministers were selected upon the basis of their ability to cooperate with, or control, parliament.

Indeed, by the eighteenth century, the monarch's "first," or "prime," minister was designated specifically for that purpose, in addition to enjoying the trust of the monarch and a reputation for strong administrative abilities. Because the entire governmental process came to depend upon this control of the revenue-raising lower house of parliament (which expanded to include all non-nobles, including the working class), political parties emerged and organized themselves for that purpose, and its members who were elected to the House of Commons increasingly were expected to practice absolutely uniform support for their leaders. Otherwise, consistent control of parliament would be impossible, as would the necessary conditions for a political party to determine the composition of the government and the policies it would promote.

Contemporary parliamentary systems that have emerged from this "Westminster model" rely upon this concept of "party discipline." The shift in sovereign authority from the monarch to the democratic polity has accented the process associated with it; the political party that succeeds in winning a majority of seats (by itself, or through a coalition with other political parties) automatically secures the prerogative of forming the government, with its leader selected, also routinely, as the monarch's prime minister and, thus, the effective chief executive of government. This executive is not separate from the legislature (unlike the American system) but is a member of, and reliant upon, parliament.

The monarch continues to symbolize the concept of a separate executive authority but now has, in fact, been relegated to the role of a "head of state," only, with extremely limited political authority but an important symbolic role of embodying the sovereign will. The precise procedures of parliamentary government are too intricate for this sort of introductory comparative constitutional analysis, although other crucial aspects of it will be addressed in another part of this chapter, especially in relation to the connection between constitutional convention and the rules of parliamentary government. Yet a very rough sketch of the origins, evolution, and current theory of parliamentary government provides an indispensable component of this analysis of British constitutional structure, even though no entrenched constitutional document exists to define it.

Principal Constitutional Themes

The British constitutional tradition rests upon a foundation of seminal political and legal events that have shaped its history and development. It also is the product of an evolution of social, political, and judicial practices that have become widely accepted, generally taught, and even expressed, occasionally, through formal legislation and regulation. A legacy of law making has become a moving force within this constitutional development, but not all laws have constitutional significance, nor is the British constitutional tradition merely a collection of laws and legal and political practices. Laws are expressions of sovereignty, but not all laws are equal, for some of them enjoy a lasting influence that allows them to shape essential constitutional values.

The most prominent theme of British constitutionalism is the principle of "convention," from which resource much of this entire system is derived. The evolution of the central political institutions of this system, especially parliament, have been pivotal, too, in this respect. Another primary theme is found within the legacy of legal practices and principles that have evolved into a contemporary understanding of the rule of law. The evolution of the legal system, especially in terms of the emergence of the modern common law system, also plays a prominent role. A diverse history of philosophical values has been, nonetheless, tied together (especially through the ideological influence of classic conservative norms and principles) to comprise another theme that helps to complete this process of British constitutional development.

Constitutional Conventions

Fundamental principles of British constitutionalism have emerged through historically significant political events, statutory enactments, and legal practices. These foundational sources are labeled generically as constitutional "conventions." They are the product of "watershed" phenomena that have accumulated for many centuries, first through the legacy of the English nation-state (with contributions from Welsh and Scottish sources) and, then, as part of an inclusive British legacy. They are not entrenched in any consistent way, yet they enjoy the same respect and force as the formally immutable clauses of a conventional constitutional document.

Seminal statutes, including royal decrees, charters, ordinances, and parliamentary legislation, offer the most conspicuous source of British constitutional conventions. Perhaps, the best known of these conventions to a casual observer is the *Magna Carta*. The constitutional principle of *habeas corpus* (demanding that an arresting authority "present the body" of a detained person and either formally charge that person with a legitimate crime or release that person from custody) was established through this 1212 royal charter. This sort of statute is considered "seminal" because a return to the previous legal or political practice or principle is generally regarded, from that point onward, as unacceptable. Further advances, consistent with the general spirit of that convention, may be introduced, but "sliding back" to a former constitutional standard is not regarded as a valid option for society and its political and legal systems.

Another good example of a statute that has become a constitutional convention, in that respect, is the Parliament Act of 1911. This statute imposed strict limits upon the power of the House of Lords to obstruct or deny legislation passed by the House of Commons, thus permanently securing the unchallenged legislative supremacy of the parliamentary lower house and the democratic sovereignty it had come to represent. The struggle for passage of this statute was fierce, and enormous political obstacles needed to be overcome. However, once enacted, it was widely acknowledged, even by opponents of this reform, that the British constitutional system never would revert to the restoration of a legislative veto for the parliamentary upper house and the aristocratic class it traditionally represented. The Parliament Act of 1911 was superseded by subsequent legislation, but those statutes (the Parliament Acts of 1949 and 2000) did not contradict the *spirit* of the original convention; instead, they represented modifications and alterations consistent with that spirit and the evolution of parliamentary government, as signified by the original statute.

Other key legislation has served a similar purpose, throughout English and British history. The Bill of Rights of 1689 advanced the principles of rudimentary civil rights and liberties, reformed parliamentary government, and advanced a sense of "share sovereignty" which prevailed from the Glorious Revolution of 1688-1689. The Act of Settlement of 1701 established the principle of a judiciary that should be relatively free from political influence and corruption. The Act of Union of 1707 joined England and Scotland together as one sovereign country. The Reform Bills of 1830, 1867, and 1883 acknowledged the gradual but, ultimately, irresistible shift of sovereign authority from an extended economic oligarchy toward a general democratic populace. These statutes, and many other laws, could be rescinded, just like any other decree or legislation. However, an overwhelming recognition of their constitutional significance, and an equally strong sentiment that these changes represent a permanent advancement of British constitutional development, has conferred upon them an aura of permanence that remains unchallenged, despite the lack of an entrenched constitutional document to reinforce it.

These "rules of the game" (and the widespread compliance with them) are such an ingrained feature of British constitutional government that it is not necessary to provide positive enactments of them or enforce their principles. Elections must be held, by statute, at least once every five years, at a time that is fixed by political circumstances and the preferences of the current government. Again, it is possible that the parliament could adopt legislation extending this period to a much longer period of time. But such action is practically inconceivable, except in time of national emergency, such as the temporary suspension of elections for the duration of the Second World War. Modifications in favor of more frequent elections might be possible as being consistent with the constitutional *spirit* of representative democracy; less frequent elections, though, are not considered an option.

Constitutional conventions also can be found within the rules and procedures that govern the parliamentary process. Many of these principles do not exist in any sort of formal-legal context. They are based upon practices and understandings that have been reinforced through repetition and the acknowledgment that parliamentary government could not continue to function without their continued observation. These expectations often contradict the technical authority that is conferred upon a particular political situation. A prime minister whose political party loses its majority in the House of Commons is expected to resign or ceremonially "advise" the monarch to authorize new elections. Technically, no formal requirement, statutory or otherwise, exists that can force a prime minister to respond in that way. However, the pressure to comply is irresistible, for failure to accede to this constitutional requirement would effectively immobilize the political system.

Other unentrenched and, often, unwritten, yet widely recognized, parliamentary procedures include the privileges of the parliamentary parties in opposition, such as guaranteeing institutional resources for their use (even though a parliamentary majority could, conceivably, retain those resources for its own use), deference to the parliamentary role of the monarch in terms of the formal (though largely symbolic) appointment of government officials (who are expected to be members of parliament) and other functions, regular consultations between the prime minister and the monarch, and the formal process of legislative enactment, despite the fact that the political reality of party discipline should make the final outcome of that process a forgone conclusion. Indeed, policy decisions really are reached through the efforts of the prime minister, members of the cabinet, and their respective ministerial departments, so the entire role of parliament might seem to be a somewhat redundant legislative confirmation of a preordained result. Nonetheless, the parliamentary process, itself, is an essential (indeed, a defining) feature of modern British constitutionalism. Dispensing with it arguably might prove to be efficient and easily accomplished, but it would offend the spirit of the British constitutional tradition to a completely unacceptable degree. Therefore, the most minor of these expectations and practices are strictly embraced and protection; any other response simply would not be "the done thing."

Indeed, one advantage to an unentrenched constitution is this greater facility of modification, not only as part of a broader evolutionary trend but also in response to special considerations and conditions that require reasonable exceptions to be made, such as the example of the temporary suspension of elections during World War II or the initiation of laws punishing "hate speech," even though such laws appear to violate the *letter* of those conventions promoting absolute protection of political expression. In both of these cases, it has been argued, the *spirit* of the constitution was maintained and, even, strengthened. Meanwhile, an entrenched constitutional approach might find such reasonable modifications frustrated by a manipulation of the constitutional documents and the construction of its clauses, and obstruction of the process (even by a small, yet determined, minority) to amend that constitution as a means of reflecting a new constitutional principle that enjoys, otherwise the consensus approval of the sovereign. A reliance upon conventions of all sorts is regarded, therefore, as a logical extension of true constitutional legitimacy, rather than being a battleground of institutional conflict that entrenched constitutional systems often experience.

Parliamentary Supremacy

A theme of British constitutionalism that is closely related to these constitutional conventions of parliamentary government is the concept of "parliamentary supremacy." It differs, though, from these conventions because it is a general principle of constitutional *sovereignty*, rather than a specific principle of constitutional *procedure*. Nonetheless, conventions regarding the parliamentary process provide a necessary context for the advancement of parliamentary supremacy as the capital expression of the will of the sovereign.

There can be no higher expression of the sovereign will than parliament. This role has facilitated historic shifts in sovereign authority, from the monarch whose decrees gained legitimacy by being declared through, or confirmed by, the parliament, to the functional oligarchies of the late medieval and early modern periods that compelled the monarch to share sovereign authority by recourse to parliamentary accommodation, to the rise of the House of Commons as the true source of parliamentary authority, as legitimized by those elected representatives to it who have been delegated responsibility for reflecting the sovereign will. But it is not just the parliamentary authority to enact legislation that enjoys this status, for the interpretation of the constitutional legitimacy of that law also is vested, exclusively, within parliament.

A statute enacted by parliament cannot be declared "unconstitutional," for parliament, as the ultimate expression of the sovereign will, defines constitutionality. Restraint, in this respect, is self-imposed by the profound deference felt for widely accepted constitutional conventions. Yet the final constitutional authority remains vested within parliament. The courts cannot claim this authority, for their independence does not confer upon them a constitutional role as a branch of government responsible for such constitutional interpretation and enforcement in the American sense. Again, conformity between legislation and constitutional principles depends upon this adherence to the "spirit" of this tradition of British constitutionalism; without it, the concept of an unentrenched constitutional tradition, itself, would be impossible. So, parliament enacts legislation in a manner consistent with the widely understood and accepted standards and limits of the British constitutional tradition.

Therefore, any act of parliament must be, by definition, constitutionally legitimate; no other authority may challenge that expression of sovereign will. Parliament may choose to delegate that sovereign authority to another body, as it has done by joining the European Union and agreeing to the jurisdiction of that confederal association's courts over certain domestic legislation. But it also retains the ultimate prerogative of reclaiming that authority, thus reaffirming (at least in theory) this constitutional theme of parliamentary supremacy, especially against judicial encroachments.

Rule of Law

Constitutional systems generally uphold some version of the principle of the "rule of law." However, the unentrenched nature of British constitutionalism gives this concept added significance. This concept has been addressed within the introductory chapter of this book, but a few observations concerning its relationship to the British constitutional tradition will be useful.

The rule of law is based upon general expectations of fairness and legal restraint. British law and politics make frequent use of this principle as a guide for legal and political participation and its process. Features of the common law system, for example, operate according to this understanding, as demonstrated by the popular expression "justice must not simply be done, it must be *seen* to be done." The adherence to consistent rules, consistently observed, conveys legitimacy upon the judicial process. This legitimacy extends to all procedural matters.

Parliamentary supremacy also is advanced through the rule of law. The fact that a particular procedure, bound by particular rules of fairness and equitable treatment, is followed, scrupulously, for every legislative enactment confers upon all legislation a widely recognized sense of legitimacy. Therefore, its authority is unchallenged, even if it is unpopular, for it was created in a manner consistent with the rule of law. The popular sovereign, in particular, requires this principle to be followed, for it also confirms the belief that this delegated sovereign authority is not being abused, misused, or withdrawn.

The British legal and political systems operate within the parameters established by the rule of law. Arbitrary actions are not constitutionally tolerated. Everything, including the command of the sovereign, must conform to established precepts and procedures. The legal realm of "equity," the requirements of "natural justice," the general requirements of legal positivism, expectations of proportionality, and limits upon the actions of government are part of this constitutional theme, and it remains an essential feature of the British constitutional tradition.

Unitary Government

The United Kingdom includes diverse regions, peoples, and national identities. By the early twenty-first century, assemblies in Wales and Scotland were created to express a sense of national self-government within those "countries" of Great Britain. Regional authorities also have been established within England, in addition to the traditional councils of the county (also called "shire") and municipal levels. The regional governance of Northern Ireland remains, socially and politically, an extremely difficult and divisive challenge that is subject to continual negotiation and revision.

Despite these diverse levels of governmental authority, *sovereign* authority remains vested solely in one place. Parliamentary supremacy, physically housed at Westminster, applies to the whole of the United Kingdom. The authority delegated to other councils or assemblies can be withdrawn, through appropriate legislation, by the British government. Indeed, during the 1980s, the scope of the powers of municipal governments regarding taxation were limited by parliament. Furthermore, the entire regional government for the greater London area was abolished, with administrative responsibility re-delegated to the separate boroughs that comprise London until a different regional government was created for greater London by the end of the 1990s.

This structure of unitary government extends to control of the judicial administration, despite the fact that England and Scotland have their own distinct legal systems. The English judicial system is firmly grounded upon the common law—indeed, England is the origin of that common law system. Scotland, however, has a "mixed" legal system. Scotland's criminal law is administered largely within the institutional context of a common law structure, but much of its "private" law is subject to the principles and procedures of a civil law system. These differences are reconciled, though, by the fact that all courts are subject to the ultimate appellate authority of an overarching British judiciary and court structure. It provides another illustration of this theme of an effective unitary system of government imposed over a diverse political configuration.

Political Culture

Great Britain and its constituent "countries" have experienced tremendous changes in political culture and values. Its philosophical beliefs and values have evolved from its tribal origins to the feudal norms of its medieval period to the modern advent of socialism and the current dominance of liberal democracy. Yet one ideological legacy has helped to unite the political and constitutional progress that has occurred through all of these cultural and philosophical transitions.

The most formative period of British constitutional development arguably occurred during the sixteenth, seventeenth, and eighteenth centuries. The influence of a class-conscious social order, dominated initially by the monarch and those peers who constituted the aristocracy, shaped many of the constitutional assumptions that have persisted from this period. The ascendancy of this social order was accompanied by the prominent presence of an ideological tradition which, while not remaining overwhelmingly dominant for very long, has persisted in its permanent effect upon British constitutionalism. This tradition, grounded upon principles of social harmony, political and economic stability, and deference to sovereign authority, and providing a philosophical link between the ideals of the medieval and modern periods, has been defined, previously (within the introductory chapter of this book), as the ideological heritage of classic conservatism.

One of the most persistent values of this classic conservatism has been a reverence for traditional institutions (including political, legal, religious, and social models), rituals, and other practices. The political philosopher and writer Thomas

Hobbes articulated these principles with strong effect, following the relative chaos of the English Civil War, particularly in terms of his vision of the "social contract" as a submission to sovereign authority in order to gain the security and stability necessary to achieve peace, prosperity, and both collective and individual aspirations. Edmund Burke argued, during the late eighteenth century, that the anarchy associated with the French Revolution (especially during the "Reign of Terror") was a product of the wholesale rejection and elimination of the traditional institutions of French society (including church and monarchy) that previously had preserved the best features of that civilization. He urged British society to preserve and revere its own traditional institutions (political, legal, cultural, religious) as part of a necessary framework for political and legal growth that could be affected peacefully, if slowly, without the negative consequences that a more "radical" approach tends to present.

The British constitutional tradition has maintained the existence of many of the same essential political and legal institutions for several centuries. Fundamental shifts in sovereignty have not been affected by an outright rejection and elimination of the institutions of monarchy and parliament but through parallel shifts in the concentrations of political power *within* those institutions. Parliament, as a political institution, has remained the central feature of English and British constitutionalism, but the ultimate source for expressing sovereign authority has transferred from the "monarch-in-parliament" of the medieval period to the House of Lords and its landed aristocracy of the early modern period to the House of Commons of the seventeenth and eighteenth centuries and the merchant and business class it represented to the prime minister and cabinet of the twenty-first century, on behalf of the current, democratic sovereign.

Many classic conservative theorists would applaud that sort of constitutional development, since it presents a "common thread" that binds together the varied philosophical and ideological contributions to British constitutional history. The relative absence of truly violent revolution as a necessary prelude to those changes has resulted in a constitutional evolution that may have been slower than many other societies but, also, more stable and enduring. That foundational principle still appears to guide the institutional development of the British constitutional tradition and the widespread deference to constitutional convention that makes it possible to sustain this sort of unentrenched system.

Legal Practice and Judicial Decision Making

Legal practitioners in England traditionally received their training though a process of internship, with many aspiring lawyers attaching themselves to the Inns of Court (traditional sites for the offices of senior legal practitioners and their professional association) until they could pass their professional examinations. Two broad categories of English lawyers exist: barristers, who represent clients "before the bar" of the court; solicitors, who engage in a more varied practice of law, primarily outside the courtrooms. Currently, professional legal preparation in England also includes university education, but the ultimate emphasis, consistent with the common law legacy, remains the examination system and practical legal experience.

Scottish lawyers achieve formal legal credentials by receiving a university degree in law, although that status now may be confirmed through other processes of professional accreditation. Lawyers in Scotland need to be familiar with both civil law and common law principles and procedures. Both English and Scottish lawyers ultimately are subject to a unified jurisdiction of professional standards and oversight for the entire United Kingdom.

The constitutional theme of parliamentary supremacy precludes the concept of British jurists exercising interpretive authority over constitutional law. That determination is left to legislative, and not judicial, discretion. The Act of Settlement of 1701 provided for independent judges who would enjoy tenure of office and not be subject to direct political pressure from governmental officials. However, it did not assign them any sort of constitutional role. Judges discover and declare the meaning of laws, but they are not permitted to evaluate these statutes in terms of their consistency with the themes and principles of British constitutional law.

Nonetheless, certain interpretive approaches and techniques have been employed by British appellate jurists that may constitute an indirect form of constitutional adjudication. Occasionally, judges may be moved to this sort of creative jurisprudence in response to a parliamentary statute or government action that seems to contravene the basic principles of British law and justice. Parliament retains, even these cases, ultimate legal authority, so it eventually can override judicial interpretations that offend legislative intent. But this sort of judicial action can generate political pressure to amend or rescind the criticized statutes or practices.

Judges rely upon the fact that all laws require some level of interpretation in order to define and apply them, completely. They rely upon common law precedent in order to include those additional legal concepts that are assumed, but not expressly indicated, within legislation, and the process of discovering these appropriate precedents and the principles derived from them involves, necessarily, an exercise in judicial discretion. The principles of "equity" (a jurisprudential field, originally with its own system of courts, established for the purpose of applying fair, or "equitable," solutions to particular legal disputes) have provided one source of interpretive discretion, since the principles of equity compel jurists to define legislation, controversies, and other legal matters in a manner consistent with rules of "fundamental fairness," including an appeal to the due process precepts of "natural justice."

Statutes that are constitutionally controversial often are the product of political expediency or compromise. Therefore, the language of these statutes can be expressed in a deliberately ambiguous way. Judges can take advantage of this condition by invoking a declaratory claim of "void for vagueness." Appellate judges who believe that the apparent meaning of a statute is offensive to essential themes of British constitutionalism potentially might declare that they simply do not believe that parliament intended to achieve such a legislative result and, in support of this belief, they may further determine that the language of the statute fails to indicate, unequivocally, that otherwise unusual parliamentary intention.

In response to such a judgment, parliament may redraft and clarify this legislation, affirming its intent and eliminating this particular source of judicial discretion, thus reasserting parliamentary supremacy. However, that action can be politically prohibitive, especially when public opinion has become aroused. Juries, sometimes, will take similar action by disregarding instructions from the judge concerning the interpretation of the statute (as part of the process of applying it to the facts of a criminal or civil controversy) because they regard that law, itself, as offending their own conception of fundamental fairness or essential British constitutional convictions.

Sometimes, laws contradict other laws. The more recent law should prevail, unless, again, the contradiction is indicative of a lack of intent on the part of parliament. Therefore, judges may have an additional reason for trying to determine whether or not parliament was aware of this contradiction and intended to give it effect. This sort of contradiction is especially apparent when a government office has been given a specific authority that normally belongs to another office or agency. These contradictions can be addressed by having the legislation declared *ultra vires*, or beyond the scope of the competence of the affected party. This same finding can be applied to other levels of government (including county and local administrations) that attempt to exercise authority over matters that normally are reserved to another level of government or to parliament, alone, including legislation that fails to provide additional statutory change to the competence and organizational scope of that level of government and its overall statutory authority.

Areas of ambiguity can be clarified by reference to precedent. Judges also rely upon the writings of eminent legal scholars, especially when the ambiguity includes a constitutional repercussion. These scholars have been instrumental in shaping the evolution of the common law, in particular, and British constitutional law, in general, and they include such eminent commentators as Lord Coke, Sir William Blackstone, Lord Bryce, and A. V. Dicey. Despite these opportunities for practicing a certain level of legal activism over constitutional matters, British jurists remain strongly constrained from violating the overriding theme of parliamentary supremacy, except in areas in which parliament has delegated part of its sovereign authority to international organizations and treaty obligations. But that delegation, again, may be reclaimed by parliament, thus affirming its ultimate supremacy over constitutional, and all other legal, matters.

Court System

The general, common law principle of a uniform judiciary has directed the formation of British courts. This fact may not be readily apparent, since the nomenclature and organization of these courts can seem, on the surface, diverse and confusing. Furthermore, the structural and historical distinctions that continue to be made between English law and certain areas of Scottish civil law can exacerbate this perception. But, despite this apparent complexity, the overriding principle of final unity remains firmly ingrained within the British judiciary, especially since final appellate authority over the entire British system is, indeed, vested within a single judicial body.

The unifying common law principle that guides the British judicial system was confirmed and clarified through the constitutional convention of the Judicature Acts of 1873–1875, making all English and Welsh courts competent to apply the rules and procedures of all aspects of common law jurisprudence and equity. But some historical archaisms of the organizational evolution of the judicial system remain, and the court system that results from it often can appear to be intricately organized and, even, confusing, especially to an outside observer. Therefore, different courts do exist for addressing different areas of criminal and civil law and their appeals, although they are subject to a single standard and a unified source of final appeal.

Criminal courts include two categories for most matters of original jurisdiction. Magistrate's Courts hear cases dealing with petty crimes, while Crown Courts have trials pertaining to most other crimes. Civil cases that involve "small claims" often are heard in county courts, while more substantive civil matters, in England and Wales, are tried in the High Court, which also exercises limited appellate responsibility for cases arising out of county courts. The High Court is divided according to areas of specialization: the Queen's Bench is responsible for cases arising generally under the common law; the Chancery Division handles most equity cases; the Family Division addresses custody, divorce, and other family-related controversies.

The Queen's Bench also serves as a first level of appellate jurisdiction for criminal cases tried in the English and Welsh Crown Courts. Appeals arising out of cases tried before Scottish courts are considered by the Court of Sessions. A similar appellate court exists for cases originating in Northern Ireland, and it is known as the Supreme Court of Northern Ireland. The Court of Appeal, Criminal Division, exercises a more general appellate jurisdiction for the system, including over criminal cases arising in Scotland. The Court of Appeal, Civil Division, assumes the same responsibility for appeals in English and Scottish civil cases. Although both this categorization and seeming specialization are imposed upon the judicial system, judges are, nonetheless, appointed to the bench upon the basis of their general maturity and experience, and they are considered competent to preside over trials and consider appeals concerning all areas of law. Administrative and military tribunals (including Admiralty Courts) also fall under this general organizational consideration.

The final court of appeal for the entire United Kingdom is the House of Lords. This upper house of Parliament provides the historic origin for English jurisprudence, extending back to the feudal *Wittenagemot*, which sat in judgment over legal disputes affecting the security of the realm and royal privilege. It evolved into the concept of a "high court of parliament" that asserted a general authority for adjudicating controversies that affected parliament as a representative body. This role preceded the general advisory and legislative role of this chamber of parliament. This original role for parliament developed, gradually and over many centuries, into a general appellate responsibility, under the authority of the Lord High Chancellor, until, by the nineteenth century, that chamber was acknowledged as having final appellate jurisdiction over all legal controversies within the country, especially those matters affecting constitutional concerns or issues of general national importance. It also can serve as a trial court for peers accused of a crime (at the discretion of the accused member of the nobility), with all members of the House of Lords serving, potentially, as jurors.

Technically, all members of the House of Lords can participate in this judicial role. Actually, that responsibility is delegated to that chamber's Appellate Committee, consisting of eminent jurists raised to a peerage specifically for that purpose and administratively chaired by the Lord High Chancellor (who also serves as a member of the cabinet and as a semi-official speaker for the House of Lords) when it meets for legislative purposes. It consists of both English and Scottish "law lords," and representatives of the latter category of jurists must participate in appeals coming from the Scottish Court of Session. The proceedings are relatively informal, but the authority it wields can be enormous, particularly in terms of reconciling statutes and other laws with conventional constitutional interpretation, in addition to the interpretive context of relevant common law precedents and, when appropriate, Scottish civil law requirements. Final rulings are by majority vote, and these appellate rulings may not be overturned, except through the enactment of new legislation by parliament.

The Future of British Constitutionalism

The evolution of the British constitutional tradition has been slow, but it has produced a remarkably stable system of law and jurisprudence. It also is responsible for much of the legitimacy that the British political system enjoys. Because of the diversity of its origins, the different phases of political culture that have shaped it, and the archaic institutional remnants of its historic development (retained, partly, through the general influence of a classic conservative bias in favor of "prudence" in affecting change), it can seem confusing and, even, somewhat chaotic, especially regarding its court structure. But its success is demonstrated by the willingness of other countries (especially former British colonies) to adopt its general principles and practices.

The British constitutional tradition continues to evolve. This ability to adapt to political, social, cultural, and economic change (including historically fundamental changes) is one of the greatest strengths of this unentrenched constitutional heritage. However, the even greater influence of legal positivism and the empirical preferences of a modern and post-modern age tend to favor the image of certainty that entrenched constitutions seem to provide. Therefore, despite its success, the British constitutional tradition is more likely to be a more broadly theoretical, rather than a strictly institutional, model for the legal development of other societies.

References

Walter Bagehot, *The English Constitution*. Boston, Little, Brown, 1873.

A. V. Dicey, *Introduction to the Study of the Law of the Constitution*. London, Macmillan, 1967.

Michael Foley, *The Politics of the British Constitution*. Manchester, Manchester University Press, 1999.

Peter Hennessy, *The Hidden Wiring: Unearthing the British Constitution*. London, Gollancz, 1995.

Geoffrey Marshall, *Constitutional Conventions*. Oxford, Clarendon, 1984.

Owen Hood Phillips and Paul Jackson, *O. Hood Phillips' Constitutional and Administrative Law*. London, Sweet and Maxwell, 1987.

William Stubbs, *The Constitutional History of England*. Oxford, Clarendon, 1880.

Colin C. Turpin, *British Government and the Constitution: Texts, Cases, and Materials*. London, Butterworths, 1995.

D. C. M. Yardley, *Introduction to British Constitutional Law*. London, Butterworths, 1990.

CHAPTER 4

Chinese Constitutional Tradition

China offers one of the most ancient civilizations on Earth. Yet its modern constitutional history is remarkably brief, being confined to two distinct episodes, beginning during the early twentieth century. The Republic of China, established after the Chinese Revolution against imperial rule, was initiated in 1912 and still serves as the constitutional model for the government of Taiwan, which still claims to represent this republic. This chapter will address the constitutional regime that displaced the Republic of China, in 1949, following the Communist victory in China's civil war.

The People's Republic of China offers a unique combination of influences that become especially apparent through constitutional analysis. It is a modern socialist state with an ancient Eastern heritage, and these diverse cultural influences are central to its constitutional development. This Chinese constitutional tradition serves as a crucial tool for accommodating the country's huge size, complex administrative apparatus, and ambitious political, social, economic, cultural, and legal goals. But this tradition differs markedly from Western (especially liberal democratic) models, so it requires a particularly critical comparative perspective.

Socialist Law Systems

Although most of the world's legal structures (excluding the legacy of tribal law) and practices are categorized as falling under the common law or civil law models, an additional category often has been acknowledged by some comparative legal scholars. A socialist law system resembles, very strongly, the civil law system, especially in terms of its structure. But differences in its underlying assumptions, in addition to its substantive content, justify treating socialist law as a distinct, though related, category.

Socialist legal systems are products of Marxist-Leninist thought. Liberal legal systems are regarded as mere extensions of economic oppression. *Bourgeois* interests use government and its law as a means of rationalizing its economic domination through legitimation of its control of the means of production and the creation of a "false consciousness" that leads everyone else to believe that they are, truly, "equal" before the law. But Marxist scholars continue to argue that liberal democratic institutions promote an illusion of autonomy while hiding the proposition that not even an elected government can overcome class oppression, unless class inequality is eradicated, also.

Socialist legal systems reject conventional liberal assumptions regarding a proprietary definition of individual personhood and the regime of property rights. Private property, in its abstract sense, is controlled by the state on behalf of the *proletariat*, so the law's primary purpose, in this respect, is the enhancement of that beneficial control. Furthermore, jurisprudence is an expression of administrative authority, rather than a source of legal protections. It also offers an orientation that differs, substantially, from the individualistic emphasis of common law and civil law institutions. Rather than serving as a form of protection, law should promote collective socio-economic goals. Therefore, legal rules and principles do not afford individual protection *from* the state but enhance the ability *of* the state to advance the welfare of all members of society.

These legal principles are found within a system of codes. These codes find their inspiration from the general directives of Marxist ideology, rather than a claim to "universal" legal principles that serves as a basis for the Roman law foundation of civil law (as represented by the *Code Napoléon*) or the nationalist assumptions associated with the formulation of a pandectist civil code. This foundation is well suited, though, to the "inquisitorial" style of the civil law system and the rejection of judicial discretion in the interpretation of law. Institutionally, the codes are devised to conform with a sovereign will expressed, on behalf of workers and peasants, by the Communist Party, serving as the "vanguard of the *proletariat*" until the people are ready to assume full political and economic control, at which point the state, including its legal system, will have "withered away" into redundancy. The codes serve, therefore, as expressions of the general policy preferences of the party, so any lack of specificity within these codes can be reconciled by reference to those party objectives, since the law cannot contradict the sovereign will of the people, under the party's ultimate guidance and protection. The legal system also is a vehicle for the state, as the principal administrative agent of the party, to determine the "process" that is "due," rather than basing this concept upon a restrictive definition of the "rule of law."

Rather than emphasizing legal conflict, socialist legal systems seek to reconcile disputes in favor of achieving a shared vision of the future. Punishment is not a deterrent, but a means of protecting important social goals. Socialist law does not protect individual people from the state (although it does seek to treat all people with similar fairness), nor is it a means for one person to engage in a legal confrontation with another person. The decisions reached by a tribunal of judges are intended to achieve a solution that is, ultimately, best for society, as a whole, within the context of the conflicting claims of the parties who appear before it. Again, though, it should be stressed that a socialist legal system closely resembles a civil law system, especially in terms of the institutional sources of legal principles (embodied, particularly, within the codes), the basic process of educating legal practitioners, its concept of statutory authority, its inquisitorial style of seeking legal truth, and its rules of procedure. The legal system of the People's Republic of China offers a typical example of that model.

Formal Constitutional Structure

This constitutional tradition is enshrined within an entrenched document, although it can be changed with much greater ease than most other entrenched constitutions. It is divided into four chapters, addressing general principles, fundamental rights and duties, the structure of the state, and national symbols. It is augmented by a separate organizational constitution for the Chinese Communist Party, which also encapsulates the party's essential political and economic purpose and goals. An understanding of the Chinese constitutional tradition needs to be supplemented by an understanding of the structure and principles of the party, particularly since it serves, primarily. as a vehicle *of* the party, and its content is shaped, ultimately, by party officials and, only then, administered by the state. It is divided into "chapters" for addressing these themes.

Chapter one of this constitution gives an explanation of the essential political, economic, and legal assumptions that provide an interpretive basis for all Chinese law. Much of its content is expressed within the lengthy preamble. It addresses the principles of socialism, the leadership role of the Chinese Communist Party, and it identifies the source of sovereign authority as being vested within a "people's dictatorship," with that sovereign will being expressed, upon its behalf, by the party and administered by the state, until the conditions necessary for a truly autonomous, classless society are achieved. This chapter also identifies and explains "Marxist-Leninist-Mao Zedong Thought," which serves as the proclaimed dominant ideology of this constitutional tradition.

Chapter two lists and briefly explains the fundamental "rights and duties" of all members of Chinese society. This distinction between "rights" and "duties," and its comparison with a conventional definition of "rights and liberties," reflects the Eastern cultural context of this constitutional tradition. In fact, it is describing a concept of human rights and liberties from the philosophical perspective of *giri*, or "reciprocal duties," especially as explained within a Confucian context. That general influence will be addressed more thoroughly within the section of this chapter of this book that deals with the political culture of this constitutional tradition. Structurally, though, these "reciprocal duties" are divided into two categories within this chapter of the constitution.

The first category is labeled "dispositive rights." Chinese citizens have the option of exercising these rights, according to their own inclination. This category of rights most closely resembles a conventional liberal conception of civil rights and liberties. It includes freedom of speech and religion, and even a right to own private property. A crucial difference, though, is the fact that, while liberal ideology permits the state to impose limits to the scope of rights and liberties upon the basis of the "harm" that exercise could present to the rest of society, socialist legal theory, as advanced within this constitution, generally instructs the state (in accordance with the general principles enunciated within chapter one of this document) to deny the exercise of these dispositive rights when they are perceived to threaten the socialist goals identified by the party. Therefore, true discretion in expressing these rights rests with the party, and not individual people. This limitation is particularly significant regarding the type and degree of "property" that is protected by that particular dispositive right.

The second category is labeled "preemptory rights." They include such features as a "right to work," a "right to democratic participation," and a "right to military service." They offer an even better exposition of *giri*, for they impose expectations upon both citizens *and* the state. The right to work, for example, is an obligation for the citizen to work in support of the collective economic goals of the greater Chinese community. However, it also imposes an obligation upon the state to provide meaningful work for every Chinese citizen. This preemptory right is related to a Marxist conception of autonomy, especially in terms of the dignity conferred upon a human being through labor. It fulfills, therefore, both a collective and an individual benefit. All citizens are entitled to the benefits of the state, but they also have an responsibility to contribute to those benefits, for the good of all and the final vision of communism.

Chapter three describes the structure of the state and its areas of responsibility. It specifies the fact that the state exists to support the mission of the party, and not the *bourgeoisie*. Since the party serves the people, the state exists to provide an overall supportive role. This constitutional chapter includes a description of the different organs of the state, including the executive authority of the presidium, the legislative responsibilities of the People's Assembly and its committees, the court system, and the general bureaucratic network. The constitution for the Chinese Communist Party offers a parallel institutional structure of party executives, policy makers, mediators, and administrators. This chapter makes clear the fact that the state is not the delegated representative of the sovereign will, as it is within other systems, but a functionary for the *party*, which *does* express the will of the people—though only, officially, temporarily.

Chapter four is brief, but important. National symbols, including the location of the capital city, serve to unite the country and its people. It also establishes a foundation for a pattern of ritual that is very relevant to this Eastern culture, as will be noted within the section of this chapter devoted to the political culture of the Chinese constitutional tradition.

This entrenched document provides a useful tool for uniting people, party, and state. Its role differs from most Western traditions, but it is typical, in certain respects, of the general ideals of a socialist legal system. These aspects of the Chinese constitutional tradition become more apparent when attention is shifted from a formal-legal description to an analysis of its principal themes.

Principal Constitutional Themes

The Chinese constitutional tradition provides an excellent example of many significant themes of Eastern legal norms. Most of these themes revolve around the philosophical relationships that are traditionally formed between people and their rulers, as modified by the modern requirements of socialist law. They also emphasize the pragmatic role of the modern Chinese constitutional tradition, especially in terms of supporting economic policy.

The Chinese constitution stresses the ideal that the people, and *not* laws, are supreme. This rejection of the conventional Western premise of the "rule of law" is one of its most important departures from contemporary liberal democratic constitutions. All of the principal themes of the Chinese constitutional tradition revolve around this central ideal.

The Constitution as a Guide

Conventional Western constitutional systems are designed to impose limits upon governmental authority as a means of protecting the sovereign will that has delegated this constitutional mandate. Liberal democratic ideology has been prominent in defining this role. But the Chinese constitutional tradition serves a very different purpose.

This constitution is an institutional resource *for* government, rather than a restraint upon it. It offers guidance to both government officials and the people. In that sense, it serves to unite the country under a single set of legal principles and goals. This orientation is consistent with both the basic underpinnings of a socialist legal system and traditional Eastern visions of socio-political relationships. This latter point will be elaborated within the section of this chapter devoted to political culture. Meanwhile, it is important to understand that the constitution is a tool of the government that assists it in the process of carrying out the will of the people, as formulated by the party. The constitution serves the sovereign; it does not limit the sovereign, even in a self-imposed way. This distinction becomes increasingly apparent within the context of other constitutional themes, particularly regarding the practical purposes this entrenched document seeks to address.

The Constitution and Economic Policy

All constitutional traditions advance the essential philosophical principles of a political community. Generally, these principles are motivated by the most pressing economic practices and desires of that community. Liberal democratic constitutional orders, for example, stress property rights and the conditions necessary for maintaining and enhancing the public marketplace of a mercantile or capitalist economy. The Chinese constitutional tradition is not different, in that respect, except that these economic goals are derived from a particularly self-conscious adherence to the vision of a Marxist ideological legacy.

The entrenched Chinese constitutional tradition has experienced several redrafted and reenacted versions. Each one was the result of a watershed shift in overall Chinese economic policy, although the socialist foundations of those policies have remained, essentially, intact. These changes reinforce the previously addressed theme of the constitutional role of providing essential legal guidance for the broader political, social, and economic will of the sovereign people, as expressed through the party and administered by the state.

Therefore, each redrafting and reentrenchment of the Constitution of the People's Republic of China has been presaged by a dramatic reformulation of general economic policy goals, and not simply shifts in economic and political strategy. The first constitution, in 1949, represented an administrative initiation of the final victory of the Chinese Communist Party during the civil war. It was preoccupied with explaining, justifying, and creating an appropriate political and legal climate for the revolutionary redistribution of property, under government control, that is an essential feature of any truly socialist state. All subsequent versions of this constitution were prompted by advancements and modifications of this initial, revolutionary directive.

The concerted desire to achieve extraordinarily rapid industrialization of the entire Chinese economy that resulted in the grand policy initiative of the Chinese Communist Party, under Mao Zedong, and that was known as the "Great Leap Forward" presaged another reformulation of the Chinese constitution in 1953. The failure of the Great Leap Forward and its threat to Mao's leadership was countered with a movement against reformers and other forces (spearheaded by powerful student organizations that were fanatically loyal to Mao) that appeared to oppose the underlying purpose of that economic plan. The chaos that resulted from this movement, known as the "Cultural Revolution," and the dogmatic economic programs it had defended were, themselves, repudiated by the party. This repudiation was acknowledged and converted into legal and political sanction through the adoption of another version of the Chinese constitution in 1975.

Another fundamental shift in economic strategy was adopted by the Chinese Communist Party by the end of the 1970s. The enactment of the constitution of 1979 reflected and enhanced this policy of greater moderation of socialist priorities. However, this constitutional change was not regarded as a final testament to the relative liberalization of the Chinese economy. Final repudiation of the more dogmatic leadership of the party, symbolized by the political trials of the group known as the "Gang of Four" was consummated through the adoption of another constitutional document in 1982. The constitution promulgated in 1993 was in response to the party's relatively increased receptiveness to aspects of a marketplace economy. These six constitutional documents represent variations upon this general, yet consistent, theme.

Furthermore, all of these six "constitutions" are variations upon other, shared basic themes of Chinese constitutionalism; they have differed only in the way each version has facilitated certain economic strategies. Generally, the essential elements of each of these documents remained the same. Differences were most apparent within those clauses describing specific aspects of government structure and policy. Often, the lengthy preamble also suggests this policy direction. Additional changes can be noted within the amended constitution of the Chinese Communist Party, especially in terms of its own policy declarations and the enumeration and description of certain party officers and the party organization.

Yet the basic themes (especially unchallenged sovereign authority, the role of the constitution as a guide to popular and administrative activity, and the reciprocal relationship among people, party, and state) have remained consistent. All of these documents were created by some sort of "entrenchment" process by the party, which initiates all such change and controls the constitutional system as a tool of its overall mission. That theme of the Chinese constitutional tradition is best illustrated by this connection between constitutional renewal and fundamental shifts in political, social, and economic direction.

Unitary Government

Despite its immense size and diversity, China's constitutional system describes a structure with, ultimately, a single source of sovereign authority. It might appear that a federal system would be better suited for a country that encompasses over one-sixth of Earth's population and physically dominates East Asia. This theme of unitary government is consistent, though, with the overall constitutional orientation of a coordinated, centralized, socialist economic mission under the leadership of the party.

The Constitution of the People's Republic of China serves a crucial role in making this unitary system function. It serves as a basic guide of party policy and government administration for all regions, political divisions, and levels of the state. It serves as a means of providing direction for carrying out specific laws and policies by giving them an interpretive context. It also offers the means for adapting local variations to laws and policies, corresponding to specific needs and conditions, that can, nonetheless, remain true to their overall, centrally determined purpose and intent. One way of expressing this theme is through reference to the colloquial expression of keeping everyone "on the same sheet of music." The Chinese constitutional tradition is like the overall musical score of the conductor that provides coherence to the work of art, even while a variety of different parts and musical schemes may be performed, in connection with it, by the individual members of the musical ensemble performing it.

That analogy is consistent with an understanding of the political culture of China as reflected within this constitutional tradition. A more specific appreciation of the complexities of this unitary system and its organization can be found through the very brief introduction to the structure of the Chinese judicial system that will be found later within this chapter. This unitary system often may need to be administered in a decentralized manner (due to those practical considerations already addressed), but discretion remains constitutionally controlled, and sovereign authority remains thoroughly centralized, particularly through the efforts of the Chinese Communist Party.

Political Culture

The preamble of the Constitution of the People's Republic of China ostentatiously proclaims the dominant philosophical role of "Marxist-Leninist-Mao Zedong Thought" in guiding constitutional interpretation, the state, the party, the people, and the country. But that formal description of this ideological heritage does not offer a substantive insight into its true principles, values, and expectations. Furthermore, it does not acknowledge the full range of the philosophical influences that contribute to the political culture of China, both in terms of the basic values promoted by the leadership of the Chinese Communist Party and the social, economic, political, and legal practices of the ordinary people throughout China.

This official state ideology of "Marxist-Leninist-Mao Zedong Thought" is more readily known simply as "Maoism." It is, in fact, an amalgamation of modern ideological influences emanating from Western sources and the traditional Eastern values which dominated China for millennia and which continues to exert overwhelming influence, even though its philosophical values, tied to China's imperial past, frequently are renounced, officially, by the party and its leaders. Despite the insistence of these elites, this diverse philosophical legacy persists.

Maoism stresses certain easily recognizable principles that are inherited from Lenin's political adaptation of Marxist ideology. Mao's particular expression of this Marxist-Leninist legacy is attributed to the practical problems of applying its assumptions to conditions within China, including the country's relative lack of industrialization at the time of the establishment of the People's Republic of China during the middle of the twentieth century. The model of the Union of Soviet Socialist Republics that had become the first practical (and constitutional) adaptation of Marxist ideology simply did not fit the infrastructural realities of China's largely agrarian, peasant-based economy within a country that remained overwhelmingly rural in character. Therefore, the need to have, within China (contrary to Marx's predictions and even Lenin's modified expectations), a revolution *before* industrialization could proceed needed to be reconciled by Mao and the Chinese Communist Party.

Mao sought to affect this sort of adaptation through a pragmatic adjustment to theoretical ideas concerning the nature and role of the socialist state that remained, nonetheless, essentially unchallenged. However, that functional approach cannot account for the myriad of political and legal practices that dominate Chinese life. These culturally singular features of Maoism are revealed and advanced by the general tone and specific mandates of the Chinese constitutional tradition, and they provide its interpretive underpinning.

Maoism advances the ideal of "revolutionary populism." Workers and peasants share a mutual class obligation that compels them to accept the leadership of the party as it leads them toward the self-sufficiency necessary for the attainment of the true communist polity, free from any need for any sort of government or property concerns. The dialectical process that Marx adapted from Hegel offers additional insights into the class struggle as it applies to China. The dialectic reveals the interrelationship of all problems, confirming a sense that this revolution is an expression of an holistic process of developing class consciousness and unity. Therefore, a focus upon one aspect of any complex problem facing the people and its party can be used to address the broader needs of the revolution, since it is a reflection of the "whole." This focus will shift from one aspect of policy or the state as the "revolution," and the conditions arising out of it, continue to develop.

Many of Mao's ideas are encapsulated within *Quotations of Chairman Mao Zedong*, more popularly known as the "Little Red Book." Mao stressed the importance of "process" in achieving the goals of a true Marxist revolution, including the process of economic policy and development and the institutional means of achieving it, as described through the constitutional tradition. Revolution is perpetual, until the final ideal of communism is achieved, marking the conclusion of the dialectic and, so, the very end (in terms of the process of conflict and struggle) of history. Unity is achieved through this continual struggle. But a reverence for traditional social and political institutions is a potential source for undermining this struggle, especially since this reverence is accepted by people, through "false consciousness," in an often uncritical or, even, unthinking manner. Mao's suspicion of a professional class, particularly intellectuals, also reflects this feature of Maoist thought that continues to be imposed upon the Chinese constitutional tradition.

But Mao Zedong's philosophical modification of Marxism, as received through Lenin's analysis, cannot be explained merely as a result of pragmatic adaptation. However, critical investigation and observation of these beliefs and values and the actual political, social, economic, and legal habits of the people who live within this environment reveal a much more textured philosophical influence. In particular, Maoism offers an amalgamation of a Western Marxism with the traditional beliefs and values stemming from the ancient roots of this Eastern civilization.

The most important of these traditional Chinese philosophical influences is, arguably, Confucianism. Its status was so important to imperial China that official mandarins and people who entered into the extremely prestigious and lucrative civil service were required to demonstrate their expertise in Confucian thought. This influence even persisted during the republican period, and it reflects a more pervasive philosophical presence throughout China that continues to be revealed, despite the official Chinese Communist Party denunciation of Confucianism and other "reactionary" traditions of thought, belief, and general practice.

Constitutional indications of this persistent influence are numerous. The responsibility assigned to the country's leadership, in particular, to provide a good model of correct behavior and respect reflects the traditional principle of *jen*. Indeed, the very role of constitutional institutions as a guide to correct legal and political action, rather than a constraint upon the ruler, echoes the traditional role of the Confucian mandarin as a teacher and mentor. The relationship of reciprocal duties among people, party, and state offers an excellent insight into the concept of *giri*. Chapter two of the Constitution of the People's Republic of China (particularly the enumeration and description of "preemptory rights," such as a "right to democratic participation") offers an excellent example of this ideal in practice, especially in its stress upon the obligations that both party and people owe each other, for the greater good of the whole community.

The principle of *li* (explained within the introductory chapter of this book) as a method of achieving harmony is extolled. The goal of a socialist regime cannot be achieved without the willing cooperation of all members of the community, so the establishment of general principles for everyone to follow becomes the preferred function of the "ritual" of the law as illuminated by the constitution. The actual constitutional language, promoting Maoism, may abandon such overt references to traditional beliefs and values and favor the lexicon of an adapted Marxist ideology, but its presence in both the lives of the Chinese people and in the unique way that the Chinese state and Chinese Communist Party reconcile these diverse needs and features is striking. Both its constitutional presence and guidance are essential, therefore, for reconciling these converging traditions, especially given China's considerable geographical and demographical size and the ambition of its transition to a modern social order, featuring a modernizing political and economic system.

This Eastern approach is compatible with the general purpose and function of a socialist legal system. Western cultures (most notably the former Soviet Union) also employed constitutional institutions as tools for promoting the will of the people through the ultimate guidance of the Communist Party. But the Chinese method of socialist law and the constitutional commitment to Maoism appear unique to its own cultural context and heritage.

One particularly revealing example of this influence is found within the preferred method for local mediators to settle disputes. These mediators encourage parties, particularly within a private dispute, to apply the principle of *jang I-tien*, which translates roughly as "yielding a little," with indirect reference to the *tao* (and the Confucian concept of the "mandate of heaven") that provides a "path" toward social harmony. Two considerations are paramount: neither party to a dispute is likely to be completely justified in its position, so each side should acknowledge its own shortcomings and the debt they owe to each other; the settlement of any dispute, including a "private" one (for a strictly legal, as opposed to a social, category of "privacy" is a *bourgeois* concept relating to the dominance and manipulation of property) can affect the community, so any settlement must try to conform to a solution that also benefits all other people. Both the principles of *jen* and *gîri* also find expression within this very popular method of legal mediation throughout China. It provides a practical example of the sort of legal behavior that may provide a more meaningful exposition of the constitutional reference to the guiding principles of Maoism.

One criticism of this political culture is that it actually may reflect the philosophical rationalization associated with the elite-driven legacy of Legalism. While its precepts (as described briefly within the introductory chapter of this book) are not formally embraced, the concept of the justification of authoritarian activity against "enemies of the state" (who are, therefore, "enemies of the people"), based upon a belief in the natural contentiousness and incompetence of people as subjects of the legal order, has been a charge made against the state and party authorities of the People's Republic of China. However, this accusation may be based upon the copious examples of apparently ruthless and autocratic behavior by the Chinese state, throughout this modern period, rather than any actual attempt to embrace the canons of traditional Legalism.

Maoism is the product of a diverse philosophical heritage, most prominently of Marxism and Confucianism. This heritage is distinctly Eastern in philosophical orientation, but it also incorporates deliberate Western influences. Attention needs to be devoted to it as a means of gaining true insight into the meaning and function of the Chinese constitutional tradition, especially in contrast to most Western, liberal democratic constitutional systems. Otherwise, many of its institutional manifestations (including its political policies, legal practices, and judicial structure) may be misunderstood or oversimplified, especially from a reliance upon a formal-legal method of analysis.

Legal Practice and Judicial Decision Making

Relatively few professional legal practitioners exist within China. These sorts of professionals represent a *bourgeois* convention of using the law as an instrument for the protection of property owners. However, lawyers do exist, particularly for the purpose of international business, with many of them operating within, or through, commercial centers of international trade, such as Hong Kong and Macao. They receive a university education in preparation for their careers, like legal practitioners of most civil law systems.

Nonetheless, these legal professionals constitute a minority of the people engaged in the legal and judicial process in China. Most law is conducted through the auspices of administrators and senior civil servants. This practice is not inconsistent with the role of judges within civil law systems, who often perform a role in applying facts to detailed codes that seems more administrative than broadly legal in nature. Furthermore, the political purposes of law within a socialist system and, particularly, the People's Republic of China make this responsibility more appropriate for political, rather than legal, officials and assistants. The mediation process, which is the level of legal administration that most people within China actually experience, is conducted by a respected elder or other social leader of the local community, which seems most appropriate for the informal purposes of this legal institution. Likewise, criminal matters of a local nature are most likely handled by administrators who may be specially trained for the task but who are not legal practitioners in the conventional, Western sense.

The judicial proceedings may seem informal, at times, but they are, in fact, performed in a manner that is quite conscious of the ritual significance of law to the community. A typical trial of someone who has been accused of a non-political offense (such as assaulting another person) will include all the elements of a normal civil law procedure in this area. If the pre-trial stage clearly seems to indicate guilt, the trial stage is performed, not so much for the purpose of verifying guilt or innocence, but for the purpose of restoring the sense of harmony and the duties of the accused toward the community that the crime has disrupted. One element of this process often included is the ritual (suggesting the principle of *li*) "confession," designed to indicate the accused persons' willingness to accept their responsibility for their actions, restore the disruption to the community they have caused, and engage in rehabilitation. This aspect of conventional criminal proceedings, often called "reeducation," is a traditionally Chinese way to conceive the role of penal law. In fact, a failure to rehabilitate a criminal through this process is regarded as a failure of, and loss to, the judges, the system, and the whole community.

A cynical image of China's legal and judicial systems may exist. However, much of that impression stems from the more overtly political uses of the judicial system at the highest levels of the People's Republic of China. In fact, for most Chinese people, the legal and judicial systems at the local level are conducted with sincerity, integrity, and competence (despite a lack of highly educated legal professionals) in a manner that is consistent with both a conventional civil law structure and the traditional political culture and values of China.

Constitutional Adjudication

The Constitution of the People's Republic of China is an instrument of the people and the power exercised, on their behalf, by the Chinese Communist Party. Therefore, the constitution serves the party and state, rather than limiting them. It also can serve as a guide for other political and legal officials to achieve a better understanding of the context of policies and their administration. Like their counterparts within civil law systems, Chinese judges do not "interpret" the constitution in a conventional sense. Furthermore, it is the Chinese Communist Party that declares the meaning of the constitution and alters that meaning to serve the needs of the political and economic systems when its leaders deem it appropriate.

Article 67 of the Constitution of the People's Republic of China, found within chapter two of that document, describes the structure and function of the Standing Committee of the National People's Congress. This legislative body is assigned the official responsibility for explaining the meaning of the constitution, especially in relationship to other laws and policies that are initiated by the party and generated by the state. It is particularly important for reconciling apparent contradictions between constitutional norms and specific legislation. It also is tasked with the responsibility for recommending constitutional changes which, subsequently, must undergo an entrenchment process initiated by the party and enacted by the government. This standing committee is the Chinese institution that comes closest to the concept of a "constitutional court."

Court System

China's judicial system is structured much like other civil law systems. Trials are conducted in an "inquisitorial" manner, before a panel of judges, who consult the appropriate codes, established by the central legislature, for applying the law to a particular set of facts, controversies, and accusations. Chinese judges have varying degrees of formal and informal legal training. Civil cases are handled in a similar way, when they are deemed to be sufficiently complicated or important to warrant formal proceedings. Otherwise, these matters generally are first referred to a Mediation Committee, which, despite its relative informality, plays a very prominent role within the overall judicial system of China.

More than 860,000 Mediation Committees serve China. The mediators who conduct these proceedings typically are respected elders of the community who do not necessarily have any legal or administrative experience and often are not even members of the Chinese Communist Party. They attempt to settle civil disputes through the previously described process of *jang I-tien*, trying to reconcile disputes, promote harmony, and find a solution that is best for all, including the community, as a whole. Nonetheless, their decisions can be appealed.

The first level of formal tribunals for China are the more than 3,000 Basic Level People's Courts. These are courts of original jurisdiction, except for appeals that come from Mediation Committees. These courts are divided into distinct divisions, in a manner consistent with civil law systems and their emphasis upon specialization. These divisions include the economic, enforcement (criminal), administrative, and specialty courts, the latter category often handling matters of a commercial, family, or policy nature.

Decisions reached by the Basic People's Courts can be appealed to one of China's 300 Middle Level People's Courts. These courts also have original jurisdiction for cases and controversies that are deemed to be particularly serious or consequential. The next tier consists of China's 29 Higher Level Courts, which are assigned, geographically, among China's provinces and autonomous republics. They are appellate courts that also may serve as courts of original jurisdiction for certain "high profile" cases, especially ones of a political nature.

Finally, the top tier is occupied by the Supreme People's Court. Although it is a single court, its 90 judges are divided according to the same divisions that categorize the overall judicial system, so it actually functions, in practice, as a *series* of final appellate tribunals. It will serve as a trial court only for very prominent state treason trials (as it did for the trial of the "Gang of Four" during the late 1970s), and it never considers constitutional challenges or any aspect of constitutional interpretation, although it will apply constitutional requirements in the same way as civil codes are administered within the judicial process.

The Future of Chinese Constitutionalism

The Chinese constitutional tradition is designed to be functional and malleable. Constitutional documents serve as tools in support of the broader goals of Chinese socialism and the socialist legal system that implements its policies. It also is a guide that brings together all people and institutions who must work with the law, so some version of this constitutional tradition will persist as long as the People's Republic of China continues to function.

A major shift in economic strategy may produce newly entrenched versions of this constitutional tradition. However, the ongoing basic structure and emphasis of the constitution, as a whole, most likely will persist. The relationship among people, state, and party that forms the core of the Chinese constitutional tradition should remain an enduring feature, as will the overall goal of achieving a communist community through the socialist phase of its development. But the value system expressed within the preamble could alter dramatically and, with it, the entire constitutional emphasis, depending upon the ongoing development of Chinese politics, economics, and society throughout the twenty-first century.

References

Jianfu Chen, *Chinese Law: Toward an Understanding of Chinese Law, Its Nature and Development.* The Hague, Kluwer Law International, 1999.

Ralph H. Folsom, John H. Minan, Lee Ann Otto, *Law and Politics in the People's Republic of China in a Nutshell.* St. Paul, West, 1992.

Ronald C. Keith and Zhiqiu Lin, *Law and Justice in China's New Marketplace.* New York, Palgrave, 2001.

Feng Li, *Constitutional Law in China.* Hong Kong, Sweet and Maxwell, 2000.

John Bryan Starr, *Understanding China: A Guide to China's Economy, History, and Political Structure.* New York, Hill and Wang, 1997.

Brian S. J. Weng, ed., *Studies on the Constitutional Law of the People's Republic of China.* New York, M. E. Sharpe, 1983.

CHAPTER 5

Canadian Constitutional Tradition

An interesting feature of the Canadian constitutional tradition is the fact that it includes both elements of an entrenched *and* an unentrenched constitutional system. The features of this sort of "partially entrenched" constitutionalism offer a fascinating exposition of legal and political ideas associated with public law, generally. The unique circumstances that created this constitutional tradition add to this sense of fascination and revelation.

Canada emerged from a colonial past, yet its independence was not achieved at one particular time. Its sovereignty was established in phases, and this fact contributes to its engaging constitutional development. Furthermore, dynamic and volatile aspects of its history and an equally diverse relationship with its southern neighbor, the United States, have been enormously influential in shaping that legal persona, including its self-conscious sense of legal values and the purposes of nationalism that constitutions frequently are designed to address and advance.

Partially Entrenched Constitutions

Two entrenched documents can be found at the core of the Canadian constitutional tradition. However, the unentrenched aspects of parliamentary government also are an integral and profound shaper of this constitutional development. They are products of constitutional conventions that are firmly ingrained and widely accepted. The Canadian version of these conventions has been largely inherited from its British imperial experience, rather than being self-generated. Meanwhile, the American example has served as an inspiration for the entrenchment of the more contentious compromises that were reached for the purpose of establishing political and legal sovereignty. The result is a mixed set of constitutional institutions, with the more firmly entrenched features emerging at a later period of this historically disparate process.

A more precise analysis of this concept of partial entrenchment will be achieved through separate examinations of the constitutional structures and themes of this Canadian tradition. This constitutional quality has affected developments in the initial attempt to impose, and the eventual structure of, an amending formula, the role of the Supreme Court, the rise of "executive federalism," and constitutional developments at the provincial level. The interplay of conventions (especially parliamentary ones) and entrenched constitutional documents (and the difficult process of entrenching them) is an often underappreciated aspect of Canadian constitutionalism, and its significance will be revealed through the evaluation of other constitutional themes.

Formal Constitutional Structure

The Canadian constitutional tradition includes two distinct documents: the Constitution Act of 1867 (entitled, prior to 1982, the British North America Act of 1867) and the Constitution Act of 1982. Additional parliamentary statutes (enacted both by the British, on behalf of Canada, and exclusively by Canada) are included as parts of the Canadian constitutional tradition (such as the formerly titled British North America Act of 1886), but they tend to have been incorporated into, or constituted transitional elements of, the two principal constitutional documents that merit most political attention. The first document was enacted by the British parliament, after having been drafted through the efforts of leading statesmen of four dominant British colonies of this region: Ontario, Quebec, Nova Scotia, New Brunswick. It was intended to provide a form of domestic self-rule that would extend limited sovereignty to a newly created federal country.

The Constitution Act of 1867 consists of 145 sections. The first part emphasizes the structure of Canadian government, while later sections tend to focus upon the nature of the federal system, including federal-provincial relations. It does not include a standard preface, although its royal proclamation of enactment serves as a functional preface that declares the guiding, unentrenched tenet that the Canadian government will be "similar in principle to that of the United Kingdom." Various sections contain considerable institutional detail.

The second principal constitutional document was created as the result of a late-twentieth century political compromise among the Canadian prime minister and nine of the ten provincial premiers. The Constitution Act of 1982 is divided into several parts. Part six describes the entrenchment formula that resulted in the adoption of this document and the formal entrenchment of the British North America Act. Part one consists of the Canadian Charter of Rights and Freedoms, including 33 sections devoted to individual civil and human rights and liberties, collective cultural rights (especially concerning language), and matters of sovereign authority at both the federal and provincial levels.

Those sections addressing the institutions of government do not explain the actual functions of a parliamentary system, the rule of law, or the principles of cabinet government. In fact, a literal explanation of these sections, from a formal-legal analysis of the Constitution Act of 1867, would indicate that the Queen of Canada, as head of state, technically runs the country as its chief executive and commander-in-chief, and that the Senate is truly more dominant than the House of Commons within the parliamentary scheme of legislative activity. The very existence of a prime minister is never mentioned. These indications are, of course, incorrect, but this knowledge depends upon an acceptance of convention as an unentrenched feature of this constitutional tradition.

Since the essential role of a parliamentary system and the principles of the rule of law are widely accepted by Canadian society, entrenchment of these constitutional features is deemed unnecessary. These principles have been explained within the chapter devoted to British constitutionalism, and they are inherited from that source. However, those sections addressing matters of federalism are based upon careful compromises which do require specification. These factors explain, in part, this diverse construction of the Canadian constitution and its institutions.

Principal Constitutional Themes

Canada's constitutional system is, as already stated, grounded upon a Westminster model of parliamentary government and the rules that guide this model, especially within a context of democratic sovereignty. It differs from its British antecedents in certain significant ways. Some of these distinctions have been inspired by the American model of constitutionalism, while other features are a product of more universal ideals of law derived from experiences of the twentieth and twenty-first centuries. Other influences, including the legal and constitutional legacy of France, and considerations of the norms and values of the aboriginal peoples of this continent, also have played a peripheral role in this development.

The most contentious and, arguably, most defining of these themes has been Canada's federal arrangement. Other specific themes include the emergence of a judicial "branch of government," the issue of competing national identities, the struggles surrounding bilingualism and multiculturalism, aboriginal rights and political representation, the protracted quest to achieve a workable constitutional amending formula, and the adoption of acceptable standards of constitutionally protected rights and liberties. These themes have made constitutional politics possibly the most volatile and dominant issue of Canadian society.

Parliament

The convention of parliamentary supremacy, described previously within chapter three of this book, was widely accepted as a constitutional principle when the British North America Act was proclaimed in 1867. The supremacy of parliamentary institutions at the provincial level (normally called legislative assemblies) also was an accepted principle, within their own defined spheres of sovereign authority. But a shift away from absolute parliamentary supremacy toward an ideal of popular sovereignty (as expressed through constitutional limits upon government during the twentieth century) culminated in the enactment of the Constitution Act of 1982.

These constitutional limits are somewhat reminiscent of the control that the British government maintained over Canada's foreign relations, trade, military policy, and a final authority (through Britain's Judicial Committee of the Privy Council) to review and interpret constitutional and other legal matters that arose under the British North America Act. Gradually, the Canadian parliament claimed, and exercised, increasing control over other areas of sovereign authority, until Great Britain officially recognized Canada's complete independence with the enactment, by the British parliament, of the Statute of Westminster of 1931—itself a British constitutional convention. But the Canadian parliament has never quite matched the level of sovereign authority over constitutional interpretation that its British counterpart has claimed.

Canada's parliament has engaged in an ongoing struggle with provincial legislatures concerning the division of federal-provincial sovereign authority. Furthermore, popular demands for constitutional limits upon parliamentary supremacy, especially in the form of entrenched rights and liberties, imposed a sense of constitutional limits, even prior to the enactment of the Charter of Rights and Freedoms. These influences prompted a greater opportunity for judicial control over the constitutional process, even under the British North America Act, and they contribute to other themes of Canadian constitutionalism.

Federalism

Originally, Canada consisted of the four provinces whose leaders negotiated the British North America Act. Gradually, additional British territories of this continent were divided into new provinces, while other established colonies joined the Canadian "confederation," until the number of provinces enjoying limited sovereignty rose to ten. The initial division of federal and provincial realms of sovereign authority was established by two sections of the British North America Act, and they remain of central importance to Canadian federalism as part of the Constitution Act of 1867. Section 91 describes the sovereign authority of the federal government, while section 92 essentially delimits the sovereign authority of provincial governments. Therefore, this constitutional tradition addresses both levels of federal power, rather than implying retained provincial powers through the express description of the confines of the central government.

Section 91 extends broad authority to the federal government over many domestic matters, in addition to those areas of external policy that gradually were surrendered to it by British imperial authority. In general, they can be described as "police powers" that conform to the liberal democratic image of a legitimate governmental mandate, received from the popular sovereign, to protect society from "harm." This authority extends to the administration of criminal law within Canada, in addition to the maintenance of armed forces and national law enforcement agencies. It has been expressed, broadly, within this section, through reference to the federal government responsibility for protecting and promoting the "peace, order, and good government of Canada," and this phrase has been cited in support of general claims of federal authority within this wide area. Furthermore, this section assigns a general responsibility to the federal government for all matters that are not "assigned exclusively to the legislatures of the provinces," which would seem to provide potentially expansive powers to the central level of sovereign authority within the federal system.

Section 92 establishes areas of provincial sovereignty, especially concerning municipal government, provincial safety, and judicial responsibility for matters pertaining to civil law. Provincial governments also have special responsibility for matters pertaining to "property and civil rights." Areas of specific provincial authority include education, commercial regulation, health services, and civil infrastructures of each province. The tone of this section seems to be relatively parochial, especially in comparison with the federal powers articulated within the previous section.

Canadian federalism generally has been more decentralized than its American counterpart. Despite the rather exclusive language used to describe the scope of provincial authority within the Constitution Act of 1867, the highest tribunal of appeal under the imperial system, the Judicial Committee of the Privy Council, issued a series of rulings (beginning during the latter part of the nineteenth century and later confirmed by the Supreme Court of Canada when it became the final court of appeal for the country) that limited the actual scope of federal government powers and placed many policy areas under the authority of the provincial governments, particularly under the "property and civil rights" clause of section 92. Although the federal government often countered this trend with its superior ability to raise revenues (especially in relation to the poorer provinces, such as the ones in the Maritime region), it could not match the dominance that its American federal counterpart could wield relative to its respective state governments.

This tendency was challenged by the process of the attempted unilateral patriation of the constitution in 1982. The provinces were able to retain their sovereign initiative, in this respect, through the successful negotiation (despite federal attempts to circumvent direct provincial participation within the process) of a constitutional amending formula that requires considerable concurrence from provincial governments. But an even more effective source of the relative strength of provincial power may have been accorded to this level of government by another clause emanating from section 92A.

Provinces maintain sovereign control over resources derived from within their borders. This fact guarantees a level of financial autonomy that often has made the provincial governments more resistant to a budgetary deference to federal policy preferences. Provincial governments that enjoy particularly good sources of resource-based revenue (such as oil in Alberta and hydroelectric power in Quebec) have been especially successful in this respect, while resource-poor provinces (especially in the Maritime region) often find themselves more dependent upon federal largesse and, thus, less resistant to federal authority and policy initiatives.

The provinces do not have their own entrenched constitutions, unlike their counterparts among the American states. This absence is explained largely by the fact that federal constitutional documents already determine provincial constitutional sovereignty. Section 93 of the Constitution Act of 1867 articulates "provincial constitutional law," especially in terms of institutional prerogatives. However, the exercise of discretion, in this respect, is possible, as an examination of Quebec's constitutional tradition, later within this chapter, should indicate.

Most of the struggle concerning federal-provincial authority and relations have been derived from matters of economic policy and the regional distribution of wealth within the country. The larger and more prosperous central Canadian provinces of Ontario and Quebec often have received greater attention and policy preference from the federal government, while the more "peripheral" provinces of Atlantic Canada, the Prairies, and the far West often have felt slighted or, even, excluded from federal efforts to promote national prosperity. The authority of provincial governments to initiate economic development has resulted in attempts to coordinate these efforts, in addition to occasional clashes among the competing regions, as well as clashes between the provincial and federal governments.

Alberta's desire to control its oil revenues, for example, has conflicted with federal efforts to control energy policy for the entire country, especially through the federal government's National Energy Policy of the 1970s.

Both positions rest upon constitutionally mandated spheres of sovereign authority that cannot be judicially reconciled. Much of this constitutional theme actually rests upon more practical struggles for political dominance among competing sovereign entities. The desire to define the constitutional process, itself (especially through the enactment and maintenance of the amending formula), has been the most conspicuous focus of this struggle, from a constitutional perspective. The failed attempt to alter this formula in a way that could achieve the concurrence of Quebec (which, in pursuit of its own claims to national identity and cultural control, was the only province to refuse to ratify the Constitution Act of 1982, though it remains binding upon Quebec) during the 1980s, culminating in the ultimate rejection of a comprehensive formula of constitutional reform known as the Meech Lake Accord, indicates the ongoing difficulties within this area and the relative strength of provincial governments, if only for the purpose of frustrating the process of constitutional change and entrenchment.

The theme of cultural identity and autonomy has been another important source of tension within this scheme of federalism. This issue will be addressed, later within this chapter, more specifically within the context of Quebec's constitutional development. However, as the only province with a majority French-speaking population, the desire to protect the inclusion of French as an official language of Canada and the desire of the Quebec government to protect and promote its unique culture, even at the perceived expense of certain absolute interpretations of certain civil liberties, has exacerbated the volatility of this constitutional theme. Other provinces, resentful of a perceived "special treatment" enjoyed by Quebec and desirous of enhancing their own sovereign authority, have interjected themselves into this conflict, including relatively recent attempts to promote the ethnic diversity of their own societies as an alternative to the traditional English-French dichotomy of Canadian politics and society.

Considerations of federalism have affected many other aspects of Canada. The evolving role of the judicial system (including the Supreme Court of Canada) has been prompted by these conflicts. The nature of all federal policy has been subject to, and affected by, these often intense pressures, both directly and indirectly. Most importantly, though, federalism and the interpretation of the federal-provincial relationship has become a constitutional struggle which generally is the first matter that any attempt at constitutional development or change must address for any chance of success to be realized.

Constitutional Entrenchment and Amendment

Canada had no formal method of constitutional entrenchment or amendment prior to 1982. Any constitutional change that needed to be made had to be submitted to the British parliament, since the British North America Act remained a statute that could be altered only by that body. Most of the Canadian constitutional changes involved procedural matters or institutional additions (such as the creation of the Supreme Court of Canada in 1878), and none of them substantively altered federal-provincial relations. Therefore, no real objections usually were raised within the Canadian political system when the Canadian parliament referred these proposed amendments to the British North America Act to the British parliament, even after Canada's full sovereignty was recognized officially in 1931.

Nonetheless, this situation was regarded as an affront to many Canadian politicians, scholars, and citizens. The desire of Prime Minister Pierre Elliot Trudeau to "repatriate" the Canadian constitution from Great Britain was, partly, an attempt to assuage Canadian national pride and identity. It also was necessary in order for him to entrench his proposed Canadian Charter of Rights and Freedoms. It would require an amending formula entirely under Canadian control.

Trudeau's attempt to achieve this result unilaterally, through a directive of the Canadian government to the British parliament, was opposed by the provincial governments, especially because they believed that the imposition of this Charter of Rights and Freedoms would have the same weakening effect upon provincial sovereignty that the "incorporation" of the Bill of Rights (through the application authority offered by the equal protection clause of the Fourteenth Amendment) eventually had upon American states under the United States Constitution. The Supreme Court of Canada ruled that the conventions of the unentrenched Canadian constitutional tradition *did* permit the federal parliament, *technically*, to assert its supremacy in this manner. However, the court also ruled that another convention was the substantive inclusion of provincial governments within any such process, especially since it would alter the constitutional character of the country. Trudeau acquiesced to the political pressure that resulted from this ruling and engaged in negotiations with the leaders of the provincial governments to patriate the Canadian constitution with the addition of an amending formula and a Charter of Rights and Freedoms.

The formula that was reached provides for constitutional amendments to be enacted when the federal government and at least seven of the ten provincial governments, representing at least half of the country's population, ratify such a proposal. Despite the refusal of Quebec's government to accept this proposal, the support of the remaining provinces was regarded as sufficient for justifying the adoption of this amending formula, the Charter, and the formal transferal of the British North America Act to complete Canadian control. It is articulated within part six of the Constitution Act of 1982. Attempts to amend it during the 1980s, as previously explained, were unsuccessful, underscoring the conventional difficulty of altering entrenched constitutional clauses, generally.

Bilingualism, Multiculturalism, and the "First Nations"

A key component of Canada's national identity has involved the issue of its original European heritage. The French colonists who founded New France during the early seventeenth century established a lasting presence, centered upon the region that is now the province of Quebec, with an additional, smaller presence in Acadia (now Nova Scotia and New Brunswick) and later migrations to small enclaves in the Prairie region, especially within the current province of Manitoba. Meanwhile, early English and Scottish exploration formed the impetus for colonization in other parts of North America. The eventual British victory over France during the French and Indian Wars of the middle of the eighteenth century resulted in the political dominance of the English-speaking population of the place that now is Canada. Yet the French population persisted, and its ongoing presence and continued adherence to its culture and language became a permanent feature of British North America and Canada.

The result has been the presence of two dominant linguistic groups within modern Canada, with an English-speaking majority within Canada as a whole, a French-speaking population dominating Quebec, a strong minority French-speaking population within New Brunswick, pockets of French-speaking (or "francophone") people elsewhere, the presence of other minority language groups, and the majority of the population consisting of English-speaking (or "anglophone") people. This fact has contributed to continuous cultural and political pressure and political conflict, including within the area of federalism.

One proffered solution had been the attempt to assimilate the francophone population. But, by the middle of the twentieth century, a more lasting solution was proposed. The Canadian parliament adopted the Official Languages Act of 1966, recognizing the equality of French and English as languages of the federal system. Meanwhile, Quebec's government continued to assert its leading role in preserving and promoting its own linguistic heritage, together with other cultural features of that province's historical roots. Agitation for separation from Canada has been a feature of Quebec politics throughout much of its history, even before union with Canada. But this agitation became so intense during the 1960s and 1970s that it seemed apparent that any constitutional change would need to accommodate Quebec's cultural, political, and linguistic desires.

However, that agenda was opposed by many people who felt that it weakened the principle of Canada as a united federal system. Other provinces and their leaders resented the "special treatment" they felt Quebec would receive under any sort of constitutional arrangement that addressed its concerns, while many Quebec leaders charged that mere constitutional change would not be sufficient for meeting the national aspirations of the people of Quebec. Many Canadian anglophones complained that Quebec might be empowered to deny language rights and, perhaps, even freedom of expression to Quebec's anglophone minority. Meanwhile, many Quebec leaders demanded a veto power for their government over any future constitutional change.

The constitutional compromise that led to the Canada Constitution Act of 1982 entrenched language rights for anglophones and francophones, including the right to have one's children educated in either of those languages. It also created an amending formula that made it necessary for at least one of Canada's two largest provinces (which include Quebec) to approve of any future amendments. While Quebec did not ratify these constitutional changes, it remains subject to them.

However, that arrangement did not end this controversy. Some provincial leaders outside Quebec used this issue as a means of expressing the concerns of ethnic minorities within their provinces who were anglophone but did not share a British heritage. Some critics charged that this interest in promoting multicultural rights seemed suspiciously sudden and may have been used more as an attempt to dilute the former emphasis upon a "bicultural" Canada than to promote a true sensitivity to a diverse ethnic Canadian heritage. Nonetheless, constitutional references to this heritage also were included with bilingual guarantees, and federal political institutions were created to address and promote this interest.

The indigenous peoples of Canada also demanded constitutional recognition. The activities of cultural and political organizations promoting this goal, particularly the Council of First Nations, have helped to spur many constitutional, and other social and political, reforms. Part two of the Constitution Act of 1982 enshrines many of these guarantees, including limited self-government, though not quite approaching the design of the American "reservation" system. The creation of a federal territory in the Arctic region around Hudson's Bay, called Nunavut, has made it possible to combine certain principles of tribal law with conventional Western legal and political practices and institutions of government. Section 25 of the Canadian Charter of Rights and Freedoms also advances this recognition as part of a larger commitment to a particular vision of a just society.

Canadian Charter of Rights and Freedoms

The cornerstone of Canada's constitutional reform in 1982 was the adoption of entrenched protections of rights and liberties. The Canadian Charter of Rights and Freedoms, which is part one of the Constitution Act of 1982, was a product of several different influences. Its presence has reshaped not only the Canadian constitutional tradition, but all of Canadian society and politics.

The Charter (as it is popularly known) received some of its inspiration from the American Bill of Rights. But that eighteenth century document's reach tended to reside within those clauses of the Canadian Charter (especially sections 7-14) that provide due process guarantees. Another source of inspiration may come from France, in the form of the Declaration of the Rights of Man and Citizen, especially the enshrinement of certain democratic rights and liberties within sections 3-5. Much of the tone of this document and its interpretation seems to be derived from the post-World War II theme of human rights and liberties, especially in terms of the Charter's treatment of mobility rights in section 6 and equality rights in section 15. Furthermore, both the scope and application of these guarantees are more expansive than traditional liberal concepts of civil rights and liberties, such as the applicability of equality rights to "every person," rather than merely "every citizen," which the Canadian courts have interpreted in that way. The attention to gender equality, as espoused in section 28, also suggests this twentieth-century influence.

Much of the Charter, though, reflects uniquely Canadian considerations. Section one's descriptions of the limitations upon these rights and freedoms in a manner consistent with the values of a "free and democratic society" suggest a more explicit legislative and popular role within this interpretive process than the American tradition has assumed. Section 25, with its guarantee of protections for indigenous peoples within Canada, and section 27, promoting multicultural policies and legislation, reflect those particular concerns, as previously noted.

But the most strikingly distinctive feature of the Charter may be found within section 33, more commonly known as the "notwithstanding clause." It was the result of a political compromise that would retain a limited principle of parliamentary supremacy and would safeguard certain provincial controls over policy matters that affect rights and liberties. Provincial leaders were particularly concerned that the Charter could be used as an instrument for aggrandizing federal power by imposing a federally determined "national standard" of rights and liberties (much like the American federal experience) that could restrict policies and legislation, accused of violating a particular right or liberty, that a provincial government might interpret differently. It applies to section two (enumerating certain "fundamental freedoms," including expression, religion, conscience, assembly, and association) and sections 7–15, which protect due process and equality rights. Section 33 declares that, "notwithstanding" the sovereign supremacy otherwise imposed by the Charter (especially in accordance with judicial interpretation), the federal parliament or a provincial legislature may override the legislative restrictions imposed by these sections for a period of five years, when a formal declaration of that intent is made.

Many critics believed section 33 could nullify the Charter in these areas. But the invocation of this override provision has been so sparse, and the political pressure not to invoke it has been so generally strong, throughout the country (except regarding expression provisions affecting the attempt to promote the French language within Quebec), that it has not undermined the authority of the Charter concerning these targeted rights and liberties. Nonetheless, the mere presence of the section 33 indicates the tension that has marked the conflicting values that underlie the Canadian constitutional tradition, especially between desires to preserve democratic sovereign supremacy and the goal of promoting liberal, and even more universal, standards of rights and liberties.

The Charter also protects English and French language rights, which protection was regarded by many Canadians as its most significant accomplishment. It has deeply transformed Canadian constitutionalism. But its true significance may be the way it has shaped the debate and self-awareness concerning the essential beliefs and values of the Canadian nation.

Political Culture

The Canadian constitutional tradition clearly identifies a liberal democratic society and sovereign. But the precise expression of those liberal democratic values is subject to debate. Many observers have contrasted the Canadian ideological heritage with the relatively libertarian image of the United States, while other observers have noted a diverse source of philosophical influences, including the legacy of the country's diverse colonial and immigrant past.

Some scholars have contended that Canada is far more collectively oriented than the seemingly individualistic United States. This alleged Canadian tendency to prefer a collective approach to social arrangements and policy choices has been attributed to the "Tory" heritage of Canada's British antecedents (bolstered by the migration of British Loyalists from the American colonies, after the conclusion of the American Revolution) and the semi-feudal legacy of the French colonial experience. It has been contended that this cultural legacy has provided, among other noted results, a greater deference to authority, respect for political and legal institutions, and a greater receptivity for social democratic policies and, even, socialist ideas. These arguments have contributed to a popular assertion of a strongly communitarian liberal democratic heritage that promotes concepts such as "group rights" and a rejection of the American "melting pot" image of ethnic absorption in favor of a Canadian multicultural "mosaic."

A greater emphasis upon democratic community over liberal rights has been an asserted result of this ideological heritage. It is supposedly reflected, constitutionally, within the "notwithstanding clause" of the Charter and its apparent deference to the democratic community, the constitutional promotion of equality and affirmative action programs, and, even, Quebec's emphasis upon its own preservation of a "national" cultural identity. Resistance to the adoption of the Charter often was expressed in terms of these communitarian values, since it potentially threatened to suppress the sovereign will of the political community in favor of individual rights and liberties and, possibly, encouraged the development of attitudes of individualism that would alienate citizens from each other as they sought to withdraw into their separate autonomous spheres, enhanced by a strong promotion of individual rights and liberties.

This interpretation of liberal democracy has been traced to the ideas of such prominent political philosophers as Jean-Jacques Rousseau. Communitarianism expresses a concern that liberal property rights actually represent a tool for a powerful minority of individual members of a community to deny that collective entity access to the resources they otherwise can provide for the greater good of the whole. It also stresses the notion that human autonomy is best achieved through associations of people who share a collective goal of fulfillment and development, so group identity becomes as important as individual identity.

But other observers have noted that Canadian liberal democratic values are more libertarian than often admitted. The popularity of the Charter has been a testament to a Canadian affinity for individual rights and liberties, even when couched in somewhat less libertarian language than its American counterpart. Also, interpretations of the Charter and other constitutional principles by the courts have tended to advance a pattern of adjudication that often seems similar (though not identical) to the American tradition.

Part of this preoccupation may stem from the needs of Canadian nationalism. Much of that theme has revolved around identifying a basis for a Canadian national identity that is truly distinct from the nationalism expressed by Canada's neighbor. The popular perception of American "rugged individualism" and the less interventionist nature of American social policy may give rise to the desire for a Canadian national self-identification that is more perceptibly compassionate, mutually supportive, and cohesive. Also, a response to the challenges of Quebec nationalism may spur a desire to identify a distinct sense of a Canadian community, rather than simply defining Canada in terms of a geographical state whose members share certain widespread liberal democratic assumptions.

This search for Canada's cultural identity has been an extremely strong motivating factor in the country's constitutional development. It influenced the move toward patriation, debates over federalism, the adoption of the Charter, and ongoing discussions regarding potential future constitutional changes. It continues to be reflected through the attempt to discern a uniquely Canadian ideological heritage within this liberal democratic constitutional tradition, and it consciously influences the judicial opinions that emanate from the ongoing process of constitutional interpretation and adjudication within the Canadian system.

Legal Practice and Constitutional Adjudication

Most of the Canadian legal system is a product of English antecedents. Therefore, the Canadian system is grounded predominantly upon a common law structure. Legal practitioners attend law school, but they are certified to practice law through the professional bar exam process. Judges are appointed on the basis of their experience and practical knowledge of law (although other political factors may influence those appointments), while legal principles are developed and preserved through the evolutionary process of *stare decisis*. Approaches to interpreting legal and constitutional precedent and general constitutional adjudication often reflect the American experience, in this respect, including references to "originalist" and "activist" options of interpreting Canadian constitutional norms and values.

Quebec's civil law system requires legal practitioners who have achieved certification through a formal university process. However, these lawyers generally must operate also within a common law context, so they, too, need to be trained in the concepts and practices of this system and be certified professionally in a similar manner. Three of nine seats on the Supreme Court of Canada are reserved for Quebec jurists, especially for the purpose of ensuring adequate appreciation of those features of a civil law system that are preserved within that province.

Canadian jurists often express awareness of the effect that their rulings have over public policy, although they strive to maintain a sense of political neutrality that is considered necessary to the independence and dignity of the judiciary. The notion of constitutional supremacy is a relatively recent one within Canada, particularly since the constitutional patriation of 1982. Therefore, a certain care is evident concerning the restrictions upon tradition parliamentary sovereignty that the actions of judges, especially within the Supreme Court of Canada, pose. Nonetheless, these constitutional rulings may not be challenged legislatively, unless they fall under the category of rights and liberties subject to override through section 33 of the Charter or unless the entrenchment process is initiated for changing the constitution.

Court System

Canada has a unified judicial system. Crown courts generally serve as tribunals of original jurisdiction and are distributed, along with appellate courts, upon a geographical basis. They follow the precepts of a typical common law system, including the accusatorial nature of proceedings, the division of trial responsibilities between judges and juries, and the competence of courts to deal with all categories of law and legal dispute. The Supreme Court of Canada, which was created by a parliamentary statute in 1878, initially did not have final interpretive authority over Canadian law. Appeals could be made to Judicial Committee of the Privy Council, in Britain, and decisions had to defer to the increasingly sovereign authority of parliament. Now, though, the Supreme Court of Canada has had its constitutional role affirmed, encouraging many Canadians to regard it as a "branch" of government in the same manner as its American counterpart, and it has confirmed its authority to exercise that role.

Provincial governments maintain their own court systems that have jurisdiction over matters falling under their constitutional authority. These courts largely are concerned with civil matters, since the federal government maintains responsibility for the criminal code. Some of these systems, especially within Quebec, may be somewhat diverse in their structure, but the unifying principle of final appellate authority is maintained, including the option of recourse to the Supreme Court as a final court of appeal over all legal and constitutional matters.

The Quebec "Constitution"

The constitutional law, structure, and sovereign authority of the provinces are entrenched within the Constitution Act of 1867, with modifications and clarifications provided within the Constitution Act of 1982. Therefore, provinces do not have separate constitutional documents in the manner of American states. However, despite this formal absence, it remains possible to articulate a concept of distinct provincial constitutional traditions through recourse to alternative modes of political and legal analysis.

Quebec offers an excellent example of this approach. The sense of a separate national identity and its unique cultural and political history has prompted the development of legal institutions that can be used to define a distinct sense of a Quebec constitutional tradition. Identification of this Quebec constitutional tradition depends upon a willingness to apply methods of evaluation that transcend the simple confines of formal-legalism and the preoccupation with entrenched constitutional documents as the only "legitimate" ones.

Quebec arguably has constitutional "conventions." The two most important examples stem from legislation addressing two themes of overriding importance to Quebec society. Although they are mere statutes, their political effect is so significant that rescinding them seems practically unthinkable. They are regarded as defining features of Quebec's social, cultural, and national identity. The first statute is the Quebec Charter of Human Rights, which duplicates many of the rights and liberties protected by the Canadian Charter of Rights and Freedoms, though from a uniquely Quebec perspective, especially as tied to a French-speaking lexicon and "continental" conception of rights and liberties that may be regarded as being oriented more toward human rights, rather than civil rights. One example is the "good Samaritan" clause of this document, which requires persons to assist other persons in immediate distress, while protecting them from civil liability if their actions should prove, ultimately and unintentionally, harmful.

The second of these conventions is the Charter of the French Language, which seeks to establish French as the only official language within the province as a means of promoting it and protecting it from being smothered by the rest of Canada and, potentially, the growing presence and affluence of the province's own anglophone community. Language is considered central to Quebec's national identity, so its overwhelming constitutional significance is apparent. This "charter" has been modified in response to federal judicial rulings that its standards violate the Canadian Charter of Rights and Freedoms. It additionally has been shielded from suits based upon alleged violations of section two of the Charter through the

Quebec government's formal invocation of the "notwithstanding clause." Yet, despite modifications, the Charter of the French Language remains a defining convention of this Quebec constitutional tradition. Again, it is merely a statute, yet its effect is the same as a constitutional convention within an unentrenched system.

Quebec has a "mixed" legal system, like Scotland. The criminal law is dominated by the federal government, so it adheres to the rules and practices of the common law system. But civil law matters fall generally under provincial authority, and these legal principles are defined through Quebec's civil code. Legal practitioners within Quebec need to be trained in both systems of law, and its presence also imposes a practical requirement upon federal appellate courts to be aware of this distinction, especially at the Supreme Court level.

Quebec's constitutional system adheres to a Westminster model of parliamentary government, as inherited from the British colonial experience. It also has borrowed certain norms from its French heritage, especially in terms of its civil code (modeled upon the *Code Napoléon*) and a general judicial interpretation of rights and liberties. Despite the charges of some critics, it clearly reflects a liberal democratic legacy that also seeks to promote its identity as a province that is *not* like the others, since it also perceives itself as the institutional expression of a special national identity for the francophones of this part of North America.

The Future of Canadian Constitutionalism

Many issues have remained unresolved regarding Canadian constitutional development. The desire to gain a full commitment to this tradition from Quebec has spurred much of this ongoing concern. Furthermore, the desires of other provinces and groups within Canada have continued agitation for constitutional change, including desires to reform the amending formula and provide additional recognition to distinct interests, such as native peoples.

But the entrenchment process makes any significant constitutional change extremely difficult to achieve. Therefore, the role of the courts in adjusting and further defining the Canadian constitutional tradition will continue to be extremely crucial to this process. Future constitutional development will require a great deal of political consensus and compromise. Otherwise, Canadian constitutionalism can become a source of ongoing social and political frustration, in addition to its more positive role as a support to Canadian national identity.

References

Louis Baudouin, *Le Droit civil de la province de Québec*. Montréal, Wilson et Lafleur, 1953.
David M. Beatty, *Constitutional Law in Theory and Practice*. Toronto, University of Toronto Press, 1995.
Henri Brun and Guy Tremblay, *Droit constitutionel*. Cowansville, QC, Editions Y. Blais, 1982.
Alan C. Cairns, *Charter versus Federalism: The Dilemmas of Constitutional Reform*. Montréal and Kingston, ON, McGill-Queen's University Press, 1992.
David Andrew Heard, *Canadian Constitutional Conventions: The Marriage of Law and Politics*. Toronto, Oxford University Press, 1991.
Peter W. Hogg, *Constitutional Law of Canada*. Toronto, Carswell, 1997.
Michael Mandel, *The Charter of Rights and the Legalization of Politics in Canada*. Toronto, Thompson, 1994.
F. L. Morton and Rainer Knopff, *The Charter Revolution and the Court Party*. Peterborough, ON, Broadview, 2000.
Christopher P. Manfredi, *Judicial Power and the Charter: Canada and the Paradox of Liberal Constitutionalism*. Norman, University of Oklahoma Press, 1993.

CHAPTER 6
Indian Constitutional Tradition

India is a vast and complex subcontinent that has struggled, throughout its extremely long history, to achieve a sense of unity. The formal 1947 declaration of independence of this federal union (the term "union" is used to refer to the Indian central government) was the culmination of centuries of struggle. It also has entailed the accommodation of varied cultural influences, legal concepts, and national identities, resulting in a remarkably ambitious constitutional project.

The Indian constitutional tradition offers another example of the reconciliation of Eastern and Western legal norms. The legacy of the British Empire has been particularly felt, here, but it has provided, largely, a structural model for shaping the substantive content of an ancient civilization and its efforts to become a modern state. The vast size and diversity of India, and its economic struggles as a developing country, have made that process difficult, especially in terms of the desire to reflect the sovereign will of an equally diverse people. India's constitutional tradition has been centered upon that formidable challenge.

Formal Constitutional Structure

India has the longest entrenched constitution in the world. It consists of a relatively brief preamble and 22 parts, divided into 395 articles. It is extraordinarily detailed for a contemporary constitution, reflecting the difficult compromises that were necessary for creating this constitutional system. Nonetheless, it has proved durable but, occasionally, somewhat unwieldy in operation.

Part one describes the Indian union, itself, while parts two and three address, respectively, requirements of citizenship and the fundamental rights and liberties enjoyed by those citizens. Parts four and four (a) impose general policy requirements upon the union government, while part five describes the institutions and authority of the union government, including its parliamentary system. Parts six through eleven address various aspects of the federal system and its various levels of sovereign government, including the states, territories, and local governmental entities. Various parts address Indian diversity, including part three (addressin rights and liberties), part four (a) and its description of social duties, and part 17, which is concerned with the constitutionally enshrined official language policy.

Other parts of the constitution address administrative and technical matters. Part 22 is particularly important, for it describes the amending formula (requiring a two-thirds approval of both parliamentary houses for adopting any constitutional change) that provides the basis for this constitutional entrenchment. The language of this constitution is legally detailed, and it has been subject to considerable amendment, much of it concerned with clarification and adjustment and some of it addressing more substantive matters, such as the amending of part 18, providing for "emergency provisions," that occurred during the late 1970s.

This constitution describes a government that follows, in many respects, the conventional norms of the Westminster model that inspired it, especially as explained within chapter three of this book. The lower house of India's parliament, the *Lok Sabha* (House of the People), has 545 deputies. This chamber's membership is based upon the democratic principle of representation by population, except for two seats set aside for appointed representatives of the Anglo-Indian community. Like most parliamentary systems, this lower house is dominant, especially in terms of financial policy and, most importantly, determining the government executive. The upper house, called the *Rajya Sabha* (Council of States), is composed of members determined through elections within each state and territory. This upper house is directed toward a representation of the federal principle within India, much like the United States Senate. In addition to its 250 elected members, twelve members are appointed by the president of India upon the basis of their perceived "special knowledge" or expertise—an arrangement not unlike the "life peers" appointed to the British House of Lords, generally in recognition of their special talents and accomplishments.

The prime minister is a member of the lower house who leads (typically for a conventional parliamentary system) the dominant political party of the *Lok Sabha*. The constitution does not express this arrangement; part five formally invests all executive authority within the president, who is elected independently of parliament. However, article 74 does refer to the assistance of the Council of Ministers, led by the prime minister, but it gives no formal indication of any considerations the president should take in making the appointment of these ministers. In fact, this arrangement is an example of the partially entrenched constitutional directives of parliamentary government, as described in reference to the Canadian constitutional tradition within chapter five of this book. It is understood that the prime minister is the leader of the party that dominates or outright controls the lower house of the Indian parliament, and the members of the

Council of Ministers are chosen from other leading figures of that same political party. The president, as head of state, is elected, directly, by the people.

The guarantee of institutional independence for India's Supreme Court is described within chapter four of part five of India's constitution, and that provision is reflective of a conventional Westminster-style parliamentary system. But this court has claimed and assumed appellate authority regarding challenges arising under constitutional law, even though the formal constitution is vague or silent on this matter. Both this action and the express language of India's constitution on this controversy are reminiscent of the controversy that initially surrounded the authority of the American judicial branch.

The Indian constitution is a single, entrenched document that can be altered only with the explicit allowance of two-thirds of both houses of the Indian parliament, as stipulated within part 22 of this constitution. Its great length and detail is a product of the enormous political conflict surrounding its drafting and enactment, reflecting the careful compromises required to affect it. This tumultuous political and social context becomes increasingly apparent, once various aspects of this Indian constitutional tradition are examined more closely.

Principal Constitutional Themes

The quest for political and social unity has been the most important goal of the Indian constitutional tradition. The Indian subcontinent is divided among three sovereign states, including Pakistan and Bangladesh, and India is the largest and most diverse of them. India's constitutional tradition has been tasked with the providing sovereign expression for this diverse and, often, volatile population. India encompasses at least five major religions, nineteen prominent linguistic groups, and dozens of ethnic and national groups, with regional, economic, and geographical differences added. These economic differences are linked to the poverty that has plagued India and affected much of its political development.

Part of the constitutional strategy for encouraging unity from this diversity has been the promotion of democratic institutions that require cooperation and advance the political legitimacy of the Indian state. Another constitutional strategy has been the attempt to institute a single official language, chosen from the most dominant religious, ethnic, and linguistic group of the country. This attempt to employ constitutional institutions for the advancement of sovereign unity is not unique to India (Canada's constitutional legacy is tied to a similar goal), but it seems particularly daunting, within this cultural and political context, for India's territorial unity has been a relatively recent phenomenon.

The establishment of a federal system also has been a prominent constitutional theme, linked to this overall goal. The detailed descriptions of the institutions and relationships of the union, state, and local levels of government within the constitution and through its added schedules is a testament to the careful consideration given to this theme. The fact that this relationship is specified within the union's constitutional document also emphasizes the overriding importance of unity and the reconciliation of considerable differences among the numerous parts of this country.

The independent judiciary has offered an additional constitutional strategy for promoting this goal. The desire to create a unified legal system and culture is reminiscent of the origins of the common law heritage (which is basis of India's legal system) and *its* somewhat similar (though much more modest, in terms of the actual diversity that it sought to overcome) attempt to achieve a similar result. It has been, arguably, an effective institution for promoting the political and social aspirations (and, with them, perhaps, a sense of potential political unity) among minority groups that feel underrepresented or, even, unrepresented within the legislative process established by this same constitutional system.

Nonetheless, the ability to forge a single polity from such a diverse culture remains the Indian constitutional tradition's most ambitious task. Secessionist conflict in areas such as Jammu and Kashmir, exacerbated by regional tensions between Pakistan and India that date back to the partition of the subcontinent, demonstrate the extreme difficulty of achieving this goal. The British imperial legacy that enforced unity upon this subcontinent may have provided institutional forms for providing a structure of unity. But the very real divisions within India (including ongoing religious conflict, especially between Hindus and Moslems, and also including Sikh militancy) continue to plague this constitutional quest.

Diversity

Part 17 of the Indian constitution, as previously explained, offers an insight into the constitutional response to the tensions inherent within India's social, religious, and cultural diversity. However, it is not the only constitutional response to this theme. Concerted efforts at political and legal secularization and the promotion of "universal" norms of rights and liberties also have been employed as part of this constitutional effort. However, the informal, though powerful, effect of a practical implementation of these institutions that continue to take these cultural distinctions into account undermines this ambitious aspiration.

Caste distinctions (a concept explained within the introductory chapter of this book), though abolished by article 15 of the Indian constitution, are an excellent example of this difficulty. The formal protection of equality by the government provides no guarantee of the removal of caste-based social distinctions and stigmas. In fact, the strength of social convention is demonstrated with particular effect by the persistence of informal caste discrimination. The actual workings of the legal and political systems, especially at the local level, also undermine this centralized constitutional goal.

One aspect of this problem is the continued, practical dominance of members of upper castes within the political, social, economic, and legal institutions of India. Despite constitutional requirements to include representatives of all scheduled castes within the political system, underrepresentation and a general political and economic deference to members of the upper castes (especially the *brahmin* and *kshattriya* castes) remain prominent features of India. Local governance is affected particularly strongly by this pattern of social distinction, including the composition of the *panchayat*, which will be addressed later within this chapter.

Constitutional guarantees of religious freedom and equal treatment often experience similar obstacles. Conflicts throughout India's history between its two most prominent religions, Hinduism and Islam (also resulting in the partition of India and Pakistan when Great Britain relinquished its imperial rule in 1947), highlight that general difficulty. Other tensions involving diverse religious groups (including the Sikhs) also are notable. But the most difficult obstacle to this constitutional goal of religious equality may occur within the legal effort to banish harmful and discriminatory practices *within* religious traditions. Failures to enforce constitutional guarantees regarding the freedom to marry and the abolition of dowries constitute one such difficulty. Discrimination against the untouchables may be constitutionally prohibited, but its enforcement is not so easily achieved. These problems are indicative of the conflicting forces within India's political culture and its relationship to Indian constitutionalism.

Despite the constitutional designation of Hindi as the official union government language for the country, linguistic differences continue to undermine unity. The commission designated by the Indian constitution for designating recognized languages finally settled upon eighteen choices, with an additional constitutionally designated status for English. This list does not include dozens of other languages spoken by smaller groups within the country. These differing linguistic affiliations affect different states and the development of regional political parties. Furthermore, while Hindi claims the largest number of Indian people who speak it as a first language (nearly one-third of the country's population), it is concentrated mainly in the less prosperous northern part of the country, thus often exacerbating economic divisions between the northern and southern populations of India. English often serves as a convenient "neutral" language of "outside" origin, especially since it often is spoken by governmental administrators and other political elites.

Constitutional enactments cannot, themselves, enforce even laudable goals. A diverse popular sovereign often can find the articulation of a single constitutional vision to be a daunting task. However, India's constitutional tradition has persisted in pursuing this ideal of accommodating the tremendous diversity of the country. Despite practical, cultural, and political hindrances, the formal constitutional foundation for this continued development remains firm.

Federal System

Part of the constitutional strategy for advancing a united India is the federal scheme. The fact that the sovereign powers of the state and local government are articulated and enumerated within the union constitution is indicative of the nature of this particular federal system. The Indian constitutional tradition describes an attempt at practical decentralization of political administration with a simultaneous attempt to enhance ultimate control at the center of the political system.

Institutionally, the state governments parallel the structure of the union government. Governors serve as heads of state, while chief ministers are the effective executive authority, and their power rests upon control of the state legislature. One exception to this pattern that reflects the union government's basic structure is the fact that most of these state legislatures are unicameral. The state-level lower house, called the Legislative Assembly, is complemented by a weaker upper house, called the Legislative Council, within only five states. Indian states do not have their own entrenched constitutions (with the unusual exception, for specific political regions, of Kashmir, due partly to its ethnic and religious challenges and partly to its disputed status regarding the claims of Pakistan), and the fact that their constitutional status is described exclusively within the union constitution is a significant reflection of other aspects of this federal system.

The judicial system retains features of a unitary structure, especially as a single hierarchy that integrates both state and federal legal systems. Many bureaucratic agencies also are centrally controlled, so certain policies relevant to state authority are administered by union civil servants. Furthermore, the union government can impose its authority upon the state governments beyond the powers expressly given to it under the seventh schedule's "union list" of powers (addressing peace and security, control over policies of general economic prosperity, national unity, legal unity, and other issues of typically national scope), particularly under the emergency powers but, also, under special provisions provided by articles 249, 256, 257, and 365. The provision of article 249 is especially telling, for it empowers parliament, if authorized by its upper house, to impose specific action upon state governments within areas that are expressly reserved to sovereign state authority by the "state list" of the constitution's seventh schedule (focusing upon internal security and economic concern) should they include problems and policies that affect the entire country, uniformly.

The union government also has wide discretion over the distribution of revenue, which gives it a considerable advantage, especially through the powers specified under the list of "concurrent powers" (including both safety and economic areas) exercised by both levels of sovereign authority. The advantages at the political center can be so great that they may seem to undermine the federal principle. But the most important purpose of Indian federalism may lie in the parallel theme of promoting national unity by recognizing diversity. The association of citizens with specific regions and areas often corresponds, within India, to identification with ethnicity, language, and, even, religion. Also, a country as geographically and demographically vast as India cannot be administered as effectively as a unitary state as it can through federal institutions. Therefore, a measure of decentralized administration is needed, despite the influence of other, centralizing tendencies within the Indian constitutional tradition.

Local Government

The strategy of a decentralized response to the practical lives of Indian citizens is underscored through the constitutional provisions for local government. Most of India's people spend their lives within a few miles of the villages of their birth, and this fact makes the more than 850,000 villages of India crucial to the country's political and legal experience. Urban municipal governments also receive constitutional sanction, but the overwhelming significance of constitutional government at the village level persists as a particularly important theme.

India is administratively divided into 476 districts. Each district is administered by an official called the "collector," which is a post inherited from the system of the former British raj. Although the current office does not exercise power as pervasively as its British antecedent, it is still the most dominant civil service presence for the vast majority of Indians. Districts are divided into *taluqs*, consisting of a few hundred villages, each, and administered by an administrator called the *taluqdar*. The government is represented at the village level by the *patwari*, whose primary responsibility is general accounting and land records. These local officials provide the connection between the typical citizen of India and the government, and the fact that they are representatives of the union government further enhances the centralist tendencies within Indian federalism.

Part nine of India's constitution enacts and describes the primary democratic councils of the local level, known as the *panchayats*. These councils also are inspired by a previous political institution that predated the arrival of the British. They had lost their significance during the period of British rule, but they had become a symbol of democratic idealism during the movement for Indian independence, so their constitutional status was not unexpected.

The exact form and composition of this level of village council government has been subject to considerable modification throughout India's constitutional history. Many of these alterations have been spurred by desires to introduce greater decentralization into this aspect of Indian government. However, the correspondingly strong desire to provide a firm link between the village and the central government and to promote union principles of diversity and equality also has been a strong factor within this constitutional development. Despite these attempts, the *panchayats* continue to be dominated, informally, by local elites, including members of the dominant Hindu castes, thus undermining part of the constitutional purpose for emphasizing this level of Indian government.

Large urban centers also have constitutionally designated governments. They are responsible for the mundane features of civic life normally associated with municipal government while, also, providing a similar link to the union government and its centralizing control of India's political, economic, legal, and social existence. It is part of the overall constitutional theme of local government that continues to be an essential feature of this enormous and extremely diverse polity.

Emergency Powers

Arguably, the most controversial aspect of the Indian constitutional tradition has occurred in connection with part 18 and its provision for "emergency powers." In one sense, this provision is not inconsistent with a conventional liberal democratic constitutional order. Many such constitutional traditions allow for the delegation of extraordinary executive authority and a suspension of normal governmental (especially legislative) oversight and civil rights and liberties during times of crisis—typically, military attack or insurrection justifies that sort of response. Those provisions often are unentrenched or implied, such as can be surmised from an interpretation of the United States Constitution. India's constitution expressly provides for this political situation.

Invocation of part 18 of the Indian constitution, in 1975, tested the assumptions associated with these emergency powers. Prime Minister Indira Gandhi advised the president to declare a state of emergency in response to severe economic unrest, militant union activities, widespread protests, and violent clashes, in addition to her own precarious political situation, resulting from a judicial finding of the violation of election laws regarding her own parliamentary seat. She observed formal constitutional requirements regarding this imposition of emergency powers, including submitting it to the approval of parliament (absent most of the members of the opposition parties, who were either arrested or abstained from the session in protest) within a few days of the declaration.

This move was widely criticized, although Gandhi insisted that her actions were necessary for preserving Indian democracy, which allegedly was threatened by widespread economic and political turmoil and undermined by "extremist" groups, including certain political parties. Tens of thousands of persons were arrested (without being charged or receiving a trial), the powers of the courts were severely curtailed, the police were granted sweeping powers, press censorship was imposed, and rights and liberties were suspended. During this period, lasting until 1977, the Indian constitution was amended to support future executive prerogatives, once the state of emergency was lifted, although India's Supreme Court later would reverse many of these changes. Eventually, the democratic process was restored, Gandhi's Congress Party was defeated in a general election, and Gandhi, herself, was convicted of criminal charges and briefly incarcerated, although she later would return to power, democratically.[1]

Many critics have been disturbed by this application of constitutional powers which seemed to undermine the same sovereign will it was designed to protect. A special commission of inquiry assessed the results and consequences of this episode, expressing concerns and making recommendations regarding the actual

---

1. A good summary of this constitutional episode can be found in Robert L. Hardgrave, Jr. and Stanley A. Kochanek, *India: Government and Politics in a Developing Nation* (Fort Worth: Harcourt, Brace, Jovanovich, 1993), pp. 241-252.

and potential abuses regarding these emergency powers. Ultimately, part 18 of the Indian constitution was retained, but the scrutiny of India's people, political parties, and judicial system may prove to be more vigilant concerning any future implementation of its provisions.

Political Culture

India's diversity is reflected within the often-conflicting beliefs and values that underlie this constitutional tradition. The formal constitutional structure resonates with an obvious liberal democratic influence. However, in practice, Indian law and constitutionalism unite this Western heritage with a strong, though not always readily evident, Eastern philosophical legacy.

The legal and political elites who dominate India's central government often are educated according to Western (especially British) standards. The framers of India's constitution clearly were subject to this ideological inclination. They imposed upon India both a Westminster model of parliamentary government and a judiciary that could exercise separate constitutional authority, like the American model of constitutional government. This influence is most evident at the federal level, but it permeates Indian constitutional government.

However, the constitutional experience of most Indians has been shaped by traditional sources of political culture, including the profound and pervasive presence of Hinduism. The essential ideals and principles of this ancient and revered religious and philosophical tradition have been assessed within the introductory chapter of this book. The implementation of policies at the local level, or the interpretation of laws within local jurisdictions, often reveals that influence. Isolated examples occasionally receive attention, in this respect, such as the mediation of sentences for crimes that allegedly were committed in defense of religious principles. These instances often involve matters of both family and criminal law, including altercations arising from marriages that cross caste boundaries or affect otherwise unconstitutional dowries. Furthermore, constitutional mandates concerning such matters as the abolition of legal and political distinctions concerning the class of "untouchables" (who lack caste status and are subject to stigma and grave disadvantages) may not be rigorously enforced or the interpretation of supporting legislation may be influenced by sentiment in favor of traditional discrimination against members of this group.

Islam also has shaped the practical workings of India's constitutional and legal systems. Private affairs within predominantly Moslem communities may be handled, informally, according to the principles of *Shari'a*, as expounded within the introductory chapter of this book. The roles of Islamic clerics and legal scholars often are as important to the political and legal processes of these areas of India as the country's constitution and the laws mandated by it. These practices often serve as a source of self-separation, not only for the Moslem community, but for all cultural and religious groups that prefer their own beliefs, values, and customs to the liberal democratic norms that the Indian constitution formally promotes. This process of separating into distinct communities (often called "communalism") threatens the ultimate constitutional goal of sovereign unity even more effectively than any actual or potential abuse of constitutionally sanctioned emergency powers.

The effects of communalism occur especially, but not exclusively, among the Hindu and Moslem communities. They also are found among other groups, most notably the Sikh community of the Punjab region, many of whom seek political separation from the rest of India. This problem underscores the broader difficulty of the relationship between the Indian constitutional tradition and its political culture, for it is actually based upon a myriad of coexisting and competing religious, philosophical, and ideological norms. Liberal democratic legal and political principles may be used as a catalyst for this constitutional tradition and its goals, but its effect, particularly beyond the political center, often can be frustrated when put into practice.

Attempts to enact sweeping social and economic reforms within India often have proved slow and frustrating. India's economic development suffers from problems that it shares with other countries within the developing world, but the country's size and complexity add to those difficulties. The attempt to manipulate or circumvent constitutional government during the 1970s was motivated, in part, by that sense of frustration, which continues to challenge, though not overcome, the democratic culture of India.

Constitutional Amending Formula

Different methods of entrenchment are available for amending India's constitution, depending upon the nature of the amendment and the part of the constitution that is affected. The amending formula is specified within part 22, which requires that all proposed constitutional amendments must first be submitted to both houses of parliament, which must approve them by at least a two-thirds vote. However, certain categories of amendment, relating particularly to the powers of the federal and state judiciary, the formal executive, and the powers and representation accorded to the states also must be approved by at least half of the state governments.

Beyond the entrenched constitution, however, the Supreme Court of India has ruled, within the 1973 case of *Kesavananda Bharati vs. State of Kerala*, that any constitutional amendment that affects the "basic structure" of that constitution is not valid. This ruling was a response to a constitutional amendment that attempted to secure an absolute parliamentary supremacy, through the amending process, itself, over constitutional government. The Supreme Court reaffirmed that unentrenched constitutional principle, following another constitutional amendment (adopted during the period of the 1975-1977 state of emergency), within the 1980 case of *Minerva Mills vs. Union of India*. The court reenforced this principle of the inviolability of certain fundamental features (including the rights and liberties protected by part three) of the Indian constitutional tradition. That distinction, though, is not always clear, making it subject to further judicial interpretation.

Legal Practice and Constitutional Adjudication

India inherited the common law system from the British colonial legacy and its English heritage. Jurists are educated according to standards first established by British authorities. They rely upon precedent, in addition to statutes (as explained within the introductory chapter of this book), for reaching their interpretation of law, including Indian constitutional law.

Those cases in which the Indian Supreme Court declared that the Indian constitution cannot be amended regarding its "basic structure" demonstrate the judicial activism often associated with its activities. It has been particularly solicitous in applying those fundamental rights and liberties enumerated within part three of the Indian constitution. However, many critics also have charged that Supreme Court justices were relatively complacent concerning abuses committed during the state of emergency of 1975-1977. Furthermore, jurists at the local levels also may allow the legal influences of other Indian cultural norms to affect their legal interpretations, as previously indicated.

It is alleged by some observers that the political controversies of the 1970s and 1980s have "politicized" the Indian judiciary. Judges have taken particular interest in interpreting broad matters of public policy, especially within social areas and in connection with parts four and four (a) of the Indian constitution, which provide directives regarding state policy. This sort of willingness to challenge legislation continues to be a defining feature of India's jurists and their approach to legal and constitutional interpretation.

Court System

Despite the presence of a federal system, the Indian judicial system operates as an integrated structure that combines federal and state-level courts. Therefore, the Indian Supreme Court exercises an appellate authority over all legal jurisdictions, throughout the country, adding to the overall centralization of Indian federalism. It can claim this authority over any case that it deems to bear any substantial relationship to Indian constitutional law. Furthermore, it has original jurisdiction over controversies among states and between a state and the union government. It has an enormous annual case load, and its members are appointed by the president, upon the advice of the prime minister and in consultation with the chief justice of the India Supreme Court and other judges who may be deemed appropriate regarding a particular high court appointment.

The Supreme Court of India consists of a chief justice and 25 associate justices. Below the Supreme Court exists the various state High Courts, below which courts are the district and subordinate courts that provide most of the original jurisdiction within the country. Again, it is a single, integrated judicial system that enjoys constitutionally guaranteed institutional independence from other government entities, including parliament. That fact, combined with the power to interpret the constitution, has made the Indian courts resemble the "branch of government" role enjoyed by the judiciary of the American constitutional tradition.

The Future of Indian Constitutionalism

The numerous amendments to the Indian constitution provide evidence of its volatile nature. Nonetheless, it has withstood many controversies and political crises, including a difficult episode of a state of emergency that often seemed to threaten the permanent status of Indian democracy and popular sovereign control. Its fundamental structure has remained essentially unaltered, and many of its amendments have been relatively technical, rather than substantive, in nature. Still, the stability of the Indian constitutional system has seemed, at various times, to be rather precarious, especially given the threat of external forces, internal dissension, political violence, and other challenges.

However, the success of the Indian constitutional tradition should not be diminished. It has established truly formidable goals, particularly in terms of promoting a sense of sovereign unity while acknowledging and fostering India's extremely diverse religious, ethnic, national, and cultural legacy. Its legitimacy has become firmly established among the people who are its source of sovereign authority, and its ideals have continued to be widely revered, even when they are breached. Certainly, in comparison with many other countries within the "developing world," India has exhibited a commendable degree of constitutional stability, although debilitating poverty, economic exploitation, and the political and legal rifts these problems cause continue to dominate its governmental process.

Therefore, the Indian constitutional tradition has been a greater success than a cursory examination might, otherwise, conclude. Considering the extremely difficult historical circumstances from which it emerged (including the violent factionalism that the British Empire could barely manage, and never abate), its imperfect triumph seems especially remarkable. It will continue to experience these problems throughout the twenty-first century. But, at least, it offers a firm constitutional foundation for India's ongoing legal, political, social, economic, and, even, cultural challenges.

References

Granville Austin, *The Indian Constitution: Cornerstone of a Nation*. Oxford, Oxford University Press, 1965.
Pradeep Kumar, *Studies in Indian Federalism*. New Delhi, Deep and Deep, 1988.
Surya Narayan Misra, Subas Chandras Hazary, and Amareswar Mishra, eds., *Constitution and Constitutionalism in India*. New Delhi, APH, 1999.
J. K. Mittal, *Indian Legal and Constitutional History*. Allahabad, Allahabad Law Agency, 1990.
G. R. S. Rao, *Constitution of India: Vision, Reality, and Reform*. Hyderabad, Center for Public Policy and Social Development, 1998.
V. N. Shukla, *V. N. Shukla's Constitution of India*. Lucknow, Eastern Book, 1990.

CHAPTER 7

Japanese Constitutional Tradition

One of the results of the tragedy of World War II was the transformation of the defeated Axis powers from authoritarian to liberal democratic states. Japan achieved this alteration in its fundamental character through the auspices of the occupying authority of the victorious Allies, particularly the United States. One of the most dramatic results of this period of political transition was the adoption of a constitutional tradition as its legal foundation. The change it helped to foster was dramatic and profound.

But Japan's new constitutional tradition was not merely a replication of American or, even, Western legal norms and values. In fact, this transformation represented a return to many of the underlying themes of Japan's traditional legal and political culture, in addition to much of the institutional structure of the previous Japanese constitutional system. The melding of Eastern and Western patterns of legal thought actually offers an insight into the characteristics of Japanese civilization that propelled it, beginning in the late nineteenth century, into a globally significant modern state. These same characteristics also are infused into Japan's contemporary constitutional legacy and continue to guide its overall development through the twenty-first century.

Formal Constitutional Structure

Japan's entrenched constitution is the world's briefest. It is organized into a preamble and eleven chapters, divided into 103, generally brief, articles. Chapter one addresses the symbolic role of the Japanese emperor. Chapter two articulates the renunciation of war, chapters four through eight explain the structure and powers of the government, including the executive, cabinet, legislature, judicial system, financial policy, and local government. Chapter nine designates the amending formula, chapter ten proclaims the principle of constitutional supremacy, and chapter eleven addresses practical matters arising under the constitution's initial promulgation. A formal-legal analysis largely would indicate a conventional, liberal democratic constitutional system that delegates sovereign authority to an equally conventional parliamentary system of government.

A substantive analysis of the cultural context of this constitutional tradition and the historical circumstances that gave rise to it is necessary to gain a meaningful appreciation of its uniqueness. Nonetheless, knowledge of the institutional structure of Japanese government that this constitution mandates remains a useful point of reference. The Japanese Diet is a bicameral parliament, with the lower house, designated as the House of Delegates, assuming the dominant role over the upper house, designated as the Senate.

Both parliamentary chambers consist of representatives who are elected upon a principle of representation by population. The difference between the two houses is found within the size of their respective electoral districts, with Senators having larger, and often more diverse, constituencies. But the House of Delegates retains authority for choosing the chief executive of government, who is actually elected by that chamber, rather than being formally appointed by the head of state. The prime minister and cabinet must, therefore, establish effective political control over this chamber, which occurs through the normal parliamentary competition of political parties and their leaders.

The brevity of the Japanese constitution was deliberate. An Allied occupation force assumed control of Japan following its surrender at the end of World War II. Its commander, General Douglas MacArthur, was tasked with the responsibility for restoring self-government to Japan within a format that would prevent the return of the sort of militarism that led to Japanese aggression. MacArthur and the commission he appointed for the purpose of drafting a suitable constitutional document believed that a concise constitution would promote its simplicity of application, making it easier to use and more useful for defending the type of democratic government it was intended to promote. That political system was based, in many respects, upon the American model, although a parliamentary structure ultimately was adopted, since it was already familiar to the Japanese people and political elites and would prove to be more practical than the admittedly more complex American presidential system. It also imitated much of the constitutional structure established during the period of the Meiji restoration, so it was not an entirely alien document to Japanese society.

Principal Constitutional Themes

The Japanese constitutional tradition combines features of Western and Eastern legal ideals in a manner that is consistent with an underlying Taoist influence. It enforces liberal democratic political institutions and norms, but it retains the culturally crucial role of the emperor, articulates rights and liberties in terms of both entitlements and obligations, and fosters a legal environment that employs a Western civil law model, yet it remains conducive to traditional Japanese legal practices, norms, and values.

The renunciation of war is a constitutional provision that was created in response to recent history. It was intended to reassure Japan's neighbors (many of whom had been victims of Japan's imperial policies) as much as it was meant to establish a peaceful domestic basis for this constitutional government. But its inclusion, and the constitutional attention paid to financial policy, helped to establish the conditions for Japan's remarkable economic recovery and eventual return to the status of an important and influential global state. This contemporary Japanese constitutional tradition has proven to be both stable and dynamic, and it draws upon Japan's previous constitutional history while, ironically, consciously seeking to displace it. Therefore, certain themes of that late nineteenth and early twentieth century Japanese constitutional legacy should be evaluated.

Prior to the mid-nineteenth century, Japan was dominated by a warrior caste of *samurai*, led by an aristocratic class, called the *daimyo*, that combined the sort of military capacity and dominance of the agrarian economy that resembled, superficially, the feudal system of medieval Europe. The emperor's position remained, during this period, largely symbolic, with real sovereign authority being exercised by his principal military advisor and minister, the *shogun*, who was the leader of the most dominant clan from among the *daimyo*. It was, in effect, a military dictatorship that seemed to function effectively while Japan remained a relatively insular country.

However, the nineteenth century intrusion of Western powers and the perceived need to modernize served to undermine this system and encourage its replacement. The undermining of the *samurai* by increasingly powerful merchants, aided by other rebellious forces, prompted the restoration of meaningful imperial authority under the Emperor Mutsuhito, who referred to his reign as "enlightened government," which translates as *meiji*. These conditions resulted in an event known as the "Meiji Restoration" and the advent of a truly modern concept of Japanese constitutional government to complement these other, modernizing developments.

The Meiji constitutional system was designed consciously upon the basis of Western models of law and government. The legislative structure was based upon the Westminster model of Britain, especially the aristocratic upper house and the limited franchise (rooted in property qualifications) for electing members of the lower house. The cabinet system was patterned after the German model of that time. The executive independence of the emperor and his prime minister was influenced by the American model of the executive branch of government. The French *Code Napoléon* provided a strong inspiration for the development of a Japanese civil code that removed the impetus for foreign powers to retain a standard of extraterritoriality for the legal status of their own nationals within Japan. Other features, such as universal public education, modeled upon the American system, and the professionalization of the armed forces (replacing the now-abolished *samurai* caste), derived from both French and German examples, complemented this constitutional development.

However, this constitutionalism of the Meiji period was susceptible to the dominance of a strong executive, especially when backed or coerced by the military, as the events leading to Japan's entry into World War II (as a member of the Axis alliance) startlingly demonstrated. Nonetheless, certain features of this previous constitutional model would resonate as themes of the current Japanese constitutional order, especially in terms of the adaptation of Western designs to an Eastern context, while imposing guarantees of a pacific system of an otherwise sovereign democratic polity. Those parallels offer interesting and, perhaps, illuminating points of analysis.

The Emperor

The first chapter of the Japanese constitution enshrines the role of the emperor. The retention of the imperial office was far from certain in 1946. Many members of the societies of the Allied countries, including prominent leaders, wanted Emperor Hirohito tried as a war criminal; even now, controversy continues regarding his culpability in the events leading to, and occurring during, Japan's involvement within the Second World War. However, General MacArthur determined that this institution was essential for gaining the acceptance of the Japanese people for the constitutional changes he wished to impose. This desire for legitimacy outweighed, therefore, other considerations.

However, Japan's previous political and legal experience warned that a strong imperial office could undermine effective and, especially, democratic government, either through the political activities of the emperor or the manipulation of the emperor's position by powerful political elites, such as the military leaders who dominated Japan during the 1930s and 1940s. Therefore, even the very limited political role of a conventional constitutional monarch within a democratic political order, typified by the British constitutional tradition, seemed potentially risky. The solution lay in a recasting of the constitutional monarch's role. Chapter one of the Japanese constitution specifies that the emperor is a "symbol of the state and the unity of the people," rather than a "head of state." This distinction is important, for it removes the possibility (extreme though it may be, normally) of the emperor making, under extraordinary circumstances, independent executive decisions.

The Diet, for example, actually appoints the prime minister, while the emperor's role in that process is declared to be purely ceremonial. The distinction may seem to be one of semantics, when examined from a functional perspective, but it remains a crucial feature of the system. The reinforcement of practical popular sovereignty through this opening chapter of the Japanese constitution stresses this democratic theme, in addition to the broader concerns of political legitimacy and cultural acceptance that originally motivated it, also.

Renunciation of War

The initial inclusion of chapter two (consisting of only one article) renouncing the use of "war as a sovereign right of the nation and the threat or use of force as a means of settling international disputes" obviously was linked to this same concern about Japanese militarism and aggression that had contributed to the Second World War. The second paragraph of that article is even more explicit in terms of prohibiting the marshaling of armed forces, with the exception of a necessarily small contingent that is designated only for domestic defense. While this chapter was necessary for reassuring Japan's neighbors and the rest of the world, it has been a source of unanticipated financial benefits for the country.

The fact that the Japanese budget is constitutionally mandated to restrict spending upon defense has allowed the country to devote public expenditures to other policy areas, including the building of economic infrastructure, public support for industry and commerce, and the maintenance of sound fiscal management. During the immediate post-war years, this mandate provided tangible assistance to the process of economic recovery and eventual prosperity, especially since the United States maintained, in response to this constitutional requirement, responsibility for Japan's physical defense, particularly through its naval and military presence, throughout this region. This advantage has not guaranteed economic success, but it has proven to be highly advantageous, since this spending option has been constitutionally prohibited.

However, the concept that a state can renounce, permanently, a specific area of its sovereign authority, while maintaining claims to full sovereign status, seems dubious. The fact that Japan's government has demonstrated an elastic interpretation of chapter two of its constitution, especially in terms of the size and activities of its "self-defense force" (as illustrated through its participation, through financial support and, even, the deployment of transport ships, in support of the Allied military effort during the Persian Gulf War) indicates this conceptual constitutional difficulty. Indeed, no formal bar exists to an amendment, or repeal, of this constitutional provision.

However, extremely strong domestic and international political pressure makes that constitutional alteration as unlikely as if it were a convention of an unentrenched constitutional tradition. Furthermore, this constitutional chapter is intertwined with the overall purpose and sovereign expression of this Japanese constitutional tradition, so its alteration would be perceived, potentially, as undermining the entire democratic order. Therefore, it seems likely to remain a defining constitutional presence of a contemporary sovereign Japan.

Rights and Liberties

The initial drafting of the Japanese constitution included an enumeration of rights and liberties that was modeled, consciously, upon many of the guarantees enshrined within the Bill of Rights of the United States Constitution. However, chapter three of this constitutional document offers an interpretation that transcends the conventional American understanding of civil rights and liberties in a couple of significant ways. The first distinction is drawn from the broader tradition of human rights and liberties that has strongly influenced the legal development of the post-World War II international community; the second distinction is a product of Japan's own unique culture and its legal value system.

Article 13's promotion of individualism, the declaration of the supremacy of rights and liberties within Japanese law and policy, and the reference to the protection of "life, liberty, and the pursuit of happiness" are obvious results of this American influence. An express exception to this influence is based upon the condition that its exercise "does not interfere with the public welfare." Nonetheless, additional references to equality rights, free expression, and the protection of petitions of grievance do reflect this direct American inspiration in the process of Japanese constitution making. Democratic participation, which was not as explicitly ordained or protected under the original American system of civil rights and liberties, receives special mention within article 15.

But other expressions of rights and liberties denote the broader human rights influence that was explained within the introductory chapter of this book. Protections of the institution of marriage were intended to overcome traditional lack of autonomy within this area, especially for women. Article 25 offers a particularly interesting expression in this respect. The guarantee, imposed upon the government, of "minimum standards of wholesome and cultured living" is an expression of human autonomy, within a collective context, that transcends a property based tradition of rights and liberties. The requirements for government promotion and protection of social and welfare policies are a further indication of the constitutional mandate of a practice that often is expressed, within other liberal democratic societies, through legislative, rather than judicial, means of delegated sovereign authority. Other examples of this broader human rights emphasis exist throughout chapter three of the Japanese constitution.

Yet another interesting feature of this Japanese theme of rights and liberties is the fact that some of these guarantees are coupled with corresponding obligations imposed upon both government and citizens. The human right to work, enshrined within article 27, also indicates an obligation to work for the economic benefit of the community. The right to an education also is expressed in terms of an obligatory requirement to be educated, generally directed toward the parents of children but implying a more general obligation toward the welfare of all members of the Japanese community. The government's obligations, which provide constitutional directives over matters of public policy, also are linked to corresponding obligations, such as the requirement, under article 30, to accept the necessity of taxation.

In practice, though, these guarantees generally do not tend to challenge government authority or policies. Japanese courts have been reluctant to uphold such challenges when presented within that forum. A more effective constraint upon government activity has been a sense of obligation to the political and cultural community of Japan. This attitude tends to promote a popular assumption that the government's actions adhere to an expectation of respecting these individual rights and liberties or, if it seems to violate them, does it out of respect for the perceived legitimate norms or needs of the broader community.

This relationship is an indication of the traditional Eastern context of Japan's constitutional tradition. It reflects the same principles found within the Confucian concept of *giri*, or "reciprocal duties," as explained within the introductory chapter of this book—a philosophical influence transmitted to Japan from China early within its history. The source of these cultural values will be addressed later within this chapter, but their influence is particularly evident within this Japanese constitutional expression of rights and liberties, and so it should be noted, now, although it will be addressed, again.

Unitary System

Historically, Japan was fragmented by feudal competition. Nonetheless, the ideal of a single sovereign was maintained through the institution and person of the emperor. That concept has been responsible for the maintenance of a unitary system of sovereign authority and government within the contemporary Japanese constitutional tradition, also.

However, as was the case with the construction of the German Basic Law, the victorious Allies were desirous of weakening the potential abuse of centralized governmental authority within Japan and its new constitutional structure. Unlike Germany, though, Japan has not experienced historical political divisions that could form the basis of an imposed federal system. Therefore, Japan's unitary system, like its relatively homogeneous culture, persists.

One exception to this system is the constitutional guarantee of the limited political autonomy of local units of government, as expressed within chapter eight of Japan's constitution. Article 95, in particular, prohibits the central government from enacting laws relating to a single local unit of government (as opposed to laws affecting *all* local units, equally), without the explicit consent of the voters of that public entity. Another exception to the unitary principle, though expressed through non-constitutional means, is the protection accorded to the aboriginal Ainu people of Hokkaido and their tribal legal norms of local governance. Otherwise, the unitary principle is maintained.

Civil Law System

Japan's legal system continues the civil law model that was adopted during the Meiji period. Japanese legal leaders ultimately favored the pandectist model adapted from the German example, as described within the introductory chapter of this book. This adaptation provides another indication of the Japanese legal tendency to combine Western and Japanese legal norms.

Rather than being based upon the "universal" abstractions of Roman law, the pandectist model derives fundamental legal concepts, principles, and values from the context of Japanese history and culture. It also extends the rights and liberties that have been constitutionally guaranteed, especially in the area of property and particularly in terms of real property, also as explained within the introductory chapter of this book. It particularly stresses areas such as obligations and family law, both of which are traditional areas of emphasis for Japanese culture.

This system's interpretive features are extended by an informal source of supplemental legal values that serves as a guide to the practical application of these otherwise detailed codes. This cultural context is a crucial part of the Japanese legal tradition and its purpose of making it uniquely Japanese, consistent with the pandectist approach to the civil law system. It is not a formal structural feature of the Japanese civil code, but it provides the same sort of guidance that the general part of a typical civil code affords to jurists of those systems.

The most distinctive principle to arise from these interpretive concepts is *jori*. It is derived from a broadly defined legal ideal that has been compared to the Western concept of a "natural law." But its true roots lie within traditional Japanese values of harmony and conciliation that are consistent with many aspects of Eastern thought. The philosophical foundation for concepts such as *jori* will be addressed within the section of this chapter devoted to Japanese political culture. However, one particularly pertinent example of this concept in operation involves the practical application of tort law under the Japanese civil code. Japanese citizens have legal recourse to an injury through civil litigation. However, that sort of confrontation is potentially combative, disruptive, and damaging to the harmony of the community. Rather than rely upon the more direct method of suing the offending party, a plaintiff often will employ the technique of invoking "shame" upon that party.

Shame is a very powerful motivating force within many Eastern cultures, including Japan. Its Western counterpart is the concept of "sin," through which a person experiences an individual sense of remorse and responsibility to redress a wrong they have committed. Sin is not based upon external perceptions but upon an internal consideration of right and wrong. By contrast, the concept of shame focuses upon the perception of other people. Regardless of whether or not a person believes that a transgression has been committed, the appearance of impropriety, from the perspective of other people or the community, as a whole, truly matters.

Shame, therefore, is a collective concept, based upon the way other people and the whole community feel about a particular person. Therefore, it can be contrasted to the individualistic qualities associated with sin, as expressed through the common retort of a parent to a child "it doesn't matter what others think about you; it's how you feel about yourself that matters!" Shame is an extremely powerful motivating factor within Japanese society, and the law informally responds to that context. Therefore, although it does not appear as a feature of this part of the Japanese civil code, it frequently is included as a defining aspect of the broader legal principle of *jori* that guides the interpretation of the law, not only for professional jurists but for non-practitioners who must make legal decisions within that context.

Frequently, the person who has been injured not only will abstain from filing suit against the injuring party, but that person will make a public declaration renouncing the legal prerogative to launch such a suit. The expected reaction of that injuring party is to be shamed into offering legal redress for this action, although, perhaps, to an extent that would be less than the amount of damages that might have been awarded by a Japanese court. Shame compels, informally but powerfully, the reaction to this legal controversy, for the burden has been placed by the community upon the perceived "correct" reaction of the injuring party toward the injured party.

Jori also is applied to legal rulings by Japanese jurists within a more formal legal process. Decisions regarding civil disputes, especially when they affect the broader community in some way, often are subject to this sort of legal discretionary interpretation. Cases involving alleged environmental violations often invoke this approach. The ruling will be made, not strictly upon the basis of a strict explication of the relevant codes and statutes, but upon the outcome of that ruling and its practical effect upon the welfare and harmony of the whole community and the well-being of both parties. That outcome may not conform strictly to the specific directives of the civil law, but it does serve the broader purpose of that legal system.

Custom is another interpretive feature of the Japanese civil law. Again, its greatest effect tends to be exerted over the behavior of people functioning within the legal system rather than the formal interpretation of jurists. It influences a general proclivity for settling civil disputes through non-judicial arbitration, rather than more confrontational institutional methods that the law, otherwise, provides. The concept of custom is particularly felicitous of the relationship between a person and a perceived "benefactor." That sense of respect (often perceived by outside observers as deference) often affects civil relationships, including the decision whether or not to engage in litigation and any remedy that may be sought. It occasionally has been suggested that this sense of custom may influence, informally and indirectly, judicial decisions regarding awards and penalties, especially when the benefactor relationship is outwardly manifested or perceived.

A formal-legal appraisal of the operation of Japan's civil law system reveals a relatively conventional example of that structure. It is through the extra-institutional functioning of law within Japanese society that its unique interpretation and application are most evident. This analysis can be frustratingly subtle, but it provides a meaningful context for evaluating the overall legal and constitutional tradition of Japan. These distinctions can be explained most effectively through an appreciation of the fundamental relationship between law and political culture, especially within the overarching context of a civilization's constitutional heritage.

Political Culture

Japan has united Eastern and Western modes of thought in a way that is consistent with its most basic underlying traditional values. The sources of this Eastern influence are diverse, including the traditional practice of Shinto and the imported religious and philosophical teachings of Buddhism, Confucianism, and Taoism. The most prominent Western influence has been liberal democracy, although the presence of Marxist ideas, especially in terms of certain socialist concepts, has offered a source of competition with this generally dominant ideological tradition. It is, however, the blending of these diverse beliefs and values that has made Japanese culture unique.

Shinto, or "the way of the gods," has prehistoric origins. It has been associated with nature worship, although it might be described, more accurately, as a holistic identification of people with their own natural environment. Many of its practices became appropriated, during the sixth century, by Buddhist priests, who associated the various *kami* (Shinto representations of the divine aspect within nature) with manifestations of the Buddha. The most significant development within Shinto occurred, though, when it became an instrument of state policy. The development of "State Shinto" advanced the belief in the divinity of the emperor and the divine mission of his government. This political variation upon the Shinto legacy was abandoned, following World War II.

Informally, certain norms emanating from the Shinto tradition seem to resemble many of the underlying assumptions of Taoism, as described within the introductory chapter of this book. The relationship between humans and their environment, as represented through the *kami*, typifies this broad philosophical relationship. Seemingly opposite forces are not really in opposition to each other; one force relies upon the other one for its very existence. The true "way of the gods" is the acceptance of this complementary relationship of all things. Otherwise, the first thing, without the presence of its opposite, would lack meaning. Shinto and Taoism share this prevailing perspective.

The ability to harmonize these contrasting forces aids the achievement of a state of fulfillment. When Japan was first exposed to Western interests, the insular reaction of the previous centuries to resist these external influences initially prevailed. However, the reconciliation of "opposites" pursued by the leaders of the Japanese state that emerged from the Meiji Restoration created a merging of often-targeted Western practices with the traditional Eastern basis of Japanese civilization, with a notable success that continues to assist Japan in its twenty-first century pursuit of stability and prosperity, as aided by its current constitutional system.

This emphasis upon harmony can be observed within the "corporatist" approach to public and private sector relationships. This approach has been employed by other political systems (Austria has offered a good example), but the Japanese variation upon this arrangement is reminiscent, again, of the holistic features of its traditional cultural influences. Government serves as an intermediary between otherwise opposing interests within society, reconciling them to a policy that serves both of their interests and the general benefit of the community. The most conspicuous example of this approach occurs within the relationship between Japanese industry and labor, in which the government harmonizes their respective, seemingly conflicting desires (such as higher wages in contrast to corporate profitability) in a manner that assures overall prosperity for all parties, ultimately benefiting the overall economic prosperity of Japanese society.

This corporatist tendency also can be related to a strong Japanese sense of communal identity. That sense of identity may be associated with an attitude of deference that has been used to explain the willingness of the Japanese people to be dominated by militarists and other authoritarian figures. But it also is regarded, within Japanese society, as a reciprocal deference, requiring the government to be respectful of the collective attitudes and needs of the community. It also puts pressure upon the individual member of society to be respectful of the attitudes and interests of the community, thus undercutting the more individualistic traits of the constitutional and legal systems, including the seeking of legal remedies regarding tortious and rights-related matters.

Constitutionally, this cultural proclivity underlies the combination of ideological values infused from the American tradition of liberal democracy with Japan's Shinto and Confucian heritage. It is expanded through the workings of the civil law system. Reciprocal duties concerning the relationship with the benefactor offer a deference to this ideal and *not*, necessarily, to the parties involved. Liberal legal norms and Western civil law structures may have been imposed or reinforced by the victorious Allies, but they have been embraced, willingly, for they are entirely consistent with this overarching philosophical legacy.

Constitutional Adjudication

The Japanese Supreme Court is a constitutional institution that was imposed by the victorious World War II Allies upon Japan for a deliberate purpose. Chapter six designates this court and its role, to the extent that it operates, practically, as a "branch" of government with ultimate authority over matters of constitutional interpretation. The fifteen justices of the Supreme Court are politically appointed in a manner similar to their American counterparts, enjoying tenure of office until the age of mandatory retirement. Therefore, they are accorded a high degree of institutional autonomy, and this independence is exercised. Cases such as the 1995 ruling on the right to privacy that upheld the government practice of fingerprinting foreign residents or the 1996 ruling that allowed for the disbanding of *Aum Shinrikyo* (the religious organization responsible for the release of poisonous gas within the Tokyo subway system), despite the claim that it violated free expression of religion, are two good examples of this role.

Often, the Supreme Court appears reluctant to undermine government policy through constitutional challenge, but it has not avoided such controversy, either. Nonetheless, Japanese jurists often are very careful regarding constitutional challenges to governmental authority and public policy. These jurists must supplement their interpretation of the constitutional and civil code texts with their own judgment and, occasionally, by making reference to previous decisions, not unlike the common law practice of *stare decisis*. But the tone of these rulings still tends to reflect the doctrinal spirit of the jurisprudence of a civil law system.

Court System

Japan's courts differ from certain other civil law systems through their relative lack of institutional specialization. The Supreme Court of Japan considers appeals regarding all areas of law and serves as an overall final court of appeal for the entire country. It meets either as a "grand bench" of the whole court or is divided into three *petit* benches, depending upon the subject matter and import of the particular controversy. The Japanese Supreme Court is responsible for making appointments to lower courts, in addition to overall administrative supervision of the entire judicial system. It serves as the apex of a unified system that reinforces the unitary structure of Japan.

The Japanese judicial system is divided into 50 districts, each with its own court that is competent to try both civil and criminal cases. Numerous summary courts address small claims and minor criminal matters. Decisions of these district and summary courts may be appealed to the country's eight high courts. An appellant has two opportunities for challenging a lower court decision: the second appeal, called a *koso* appeal, is a request for reconsideration after a high court has considered the first, or *jokoku*, appeal. Again, appellate and trial courts are not specialized in the normal fashion of a civil law system, with the exception of the separate family courts.

The Future of Japanese Constitutionalism

Although it was imposed upon the country, the current Japanese constitutional tradition has enjoyed enduring legitimacy. The fact that it perpetuates legal ideals and values that precede the Second World War and even resonate with Japan's ancient history may account for part of that success. However, it also has provided a successful foundation for the post-war recovery of Japan's economy and society.

The Japanese constitutional tradition combines features of both Eastern and Western constitutionalism. It reconciles these features in a way that has promoted a harmonious political and legal system, contributing to Japan's ongoing stability and prosperity. It promises to be an important part of the ongoing legacy of Japan as a dominant member of the global community throughout the twenty-first century. Its initial purpose may have been political expediency, but the Japanese constitutional tradition is an impressive tribute to the powerful appeal of this democratic institution to the popular sovereign it now serves.

References

Koichiro Fujikura, ed., *Japanese Law and Legal Theory*. New York, New York University Press, 1996.
John Owen Haley, *The Spirit of Japanese Law*. Athens, University of Georgia Press, 1998.
Glenn D. Hook and Gavan McCormick, *Japan's Contested Constitution: Documents and Analysis*. New York, Routledge, 2001.
Kyoko Inoue, *MacArthur's Japanese Constitution: A Linguistic and Cultural Study of Its Making*. Chicago, University of Chicago Press, 1991.
Percy R. Luney, Jr. and Kazuyuki Takahashi, eds., *Japanese Constitutional Law*. Tokyo, University of Tokyo Press, 1993.
Hiroshi Oda, *Japanese Law*. New York, Oxford University Press, 1999.

CHAPTER 8

Nigerian Constitutional Tradition

Most of Africa found itself, during the mid-twentieth century, continuing to exist under the control of European imperial systems. But the difficult struggle for independence began to yield positive results, so, by the latter part of that century, that situation changed and new African states emerged. But many African countries have found the transition from colonial control to full sovereignty to be exceptionally difficult. These problems have posed a particular challenge to the establishment of constitutional government, throughout the continent.

Nigeria is a prime example of this challenge. It is a country with borders that were artificially (indeed, almost indiscriminately) drawn as a result of competition and agreement among colonial rulers, including the British Empire. It included, excluded, and divided peoples of diverse ethnic, religious, and other cultural identities. Therefore, it lacked the immediate sense of unity that many other emerging countries have enjoyed. Its contemporary legacy of political conflict and military interference can be attributed, in large part, to this core dilemma, in addition to the daunting socio-economic problems that African states have experienced, generally, especially in relation to the tragedy of underdevelopment and economic exploitation.

Nigeria's equally complex constitutional heritage is a product of these conditions. Its very complexity is an indication of the desire to impose stability upon the country while, simultaneously, establishing and promoting a sense of popular sovereign control. Its democratic goals have experienced enormous obstacles, culminating with the suspension of constitutional sovereignty, itself, and its displacement with military rule. Nonetheless, that constitutional system has persisted and, with it, hope for the Nigerian people who seek to claim the sovereignty it represents.

Formal Constitutional Structure

Nigeria is grounded upon an extremely long and detailed entrenched constitutional document. It is divided into eight chapters, consisting of a total of 320 articles. Many of these articles consist of relatively lengthy and detailed sections, especially regarding the policy directives and powers of the various government institutions. This constitutional document replaces the supplementary written provisions that described the "emergency conditions" of the military government that displaced constitutional government for several years.

Chapter one encompasses "general provisions" that describe the basic principles of Nigerian constitutionalism and the ultimate basis of its sovereign authority. The second chapter addresses "fundamental objectives and directive principles," providing constitutional guidance to the government concerning public policy, while chapter three addresses the status of citizenship and chapter four enumerates basic rights and liberties. Chapters five through seven describe the sovereign power delegated to the legislative, executive, and judicial institutions of government at both the federal and state levels. Chapter eight concludes with the legal status of the federal capital territory and other supplemental matters of institutional and policy concern, followed by numerous constitutional schedules, many of a procedural or technical nature.

Nigeria's constitution differs from the Westminster model of British government in terms of the presence of a federal system, the presence of a separate *and* effective political executive, and the greater constitutional role that appears to be accorded to the judiciary. Furthermore, various aspects of the public administration also are addressed within this constitutional document, including the specific enforcement sector of the independent executive, devoted to both the country's police force and the armed forces.

Principal Constitutional Themes

The role of the independent executive is key to this constitutional system. This role is consistent with certain aspects of traditional life and culture among the peoples of this part of Africa. It also is indicative of the instability provided by the colonial legacy and the conflict arising from the country's diversity. These features have interacted, throughout Nigeria's modern history, to produce a complex and, often, volatile constitutional experience.

Independent indigenous states shaped the culture and social existence of the present Nigerian state. The Kanem-Bornu Empire of the eleventh century adopted Islam and brought order, prosperity, and cultural prestige to the region. It competed with the Hausa (who would continue to flourish until the nineteenth century) and Songhai peoples, who added to the diversity and general strength of the region. By the late sixteenth century, the Fulani presence became a prominent force within the region. These "states" were much more fluid than this Eurocentric term might suggest, but they were sophisticated, advanced cultures that belied the Western stereotype of Africa as a "savage jungle." They also would help to establish the presence and interactions of the various peoples who dominate contemporary Nigeria.

The area that is modern Nigeria was undefined by any sense of Western political geography prior to the arrival of colonizing Europeans, especially from Portugal and Great Britain. Its boundaries were determined by agreements with other foreign powers, especially France. This foreign presence was instituted through trade (including slave trading), resource development, and, finally, military and political forces. Two late-nineteenth century protectorates were established. They were consolidated into a formal colony of Nigeria, by the beginning of the First World War, and divided into a northern and southern province and a separate colony of Lagos.

British imperial administration was noted for being highly professional and effective. The area these administrators served, however, was artificially constructed and lacking in uniformity, including the heterogeneity of the people of this large area of Western Africa. One of the approaches toward administering this colony, under these circumstances, was the delegation of many political and social responsibilities to traditional tribal leaders. This practice would have an influence upon the later development of local constitutional practice under an independent Nigeria.

The administrative division of Nigeria into northern and southern divisions would become a basis for part of the initial federal division of the independent country. These areas were divided, further, into provinces, which were granted, after the conclusion of the Second World War, limited self-government. Colonial experiments in constitutional government delegated to these provinces limited authority over local matters that sought to include the participation of the various ethnic groups of the colony. British authorities eventually consolidated these provinces into the Northern, Eastern, and Western regions, each one enjoying a degree of political autonomy that also attempted to correspond to the three most dominant ethnic groups within Nigeria. These arrangements provided a basis for the constitutional transition from colonial to sovereign government.

This colonial experience established conditions that would affect Nigeria's subsequent constitutional development. Despite experiments with legislative autonomy, the executive style of decisive colonial administration would maintain an enduring appeal. Colonial attempts at including the participation of the various ethnic and religious groups foreshadowed similar concerns addressed by the

Nigerian constitutional tradition. Provincial and regional experiments under British authority presaged approaches to Nigerian federal demarcations and powers. Nigerian constitutionalism was not generated spontaneously.

Diversity

Nigeria includes over 250 ethnic groups. It also encompasses a variety of religious faiths, including Sunni Islam, the largest religion, Roman Catholic, Anglican, and Methodist Christianity, and traditional Animist beliefs and practices. The official language is English, which also serves as a bridge among many indigenous languages, corresponding to some of the most dominant ethnic groups.

The Nigerian constitutional tradition formally attempts to address and accommodate this diversity. Part of that strategy can be found within the federal system, particularly in terms of the shifting boundaries and numbers of states that correspond, primarily, to the broadly defined domains of the various ethnic and religious groups, especially the largest and most prominent ones. The significance of this approach will be considered, further, within the section of this chapter that addresses the Nigerian federal system.

Another approach concerns the election of the president, as described within chapter six, part "A" of the Nigerian constitution. The successful candidate must not only receive a plurality of the overall vote, but that plurality must include at least one-fourth of the vote cast in a minimum of two-thirds of Nigeria's states. This requirement is intended to promote a more widespread acceptance of the legitimacy of the president among as wide a range of ethnic and religious groups as possible, since they tend to be concentrated within the separate states.

Chapter two of the Nigerian constitution also directs the government to be organized according to a principle of inclusion. It also advances provisions that encourage policies and programs to promote "national unity" over "sectional" interests, exhorting the Nigerian people to behave in a similar manner. Chapter four of this constitution, dedicated to fundamental rights and liberties, devotes considerable attention to the subject of freedom from discrimination. Section 42 prohibits such discrimination by specifying, first, the protections accorded to citizens of "a particular community" and "ethnic group," but also including religion, gender, place of origin, and "political opinion." In addition to forbidding "disabilities or restrictions," it also disallows any "privilege or advantage" upon that basis.

This constitutional provision may seem conventional, particularly by Western standards, but its significance is made more apparent through a reconsideration of the socio-political context of Nigeria's political and legal experience. Nigeria is Africa's most populous country, and certain ethnic groups within the country are particularly prominent. The Fulani and Hausa peoples are dominant within the northern part of the country, while the Ibo dominate the southeastern sections and the Yoruba are dominant within the southwestern part of the country. Complicating this ethnic distribution is the presence of many other groups, including, among the more conspicuous ones, the Kanuri people of the northeast, the Nupe and Tiv peoples of central Nigeria, and the Edo, Ibibio, and Ijaw of the country's southern region. Furthermore, the Fulani, Hausa, and Kanuri peoples who dominate the northern part of Nigeria are predominantly Islamic, while other parts of the country are more heavily Christian and practitioners of traditional Animist beliefs are found throughout the country. Religious differences exacerbate these ethnic differences.

The most violent expression of these differences occurred, during the mid-1960s, when the predominantly Christian Ibo people rebelled against a planned reorganization of the federal system that would have been severely disadvantageous to them. This plan coincided with a massacre of Ibo people by members of the Fulani and Hausa groups. The leadership of the state known as the Eastern Region, dominated by an Ibo population, declared the creation of a separate sovereign state, the Republic of Biafra, which was resisted by the Nigerian government, then under military rule but dominated by Islamic and northern Nigerian groups, especially the Fulani and Hausa. The resulting civil war was one of the most bloody in African history, and it only ended when, in early 1970, the Ibo leaders surrendered and agreed to dissolve the separate Republic of Biafra.

Much of Nigeria's constitutional development has been a response to this overwhelming problem of discordant ethnic and religious conflict and competition. The rise of military governments has been linked directly to the inability of the democratic constitutional order to deal with this problem, effectively. Another constitutional strategy in relation to this theme has been the creation of *Shari'a* courts exclusively for the private legal relationships of the Islamic peoples of Nigeria, which will be addressed later within this chapter. However, the general attempt to impose a sense of national identity upon the diverse population of this country has been an extremely difficult one, despite the guarantees and exhortations of the constitutional tradition. It has been a factor underlying most of its other constitutional themes.

Federal System

Nigeria has experienced a relatively weak form of federalism, aided by the apparent design of its constitutional tradition. The delegation of sovereign authority to the state level is expressed within the federal constitution, and its practical implementation has been left, largely, to the discretion of the federal government. The number and size of these states have varied, widely, throughout Nigeria's history, undermining the traditional principle of a federal union as composed of sovereign states that have voluntarily surrendered some of their sovereignty for the purpose of creating a permanent union. The reality, within Nigeria, is very different.

The entrenched Nigerian constitutional document does not devote a particular chapter to the subject of federalism or the state governments. Instead, these matters are addressed within chapters that are dedicated, primarily, to the federal government, especially the general provisions of chapter one and the institutional descriptions provided within chapters five through seven. This structural nature of the constitution, itself, provides an indication of the highly centralized nature of Nigerian federalism. Additional observations reinforce that impression.

The powers assigned to the federal government are addressed within the Nigerian constitution's chapter one, with a more specific articulation provided through a description of the legislative authority of the National Assembly, as provided within chapter five of the Nigerian constitution. These powers are embraced by the sovereign authority to ensure the "peace, order, and good government" of the country—a phrase reminiscent of the general responsibility delegated to the Canadian federal government (as discussed within chapter five of this book) yet also assigned, constitutionally, to the state governments. But combined with the specific powers enumerated within part one of schedule two of the Nigerian constitution, it gives the federal government a predominant role, accentuated by the provision within this same section that the laws of the federal government will "prevail" over state governments when the two levels are found to be in legislative conflict, even though these state laws have been enacted, otherwise, within their respective spheres of sovereign authority.

But an even more powerful authority of the Nigerian federal government emanates from its strong presence within the process of constitutional amendment. The constitutional document that emerged after the return, in 1999, of democratic sovereign rule provides an amending formula designed to address this problem regarding any amendment that would change the boundaries or number of Nigerian states. However, other amendments may be enacted solely by the federal legislature, reaffirming the dominant position of the federal government, generally.

Nigeria has experienced, in fact, a somewhat chaotic history regarding the size, number, and disposition of its states. Prior to gaining independence, British authorities divided the country into three principal regions: the Northern Region, dominated by the Fulani and Hausa people; the Eastern Region, dominated by the Ibo people; the Western Region, dominated by the Yoruba people. But unrest among other ethnic groups led to the further division of the federal system into a larger number of smaller states.

The number of states has altered according to political circumstances; under the 1999 constitution, 36 states exist within Nigeria. The constitution also describes and entrenches the authority of local governments and places administrative responsibilities overwhelmingly under the control of the federal government. Yet the central government remains the competitive focus for economic benefits and patronage, undermining these institutional features of a federal system.

The states often have provided an institutional framework for ethnic groups, especially in terms of their collective competition for power and influence. The proliferation of states also has been intended to provide more diversity among states and deter the use of states as political bases for the advancement of the interests of a ubiquitous ethnic group that might seek to dominate a particularly large and powerful state. It has proven to be, therefore, both a constructive and a destructive force. The constitutional centralization of power has, like the imposition of military government, been a response to this promise and conflict. The elimination of the federal system and its sovereign states under military government demonstrated this focus.

Strong Governmental Executive

The Nigerian constitutional tradition divides governmental responsibilities between the executive and the legislature, with provisions for a strong, independent judiciary also being constitutionally described. Superficially, it seems to resemble the "branches of government" arrangement found within the American constitutional tradition. However, the actual practice of Nigerian constitutional government has accorded a overwhelmingly dominant influence to the executive authority, even during periods of democratic sovereign control. Nigeria's constitution offers insights into this condition.

The Nigerian president enjoys powers of law enforcement similar to the constitutional authority found within both the French and American constitutional systems. Although the president's authority does not extend to the creation of policy through edict, the ability to shape policy through enforcement and regulation is immense. That capacity exists for any political executive (even within a democratic system of government), but the Nigerian constitutional tradition has provided additional support for the extension of that authority, both through features of the entrenched constitution and the political culture that shapes it.

The Nigerian constitution expresses detailed institutional support for the president throughout chapter six of that document. Perhaps, the most significant sections address the delegated authority of the country's civil service, police forces, and military. Usually, the inclusion of these sections would indicate constitutional limits upon these enforcement agencies by expressing the limits of their authority. However, the constitutional connection between the president and these agencies and administrators may, instead, reinforce their executive role and their effective use as instruments of executive authority. Furthermore, the constitutional role assigned to the president and vice-president concerning the various commissions that serve the country (including the National Election Commission) also suggests the possibility that they can be used, potentially, as instruments of executive power, rather than a check upon that power.

This interpretation is supported both by historical experience and an indigenous way of envisioning the role of the Nigerian leader. The role of the "strong leader" is consistent with a traditional perception of tribal leadership that is familiar to many people throughout this region of Africa. Those sentiments are explained within the introductory chapter of this book, and they relate to the responsibility of the family, kinship group, or tribal leaders to distribute resources, share largesse, and coordinate the security and prosperity of their people. The traditional political role of the Nigerian president, especially in terms of such matters as patronage, safeguarding the country, and being the focal point for administering and distributing all resources may be based more firmly upon traditional cultural expectations than upon the powers and institutions (which may be extensive but, also, comparable to the experiences of other democratic constitutional systems) that are expressly linked to that office. Certainly, the dominant role of the Nigerian president remains pervasive, even during periods of effective democratic sovereignty and civilian control of the government.

Military Rule

Nigeria has experienced, since achieving independence in 1960, two sustained periods of military rule that have suspended constitutional government and supplanted any semblance of democratic sovereignty. Political infighting, corruption, and ethnic unrest motivated young army officers to stage a *coup d'etat* in 1966 that replaced civilian government with their commanding general, who abolished the federal system. Another coup replaced this military leader with a general from the Northern Region, who reestablished the federal system but not the democratic constitution. It was during this period that relations between the Ibo people and the rest of the country deteriorated to the point of civil war and the attempted establishment of the Republic of Biafra.

Promises made during the early 1970s to return to civilian rule were not kept, despite increased economic stability (due largely to oil revenues), and other military coups ensued, with different military leaders assuming control of the government. Political parties were allowed to organize, again, and the last of these military leaders finally prepared for the restoration of democratic government with a redrafting of the Nigerian constitution. Elections finally were held, under the restored constitution, in 1979.

The deterioration of the economy spurred, in 1983, another *coup d'etat*, despite the apparent sovereign popular support for the civilian government. Another series of military governments ensued, with a 1993 election, preparatory to a return to civilian rule being nullified by the military leadership. The following year, attempts by this leadership to hold elections for a national constitutional conference were boycotted, and the ensuing unrest led to a gradual easing of this dictatorship until in 1999. At that time, a new constitution, based closely upon the old model, was drafted and enacted and civilian government was restored through democratic elections.

The nature of these military governments reflects a broadly patriarchal theme that often has influenced Nigeria's constitutional development. However, the legitimacy of these governments never was fully claimed or accepted. The legal documents drafted in support of these governments always posited them as "temporary" and "interim" responses to economic and political emergency, with a stated or implied promise of a return of sovereign authority to the democratic population. This attempt to provide some veneer of constitutional legitimacy, especially through the appearance of the sanctioning of military government by a formally amended constitution, demonstrated the contention of the military that its rule was imposed purely for the benefit of "the people" of Nigeria.

A political tradition that values, and becomes dependent upon, strong personal leadership may be more prone to this sort of military intervention. Furthermore, conflicts arising from ethnic and religious diversity, as addressed, partially, by the federal system, may enhance the image of the military forces as being much better organized, more stable, and less partisan than the political parties whose leaders compete for elective office. Political corruption and ineffectiveness also contribute to this development. However, the extensiveness of these periods of military rule undoubtably has a cumulative effect upon the overall tone of the Nigerian constitutional tradition.

Political Culture

Nigeria's core political and legal beliefs and values are a mosaic of disparate sources. The traditional African way of life has been subjected to the introduction of modern institutions and activities. Historical introductions of Islamic and Christian theologies also have induced changing beliefs and values throughout this part of the world. These various and, often, competing cultural forces have shaped Nigeria. But they also have made it difficult to identify a uniform cultural foundation for its constitutional tradition.

A formal-legal analysis of the Nigerian constitution prompts the superficial impression that it is grounded upon conventional Western liberal democratic principles. This formal constitutional tradition is, indeed, strongly influenced by those beliefs and values, particularly as they were transmitted through the British colonial administration. Experiments in limited constitutional government began prior to 1960, when Nigeria received full independence, and these earlier models, which included rudimentary practices of a federal division of powers, provided an ideological basis for subsequent constitutional developments. The fact that Nigeria's political and legal elites who dominated the initial constitutional process often were Western educated reinforced this ideological influence, especially at the federal level of government.

However, most Nigerians have not been affected in the same way, so the beliefs and values they bring to the daily implementation of these constitutional features reflect a strong influence of traditional African values. Tribal norms have influenced the approach toward the distribution of government services and resources that the Nigerian constitution mandates, particularly within chapter six of that entrenched document. It also has affected, as previously noted, attitudes toward political leadership, as constitutionally constructed.

Social, political, and economic activities at the local level, including party, state, and ethnic loyalties, strongly affect this constitutional implementation. The interpretation of Nigerian law at the local level also can be influenced within this cultural model, even when implemented by jurists of this conventional constitutional system. Furthermore, tribal units flourish, throughout the country and beyond its boundaries, providing a daily experience far more real than the abstract constructs of the Nigerian state and its constitutional system provide.

These tribal practices, described within the introductory chapter of this book, include a collective identification, despite the presence of constitutionally guaranteed individual rights. They also tend to promote a sense of shared resources and particular loyalties that can reinforce yet, also, undermine the centralized goals of Nigeria's federal system. Those values are demonstrated through the activities of courts specially designated for addressing controversies arising under "customary law," as described later within this chapter. The interaction between Western liberal democratic and traditional tribal norms is a distinctive feature of the functional Nigerian constitutional tradition.

Islam provides a strong cultural influence, also. Chapter one of this book describes some of the features of this influence and its affect upon a Western understanding of law. The search for consensus is one of the most dramatic results of this Islamic approach to law, and it becomes particularly manifested through those parts of the judicial system provided as a formal outlet for it. Certainly, this influence also adds to a compartmentalization of political culture that makes a sense of true constitutional unity for Nigeria difficult to effect.

Court System

Nigeria inherited, from its British antecedents, the English tradition of the common law system. The judicial system relies upon the appeal to precedent, the factual evaluations of jurors, and the accusatorial approach to settling legal controversies, as explained within chapter one of this book. Nigerian legal practitioners generally are educated and trained from a Western perspective, and jurists who function at the highest levels of the judicial system often have received at least some of their formal education within Western societies. However, this Nigerian legal profession has not had a good opportunity to establish a coherent judicial legacy, especially given the dominance of strong executive leaders and the frequent imposition of martial law.

The Nigerian constitutional tradition provides, within chapter seven of the entrenched document, for a unified, hierarchical court structure that is consistent with the common law system. The apex of this structure is occupied by the Supreme Court of Nigeria, with the Nigerian Court of Appeal occupying a place directly below it. The Federal High Court has exclusive jurisdiction over matters involving revenue, customs, economic regulation, and other economic laws, according to section 251 of the Nigerian constitution. Each state also has a High Court that serves as a court of original jurisdiction for most civil and criminal matters falling under both federal and state jurisdiction, as indicated within section 270 of the Nigerian constitution. This relationship between the state and federal courts is the structural basis for this unified judicial structure for the country.

Section 286 of chapter seven of the Nigerian constitution clarifies the nature of this coordinated jurisdiction, with state courts designated as competent to try matters, both civil and criminal, that fall under both state and federal laws. But the federal Supreme Court maintains ultimate appellate jurisdiction over most legal matters at both state and federal levels. Section 233 of the Nigerian constitution confirms that jurisdiction (especially over all rights and liberties protections provided within chapter four of the Nigerian constitution), as does section 240 regarding the Nigerian Court of Appeal. Therefore, Nigeria's judicial system affects the overall centralization of the federal system and suggests the potential weakness of state governments as sovereign units of constitutional government within Nigeria.

One of the most interesting features of Nigeria's judicial system is the presence of separate jurisdictions addressing both Islamic law and the "customary" law derived from traditional sources of African jurisprudence. *Shari'a* courts, including the state *Shari'a* Court of Appeal as described within section 275 of the Nigerian constitution, exercise jurisdiction over civil affairs (especially within the area of family law) according to principles derived from a well-established legal tradition of Islam as previously described. The role of the *kadi* as the traditional Islamic jurist also is constitutionally sanctioned.

Additionally, the Customary Court of Appeal requires the presence of jurists certifiably trained within this area of law, including an understanding of tribal law. Customary courts also address matters of civil affairs from a traditional African perspective (as previously described), including matters relating to the area of family law. Recourse to these courts is provided for their respective communities and they are particularly favored among the Islamic and traditional tribal populations of certain regions and states. Appellate courts for both Islamic and customary law exist for both the Federal Capital Territory, Abuja and the state level, with the former judicial level providing overall appellate jurisdiction over both Islamic and tribal law for the entire country.

The presence of these special courts addresses the diversity of Nigeria, in addition to the conflicting sources of political culture that contribute to the fundamental norms and ideals of Nigerian constitutional law. They complement the conventional Western judicial system of Nigeria that reflects the imposition of liberal legal norms and values and a common law order derived from the country's colonial legacy. It is based upon a relatively complex structure that attempts to provide safeguards for individual Nigerian citizens and limits upon the delegated authority of the Nigerian government.

The Future of Nigerian Constitutionalism

The complex structure and depth of detail found within the entrenched Nigerian constitution may provide certain contrasting indications. The specificity of these constitutional provisions suggests a distrust of government and the delegation of sovereign power to it. Yet, it also intimates a desire to define, as carefully as possible, the difficult political arrangements that make such a delegation possible. These arrangements are the result of conflict: ethnic, religious, cultural, regional, economic. Constitutional attempts to ameliorate this conflict are reflected within the various permutations of the federal system, the attempts to provide entrenched guarantees of rights and liberties, the creation of *Shari'a* and customary courts, and provisions regarding the need for some level of state and regional presence in the vote that determines the president.

But the tradition of the strong leader, represented, at best, by the powerful constitutional role of the government executive and, at worst, by military subvention, threatens the continued success of Nigeria's constitutional accord. The 1999 restoration of sovereign constitutional authority heralded a desire to return to the goals that had been established when full independence initially was achieved by Nigeria in 1960. But the ability for Nigerians to maintain that sovereign constitutional order cannot be entirely certain.

Nonetheless, the constitutional structure first established for Nigeria has persisted despite specific changes added to each redrafting and renewed entrenchment. It is a monumental document and a testament to the continued aspirations for the future of an eventually stable, united, and truly democratic Nigeria. The formidable problems (including poverty, lack of indigenous control over resources, external economic dependency, ethnic conflict, extremely uncertain health and safety conditions, and a very fragile infrastructure) of this African state remain daunting. But the political and legal foundation provided by the Nigerian constitutional tradition offers some basis for hope for real and sustainable success for the twenty-first century.

References

Bamgbose J. Adele, *Fundamentals of Nigerian Politics*. Lagos, 1998.
Epiphany Azinge, *Law-Making Under Military Regimes: The Nigerian Experience*. Benin City, Oliz, 1994.
Billy Dudley, *Introduction to Nigerian Politics and Government*. London, Macmillan, 2000.
William D. Graf, *The Nigerian State*. London, James Currey, 1988.
Benjamin Obi Nwabueze, *Nigeria's Presidential Constitution*. New York, Longman, 1985.
Sir Egbert Udo Udomo, *History and the Law of the Constitution of Nigeria*. Lagos, Malthouse, 1994.

CHAPTER 9

French Constitutional Tradition

The French constitutional tradition often has been described as a model of constitutional development. It served as a herald of political freedom and the democratic assertions of a sovereign people. It includes many features that offer significant sources for comparative constitutional analysis, especially in terms of its approach to diverse influences and sources of sovereign authority and its attempt to reconcile conflicting forces of political, social, and economic interests.

The current French constitution is the fifth republican version of this tradition. These constitutional republican documents have been interspersed historically with expressions of monarchical and oligarchical sovereignty. They are, indeed, the culmination of this diverse and, often, volatile history that, ultimately, has shaped this constitutional result.

Formal Constitutional Structure

The French constitutional tradition is based upon an entrenched document, adopted in 1958. It is divided into 14 titles, plus a brief preamble. The first title defines political sovereignty, citizenship, and voting rights. Titles two through five describe the different parts of government. Title two addresses the executive authority of the president of the republic, while title three describes other executive offices and administrative authority, especially the premier, and title four is concerned with the constitutional and political role of parliament.

Another historical document plays a constitutional role. The preamble to this constitution makes reference to the Declaration of the Rights of Man and Citizen, which legally inaugurated the French Revolution in 1789, and the preamble of the 1946 constitution of the Fourth French Republic. They serve as unentrenched features of this constitutional tradition, especially providing a guiding role for purposes of application and interpretation and an inspiration for the French protection of rights and liberties found within the civil code. Their guidance remains informal, but the practical effect is politically and culturally strong.

As an entrenched document, the legitimacy of this constitution as an expression of a popular sovereign will is provided by the amendment process that is described within title 14. Either the president or parliament may initiate this process, which then must either be ratified through a popular referendum or subject to a special parliamentary session, convened as a constitutional congress, whose deputies must approve it by a three-fifths majority. Other titles address matters such as guidelines regarding treaties, international covenants, foreign relations, the structure and authority of an independent judiciary (which is not vested, however, with a role of constitutional interpretation), the structure and role of the Constitutional Council, and the role of the Economic and Social Council, especially in terms of the development and enforcement of public policy.

Parliament consists of a Senate that is indirectly elected by the various territorial administrative units of France and a National Assembly of deputies elected directly by the citizens of France, whose numbers and specific constituency are determined through the principle of representation by population. The premier wields certain defined executive responsibilities, in conjunction with a constitutionally specified cabinet. The premier is appointed by the president but, in fact, is the legislative leader of the political party that dominates the National Assembly, consistent with the general theory of parliamentary government. It is not representative, though, of a typical parliamentary system of government. The president is a separate executive official who exercises genuine political powers, independent of the legislature, like the American president. Popular sovereign supremacy, therefore, is delegated to both the president and parliament.

Principal Constitutional Themes

This French system of government, as constitutionally expressed, does not fall neatly under the categories of either a parliamentary system or an American-style presidential system of divided government. Instead, it exhibits qualities of both of these categories, so scholars often refer to it as a "quasi-presidential" system of government. Its construction is a consequence of one of the most prominent themes of the French constitutional tradition.

The creation of the Fifth French Republic and its constitution resulted most immediately from the need to overcome a political and constitutional crisis arising from the threat of civil war. Indirectly, it has been a response to a series of historical cycles of social movement, shifts in sovereign authority, and experiments in constitutional government. A related theme is the persistent and pervasive influence of the French Revolution and its civic purposes—a source of inspiration for other political systems, including emerging nation-states, throughout the world.

A conspicuous reverence for law and legal institutions permeates French constitutionalism. Its civil law system, first codified through the creation of the *Code Napoléon*, has been a source of pride that often affects the perception that other constitutional issues are tied to this source of law and legal principles. The French constitutional tradition is a paragon of social and political compromise, and it serves as a strong source of popular pride in addition to being the ultimate expression of French sovereign identity.

Cycles of Historical Constitutional Development

Three political and legal phases of French history can be detected as having emerged and repeated themselves. They correspond to the assertion of sovereign control from the monarchy, different elite sources, and the democratic polity. These cycles have produced periods of great turmoil and great opportunity. The most dramatic of these periods have produced great events that have, in turn, generated a tremendous sense of national pride among French people, especially in terms of a perception of political, cultural, legal, and military achievements associated with the ideal of *la gloire*, or "glory." Each phase has produced a constitutional system to express the ideals of each cycle, assist in the process of imposing political order and the pursuit of political, social, economic, cultural, and strategic goals, and conferring legal legitimacy upon the sovereign.[1]

The first cycle could be described as "authoritarian." It is revealed, first, through the constitutional activities of the Bourbon monarchy, especially under the direction of King Louis XIV. The deliberate concentration of all sovereign power for the benefit of a single leader was not a novel development in French history, but the later Bourbon monarchs sought to institutionalize this process, especially through the centralization of all administrative functions, including the judicial role of the *parlements*. The famous statement attributed to Louis XIV, "*l'etat, c'est moi*," was indicative of this approach to constitutional government. It was displaced by the French Revolution, but revived under the First and Second Empires and, briefly, under the Vichy government that ruled southern France, under Nazi auspices, during World War II.

The second cycle could be described as "oligarchical." It represents the efforts of certain prominent groups, distinguished by elite status or regional affinity, to

---

1. An overview of this approach to French constitutional history is offered in William Safran, *The French Polity*. New York, Longman, 1998.

assert sovereign control over France. Phases of this cycle often have been relatively brief and chaotic, especially since the establishment of these sorts of constitutional government has been the result of struggles among competing groups and interests. They have included the rule of the Directory and Consulate during the French Revolution, the cooperative process of the Orléans constitutional monarchy of the 1830s and 1840s, and the somewhat eccentric division of powers established under the Third Republic.

The third cycle could be described as "republican." Admittedly, though, this label is somewhat a misnomer, since this cycle has been the product of attempts to establish popular sovereignty through the complete dominance of a legislative system of government. A true republic is closer to some of the French experiments with limited oligarchy, since that sort of government seeks to accommodate the interests of various classes, groups, and regions. This use of the term "republican," within this context, is more simply directed toward democratic government, and it has been represented particularly by the constitutions established under the First, Second, and Fourth Republics. In fact, it is the attempt to combine these three cycles of French constitutional history, under the Fifth Republic, that could be described more accurately as "republican."

These cycles promote an image of French history as being subject to constitutional confusion and volatility.[2] It reflects a struggle over sovereignty that was not definitively settled until the latter part of the twentieth century. Each cycle has produced certain political and legal advantages and problems, and the lessons of this theme were not lost upon the framers of the constitution of the Fifth French Republic, including its leading proponent, Charles de Gaulle.

Quasi-Presidential System of Government

The current constitution was a product of political, social, military, and constitutional crises. The weakness and indecisiveness of the constitutional model of the Fourth Republic were revealed throughout the 1950s. But that sense of inadequacy became intolerable when French armed forces in Algeria, reacting to this weakness and against the insurrection of Algerians rebelling against French colonial rule, threatened to plunge the country into civil war. The leader of the Free French

---

2. Perhaps, the best description and explanation of this cycle has characterized these phases as "moderate monarchy," "conservative reaction," and "liberalization," Dorothy Pickles, *The Fifth French Republic* (New York: Praeger, 1965), pp. 3-5.

during World War II, Charles de Gaulle, was recalled from political retirement to provide stability. Subsequently, he drafted a new constitution that would restore the executive authority that had been deliberately excluded from the constitution of the Fourth Republic. This constitutional concentration of delegated sovereign power within the legislature had been a reaction to the authoritarianism of the Vichy regime, but many of its critics regarded it as an overreaction that resulted in a lack of political cohesiveness, especially since no political party could effectively exert control over the government or public policy.

De Gaulle's constitution was ratified by a plebiscite in 1958. It restored a strong executive to the constitutional scheme. It also made some attempt to create an upper house of parliament, called the Senate, that would informally represent certain socio-economic and professional sectors of society, through a process in which local political leaders from the various regions of France would select its membership. But it also retained (as other political leaders had insisted) an effective parliamentary system. Therefore, it sought to rectify the weaknesses of the Fourth Republic through a strong and independent executive, a role for certain elite members and interests of French society, but also by upholding the principle of popular sovereignty as represented by legislative representatives.

This system has worked most efficiently when the executive, represented by an elected president, is controlled by the same political party that dominates the parliament, particularly its lower house, the National Assembly. A separate executive, the premier, is appointed by the president, but that choice is, for practical purposes (consistent with the traditional principles of parliamentary government), limited to a person who is acceptable to the political party that controls the National Assembly. Members of the cabinet also are appointed by the president but upon the recommendation of the premier. In practice, when the president and premier come from the same political party, the president is regarded as the more senior party leader and the most dominant executive presence within the governmental system.

This system does not work as smoothly when the National Assembly is controlled by a political party that differs from the president's affiliation. The president's powers over foreign affairs, diplomacy, and the actual disposition of the armed forces are expressly provided by the constitution. However, the constitutional description of executive powers was left vague in many areas, particularly the identification of the ultimate source of authority for domestic (including economic) policy development and implementation. Therefore, it is possible for both the president and the premier to claim that authority and the responsibility for directing the activities of members and their respective departments. This pattern of a "dual executive" in competition with each other is best revealed through the informal relationship known as "cohabitation."

Generally, under this arrangement, the president loses enormous initiative regarding domestic policy. But the independence of the president from requiring a parliamentary mandate in order to hold office (being directly elected for a seven-year term) provides a secure and prominent political platform for shaping public opinion, criticizing and advising the cabinet and parliament, engaging in political negotiations, and even threatening to exercise the president's constitutional authority of dissolving the National Assembly and dismissing the premier and cabinet, although that last action is regarded as being politically extreme and potentially costly. Therefore, some form of compromise often is reached for the purpose of facilitating this awkward relationship.

The ultimate purpose of this system was the restoration of a strong, decisive, independent executive, reminiscent of the monarchical phase of French constitutional history. Yet the retention of strong republican features protects the principle of popular sovereignty and the parliamentary traditions of the republican cycle. Reconciling these conflicting interests into a workable system is advanced by other constitutional features that also will be addressed within this chapter.

Declaration of the Rights of Man and Citizen

One unentrenched constitutional feature has exerted a particularly strong influence over the entrenched French constitutional process. The Declaration of the Rights of Man and Citizen was a cornerstone of the French Revolution. Its principles have not remained a formal part of the French constitutional tradition. However, its spirit, in addition to many of its specific clauses, has become an integral part of the ideals of French constitutionalism.

This declaration asserts fundamental civil rights and liberties, including freedom of speech and conscience, the right to vote, freedom of assembly, and due process guarantees. It embraces liberal principles and liberal democratic values, and it makes this statement even more strongly, perhaps, than the Bill of Rights of the United States Constitution. It has served as an inspiration for other civil libertarian traditions and a model for constitutional development.

This declaration is explicitly mentioned within the constitution's preamble. Its true constitutional significance was not recognized until the 1970s, when it was invoked by the Constitutional Council for the purpose of evaluating policies and legislation. Furthermore, its political effect remains even stronger, since it has become a symbol of both French constitutional development and French national identity. Therefore, its effectiveness is due to both legal interpretation and more intangible political considerations.

Unitary System

The French system is centralized. The provinces have been delegated a degree of administrative autonomy which corresponds to their historical significance, but final sovereign authority continues to reside in the central government. Cultural and linguistic distinctions contribute to the importance of France's regional governments, so their role remains politically significant, despite the centralized structure of the French polity, which is reinforced by the constitution. This centralization is especially apparent within the administrative structure, for policy remains firmly under the control of the central government, but the administration of social policy, in particular, is delegated to decentralized authorities.

One exception to this unitary trend is Corsica. Strong nationalist sentiment within that province, tied to its island geography, cultural and political ties to Italy, and prominence as the home of Napoléon Bonaparte, has compelled the central government to grant more local autonomy to officials representing Corsica. Nonetheless, the federal principle has not been introduced, despite this greater local autonomy, and the unitary principle remains firmly in place.

Political Culture

France has emerged as a leading example of a liberal democratic society. Despite an authoritarian legacy and an association with classic conservative thought, this cultural heritage remains a driving force within French social, cultural, legal, and political development. The central significance of the National Assembly, the Declaration of the Rights of Man and Citizen, and the concept of equality before the law are testaments to the dominance of this ideological tradition. Yet the French expression of liberal democracy has not been as fiercely individualistic as can be found within some other liberal cultures such as the United States.

Many observers associate French liberal democracy with a communitarian interpretation of its basic principles and values. This ideological perspective can be found expressed within the French constitutional tradition. The maintenance of legislative initiative, even in the presence of a strong executive, is a broad testament to that influence. The specific interpretation of the Declaration of the Rights of Man and Citizen by the Constitutional Council offers another insight, especially in contrast to its usual deference to parliamentary desires to limit the scope of such rights and liberties when they are deemed to undermine genuinely and widely beneficial public policy. This emphasis can be traced to the theoretical writings of Jean-Jacques Rousseau and his advocacy of the ideal of a "social contract" as the basis for a society that promotes the popular will against the selfish or fearful interests of entrenched minority interests. It has been a motivating force for the central role of the legislature throughout the various phases of the republican cycle of French constitutional history.

But this constitutional tradition also reveals an obvious republican perspective upon liberal democratic ideology. The inclusion of the plebiscite as the preferred method of constitutional entrenchment may seem to be a reflection of a communitarian principle, but it also can be regarded, within the overall context of the constitution, as a reflection of an ancient republican principle (as it has evolved into a variation of modern republicanism) of providing an institutional role for the common people within the process of government. The republican emphasis upon the organic image of the community, with various component parts that need to be included, is strongly reflected within the French constitutional tradition.

The principle of the strong magistrate found in the presidency, the geographical representation that the Senate provides (along with its implied role as a venue for elite socio-economic and professional classes), the chamber of the people provided by the National Assembly, are all indicative of this philosophical influence. Therefore, the term French Republic may echo an actual ideal, derived from an historical need for social, political, and ideological compromise among monarchists, conservatives, libertarians, communitarians, and other competing visions of French government and society. It is an indication of a liberal democratic national identity that is not quite as homogeneous as outside observers otherwise may conclude.

Legal Practice

France offers, for many people, the epitome of a civil law system. The creation of the *Code Napoléon* in 1804 advanced the revolutionary principle of equality before the law by making the law knowable and accessible through codification. Other key civil law features have emerged from that process, and a respect for the rule of law remains a guiding principle of French constitutionalism.

Various categories of legal practitioner exist within France. Each one is specially trained through the university system and is certified, after receiving their respective degrees, through a separate examination process. This process produces *avocats*, who try cases before tribunals, *notaries*, who prepare certain types of legal documents, *fiduciaires*, who address taxation law, and *conseilleurs juridiques*, who provide general legal advice. Additionally, judges are produced through this process, rather than the common law practice of elevating experienced jurists from the ranks of the legal profession. Given the restricted role of judges within a civil law system, as described within the first chapter of this book, it is not surprising that these legal professionals often are regarded more as legal administrators or civil servants than as distinguished guardians of the law and its principles. Their main task is an inquisitorial process of discovering truth, rather than law.

Other aspects of French legal practice have been addressed within this book. However, the adjudication of constitutional disputes is handled differently. In that case, law is categorized according to its purpose or relationship to the political system. These categories include "ordinary laws," which address public policy, "organic laws," which affect the institutional structure and powers of government, "constitutional amendments," "regulations," which put ordinary laws into actual effect, and "decrees," which are made by the executive (either president or premier) for the same purpose as regulations, but without the need for legislative sanction. This last category largely corresponds to the category of "administrative law" as it is practiced in other democratic systems, including the United States. The legal system for adjudicating these laws is complex and rigorously applied, but it cannot challenge the ultimate propriety of these laws. That process is left to another institution of French constitutional government.

Constitutional Council

The French constitution provides, within its title seven, for the presence and participation of a Constitutional Council. This council falls outside the direct control of executive and legislative authority. A third of its nine members are appointed by the president, three of them are appointed by the National Assembly, and three of them are appointed by the Senate. This council enjoys independence from direct government authority.

Unlike common law systems, French constitutional law is not subject to the interpretive domination of jurists. The Constitutional Council is dominated by political scientists, who have traditionally been regarded (even outside the civil law tradition) as the true interpreters of public law. This presence is especially important because of the broader social science context that is applied to this understanding and application of French constitutionalism. Furthermore, it provides an acknowledgment of the particular governmental purposes of the French constitutional tradition in a way that does not interfere with the normal process of the legal system.

The most important purpose of the Constitutional Council is the adjudication of disputes among governmental institutions, particularly regarding the scope of their delegate sovereign authority. Therefore, a considerable amount of this council's attention is focused upon the organic laws passed by the parliament (which must be submitted to the Constitutional Council, automatically, for its consideration), since these laws pertain most often to the relationship between executive (including administrative) and legislative sectors of French government. However, other laws also fall under the interpretive control of the Constitutional Council. Since the 1970s, this council has been active in upholding the tenets of the Declaration of the Rights of Man and Citizen (especially those protections that have since been codified) against claims of parliamentary supremacy or executive prerogative. This sort of action has been especially true in terms of protecting freedom of expression from governmental policies, laws, and regulations that seek to facilitate political goals by muting the alleged "interference" of the press.

The Constitutional Council does not fulfill its role through the judicial appellate process. Controversies are referred to it in different ways. All organic laws are submitted to it, automatically, prior to being promulgated. The president, the premier, or a designated number of parliamentary members may submit laws and regulations for its examination. Any invocation of article 16 of the French Constitution (which grants emergency powers to the president under "grave and immediate" circumstances) must be reviewed by this council. The decisions of this council may not be appealed. It has provided a source of constitutional protection, and ordinary citizens have been able to use it, through their parliamentary representatives, to protect their rights and interests.

Court System

The French judicial system is a typical example of the civil law model. It is relatively specialized, with a separate structure for civil, criminal, labor, commercial, social services, and rent controversies, in addition to other administrative courts in which citizens seek redress against government agencies that fail to fulfill their obligations, especially in matters of enforcing public policy. The juries of the common law system are almost entirely absent, with judges considering matters of both fact and law in cooperation with other participants in the proceedings. Each sector of tribunals has its own system of appellate court, with the judges considering potential errors of both fact and law committed by the trial courts, should they agree to consider them.

The final court of appeal is the *cour de cassation*. This "supreme" court also is subject to specialization. It is divided into six chambers, each one composed of at least seven judges who consider appeals of the various specialized civil and criminal judicial divisions. Again, this appellate level may not consider challenges to the specific laws. They apply the law, as transmitted through the legislative process and the civil code, as accurately and as free of bias as possible, and the decisions of this judicial level are final.

The Future of French Constitutionalism

Enormous change has marked the development of the French constitutional tradition. It has proven to be one of the most remarkable legal experiments in Western history. Despite all of the fluctuations in its composition and sovereign expression, the French constitutional tradition has been guided by an underlying faith in, and reverence for, the law as an institution and an expression of justice. This theme continues to direct it.

The constitution of the Fifth Republic has sought to achieve an overarching compromise of these volatile forces. This process provides an opportunity for a lasting constitutional settlement that offers strength and decisiveness, together with freedom and popular sovereign control. The persistent role of the Declaration of the Rights of Man and Citizen symbolizes this process and progress. Therefore, the French constitutional tradition remains an important model of constitutional government that continues to inspire other aspiring political and legal systems.

References

John Bell, *French Constitutional Law*. Oxford, Clarendon, 1992.
Christian Dadomo and Susan Farran, *The French Legal System*. London, Sweet and Maxwell, 1996.
Guillaume Drago, *Contentieux constitutionnel français*. Paris, Presses Universitaires de France, 1998.
Pierre Esplugas, *Le Conseil constitutionnel et service public*. Paris, L. G. D. J., 1994.
Marcel Morabito and Daniel Bourmaud, *L'Histoire constitutionnel et politique de la France, 1789-1958*. Paris, Montchrestien, 1991.
Anne Stevens, *The Government and Politics of France*. New York, St. Martin's, 1996.

CHAPTER 10
German Constitutional Tradition

The legacy of the Second World War deeply affected the globe, including in terms of its constitutional consequences. Germany has sought to transcend its terrible role in this conflict partly through a reaffirmation of many enlightened values that were suppressed under its militarist and fascist experience. The contemporary German constitutional tradition offers a dramatic rejection of this terrible legacy and has sought to replace it with a legal heritage that aspires to embrace many of the most noble ideals of the post-World War II period. The unification of its eastern and western parts has posed a particularly daunting challenge to this new constitutional development, requiring both innovation and a respect for the liberal democratic principles that have been its goal.

The Basic Law of Germany, which continues to serve as this country's constitution, may have been imposed upon it by the victorious Western Allies. However, it has assumed characteristics and concepts that embrace features of an historical German legal development that had been nearly lost through the tragedy of autocratic governments and two world wars. It is a model of constitutional reconstruction that deserves special attention, especially for many of the emerging nation-states and the political challenges of the twenty-first century.

Formal Constitutional Structure

The German Basic Law was not intended to be an entrenched constitution, although it has assumed that status since the adoption of the amendment that united the eastern and western parts of the country. The occupying Western military powers (France, United Kingdom, United States) required the civil government of West Germany to enact this document to provide an interim constitutional structure for this part of Germany, in the anticipation (really, more of a hope) of uniting the eastern and western parts. But once a separate communist government, under the direction of the occupying forces of the Soviet Union, was established for East Germany, this supposedly temporary measure became a permanent constitutional institution.

This Basic Law was drafted by a constituent assembly and ratified by elected legislative assemblies of the *länder*, or German states. This entrenchment process was preferred over a popular referendum, because it suggested that this document was not a permanent constitution, so the division of Germany was not intended to be permanent, either. It has not been replaced, even after the 1990 unification of the two parts of Germany occurred.

The Basic Law consists of 146 articles, divided into nine sections. Significantly, the first section is devoted to guaranteed rights and liberties, which are derived both from a civil rights and a human rights tradition. The second section describes some of the basic conditions of the political system, political parties, security (including limitations of defense) policy, and federal relations. Sections three through eight describe the structure and authority of the government, including both houses of parliament, the chancellor, the presidency, and the federal administration. Section nine is devoted to the legal system, the court structure, and constitutional legitimacy.

This Basic Law describes and empowers a governmental system that adheres to a conventional parliamentary model. A separate executive, in the form of the president, exists as a largely ceremonial head of state. True executive authority resides in the chancellor, who is selected by the lower house of parliament, the *Bundestag*, which consists of deputies elected upon the basis of representation by population. The upper house of parliament, the *Bundesrat* (council of states), consists of members elected by the *länder*. The rules of parliamentary government, including such features as the dissolution of parliament and the calling of new elections in the event that the chancellor's political party loses its control of the *Bundestag* (as indicated by a "vote of no confidence") are not left to unentrenched conventions or shared understandings. All of these features are express provisions of the Basic Law, with little implied power derived from it.

Despite the presence of this sort of explicit detail, the Basic Law is not very lengthy. It is, however, a testament to the environment of political mistrust that followed the end of World War II, requiring, in the opinion of the victorious Allies and many Germans, a specific constitutional document that ensured the ultimate sovereign authority of German citizens. This goal is advanced further by the detailed description of a federal system and a guarantee of the limited role of the *länder* as a delegated source for expressing the sovereign will. But this spirit of mistrust would be replaced by a more genuine spirit of constitutionalism and a desire to embrace the progressive values of the late twentieth and early twenty-first centuries, and judicial interpretation of the Basic Law would confirm this trend.

Principal Constitutional Themes

The Basic Law was intended to be a testament to Germany's rejection of its authoritarian (especially its Nazi) past. It also offered a constitutional outline for a future state that would united the two parts of Germany without the threatening prospect of German expansion or any promotion of the idea of a "greater" German realm. This theme is as much a reflection of the concerns of Germany's neighbors and the world community as it is a testament to the renewed spirit of German political freedom and benevolence. It is particularly reflected in its constitutional provisions regarding the renunciation of military aggression and the limitations imposed upon the German government's powers to develop and implement defense policies.

Other constitutional themes proceed from that prime consideration. The imposition of express parliamentary institutions and procedures is intended to guarantee democratic sovereignty and the divided delegation of that sovereignty between federal and *länder* levels. The conspicuous protection of basic rights and liberties also reflects this overriding concern, especially in terms of defining the nature of sovereign limitations upon government through constitutional and other legal means. The German constitutional tradition continues to be predicated upon these themes, and the result has been a remarkably stable, successful, and well-regarded system.

Parliamentary Government

Many of the most important constitutional features of the German parliamentary system already have been considered. However, the way it reconciles legislative and executive governmental roles merits further consideration. The efficiency of a strong chancellor and cabinet is consistent with German historical practice, but it also offers a potentially foreboding reminder of the excesses that such executive authority can effect. Therefore, the dependence upon the political support of the legislature is a scrupulously protected and promoted principle.

Section six of the Basic Law outlines this relationship. It provides the chancellor with considerable discretion in appointing federal ministers who comprise the cabinet. It also affirms the authority of the chancellor to establish guidelines for the implementation of public policy, the general conduct of government administration, and the executive responsibilities of federal ministers, especially as articulated within articles 64 and 65. However, articles 67 and 68 reinforce the ultimate political supremacy of the legislature as the representative of the sovereign people. The authority of the *Bundestag*, in particular, is made clear, in this respect, as is its primacy in the creation of legislation and public policy, as expressed within articles 70 through 78.

The role of the parliament in amending the Basic Law offers an interesting insight. This entrenchment process officially is left entirely to the parliament. Article 79 of the Basic Law requires a two-thirds vote of both parliamentary chambers in order to affect this result. The fact that this entrenchment process does not require popular referenda or recourse to the *länder* (although they are, supposedly, represented through the *Bundesrat*) is a further indication of the supposedly temporary nature of this constitutional document. Nonetheless, the fact that this article also nullifies any attempt, under any circumstances, to change the constitutional powers of the *länder* or the basic principles enshrined within articles one and twenty of the Basic Law also confirms the broader theme of protecting the sovereign integrity of the system that the government has been delegated to provide.

The parliamentary system of Germany seems typical and unassuming. It adheres to the principles and procedures of parliamentary government, within the context of liberal democratic beliefs and values, in a rather unremarkable way. But that very fact is a testament to the success of the Basic Law in helping Germany recover from its authoritarian past and the tragedy it produced, and it offers considerable promise for its further democratic development.

Rights and Liberties

The first twenty articles of the Basic Law address the fundamental rights and liberties that are considered essential to German constitutionalism. They include guarantees that can be classified as both civil and human rights and liberties. They range from freedom of expression, belief, and association to a freedom of work and profession and the inviolability of the home. The Basic Law makes reference to property rights but, also, to a general principle of human personality (especially within article two) that underscores a relatively broad interpretation of these protections.

Article one offers the most significant expression of these principles. Its commitment to the "protection of human dignity" makes express reference to the human rights tradition. It provides an obvious reaction against the violations of the Nazi regime, and it makes assurances beyond the scope of its sovereign constitutional authority. Its acknowledgment of "inviolable and inalienable human rights as the basis of every community, of peace, and of justice in the world" lies at the core of a trend of constitutional interpretation that has been notably expansive. The very definition of a "human," for example, has been interpreted by the Constitutional Court as including a foetus; the legacy of restrictive legal definitions of "human" existence (such as the "subhuman" labels attached by the Nazis to certain ethnic and religious groups, including Jewish, Slavic, and Romany people) has motivated politicians and jurists under this constitutional system to err on the side of this enlarged approach, even though it has been opposed by some Germans as imposing restrictions of abortion policy and the associated rights of women over reproduction.

Perhaps, the most dramatic guarantee can be found within an article that falls, technically, just outside this first section of the Basic Law. Section 20 encompasses a "right to resist." It reaffirms the principle of popular sovereignty and empowers all German citizens to oppose any force that might seek to overthrow the constitutional order. This clause would have sanctioned attempts to assassinate Adolf Hitler, for example, and it can apply to any other despot. It also implies a duty to resist all assaults upon democratic constitutionalism. This idea that the human rights tradition also imposes obligations is further reflected within articles 12a and 19, especially in terms of the duty of military service in the legitimate defense of the country and the legitimate limitations upon rights and liberties when they present a valid threat to the freedom and security of other Germans, consistent with the theoretical guidance of the liberal democratic "harm" principle.

This German approach to rights and liberties reflects both the American civil rights tradition (as provided through its leading role in the post-war occupation and administration of the country) and the broader human rights tradition embraced by the United Nations. Most of these rights and liberties apply to anyone residing within Germany. However, certain specific political rights and liberties (including voting rights) are extended only to German citizens. This consideration is made more restrictive by the definition of German citizenship, as expressed within article 116 of the Basic Law and consistent with an overall legal heritage of this concept.

Two categories of citizenship tend to predominate among the world's constitutional traditions. The most common category is a "citizenship of the land," in which this status can be obtained upon the basis of a person's place of birth. A person who is born within the territorial boundaries of the United States is, for example, a constitutionally recognized American citizen. The second category is "citizenship of blood," in which this status is attained by virtue of being descended from other citizens. Many legal systems combine these sources, so a person can be recognized as a citizen through either birth or descent. But the Basic Law continues the German tradition of grounding citizenship upon an ethnic definition of German identity.

The consequences of this relatively restrictive definition can be telling. Although Germany provides generous protections to refugees, they, and their descendants, may not obtain German citizenship, regardless of the fact that they may have been born within the territorial boundaries of Germany and represent many generations of this residence. This requirement is consistent with the general nature of German political culture and its historical context, but it has been opposed by some critics as being unnecessarily parochial and a disturbing reminder of the ethnic and racial policies of a previous age.

Nonetheless, the German commitment to rights and liberties within its constitutional tradition has been genuinely strong. The reference to the "inviolable and inalienable" nature of these rights and liberties introduces an impressive libertarian emphasis that has not, historically, been a prominent feature of German legal and political culture. Its importance is revealed through its prominent place at the beginning of the Basic Law. Furthermore, the creation and special role of the Constitutional Court in safeguarding and interpreting these principles and using them to limit the scope of German governmental authority reinforce this constitutional commitment.

Federalism

The modern German nation-state, once finally established during the latter part of the nineteenth century, was formed as a unitary system. However, its antecedents were extremely fragmented, especially in the form of the myriad kingdoms, electorates, palatinates, duchies, archbishoprics, counties, and numerous other petty states that comprised the German territories of the Holy Roman Empire. The centralization of authority under the German Empire facilitated its military and political dominance, prior to World War I. Hitler's centralization of authority, following the rise of his Nazi party, and the subsequent demise of the Weimar Republic aided him in the quest for national and, then, world domination. This memory was key to the demands of the victorious Allies that this German unitary structure be replaced with a federal system of shared sovereignty.

The Basic Law identifies the resulting states, or *länder*, and acknowledges the historical basis for many of them, particularly since they often represent regional and cultural variations upon a German national identity that often is mistakenly regarded as rigidly homogeneous. Sections two, eight, and nine of the Basic Law define the constitutional relationship between the federal and *länder* levels of government and imply the goal of limiting the potential for autocratic government that prompted this development. Articles 28, 29, and 30 are particularly important, in this respect, for they impose a responsibility upon the federal government to guarantee that all *länder* conform to the same "principles of republican, democratic, and social government based on the rule of law" that is constitutionally expected at the federal level.

Each *länder* has its own constitutional institutions. They enjoy the same sort of "reserved powers" that constitute the sovereign jurisdiction of the American states under the United States Constitution. These powers are directed especially toward local administration, public services, certain areas of domestic policy, and those "police powers" not expressly delegated to the federal government. Each of the *länder* has its own court system to address laws created by their respective legislatures, but the legal principles that guide these courts are the same for both sovereign levels, reinforcing a judicial unity that will be addressed later within this chapter.

Articles 91a and 91b describe an interesting cooperative relationship between the federal and *länder* governments. They recognize, explicitly, shared policy areas that other federal systems address on an implicit level. These policy areas include higher education, regional economic development, agricultural and marine interests, and general matters of educational planning, including scientific research. These policy areas are of particular interest to the *länder* governments, but they also affect the national goals. Criminal law enforcement and a variety of social welfare programs also tend to fall under this category of shared governmental responsibilities.

The *Bundesrat* provides a federal institution that represents *länder* interests. Its representatives are elected by the *länder* governments, as a bloc of votes, and the number of each *länder's* representation (between three and six members) is determined by a system that provides a disproportionate representation in favor of the smaller *länder*. This principle of intrastate federal representation is similar to the arrangement provided by the United States Constitution for its Senate prior to 1912. Although the *Bundesrat* is less dominant than the parliamentary lower house, its role is significant within the legislative and governmental process and necessary within the constitutional amendment process.

The federal principle is crucial to the success of contemporary German constitutionalism. It is not inconsistent with historical precedents, particularly under the German Empire of the nineteenth century in terms of the tendency to defer the creation of certain policies to the central government while allowing local governmental units to administer them. However, in this case, the *länder* also have sovereign authority over certain areas, especially the "reserve powers" not expressly provided to the federal government. In this way, the larger themes of limited government and the guarantee of popular sovereignty are advanced.

Political Culture

The Basic Law describes practices and institutions that clearly are compatible with liberal democratic norms and values. Interestingly, reference is made to a respect for inalienable rights and liberties in a manner consistent with a libertarian interpretation of that ideological tradition. However, German society is part of a continental tradition that may be more conformable to a communitarian interpretation, especially in terms of a strong deference to the goals of the community as expressed through the legislature.

But a clearer indication of a collective German system of thought may be derived from its tradition of nationalism. This ideal, expressed as an ideology, has inspired a sense of common identity, values, and purpose for the German people, throughout their history. It has been articulated by such eminent philosophers as Georg Wilhelm Friedrich Hegel, especially in terms of his theoretical exposition on the dialectic and its role in shaping a collective human history. The notion that a common "idea," or *geist*, guides a community toward a collective purpose inspired the emergence of the German nation and nation-state, especially in terms of the development of institutions and the activities of social, economic, cultural, and political elites who have sought to define the German "soul."

Unfortunately, this concept of German nationalism also has been subject to manipulation, particularly as a reaction to collective misfortune and the frustration of common goals and values. The rise of fascism represented a perversion of these ideals, fostered by military defeat, political humiliation, social unrest, and economic deprivation, especially during the inter-war years of the 1920s and 1930s. The Basic Law deliberately has sought to mute this expression through the promotion of both general liberal democratic ideals and the attempt to safeguard popular sovereignty. The fact that the articulation of rights and liberties has adopted the language of a libertarian interpretation of this widespread ideological tradition may be an indication of this desire, since this individualistic approach could be regarded as an antidote to any possible abuse of the uniformity that a more collectivist national identity could impose.

This German tradition of national identity has focused upon the institutions of the state. As the interests of the state and its leaders have shifted, so has the definition of this national focus. Now, though, national identity and liberal democracy have merged through the Basic Law and the general reform of the German polity. Therefore, nationalism and a liberal constitutional tradition have become the same thing. The goals of the state are the goals of the sovereign people, and the purpose of the Basic Law is to direct the state toward fulfilling that renewed sense of German national purpose.

This historical development of German nationalism as an ideological expression is important for gaining insight into the evolution of contemporary German constitutionalism. It is especially present within such features as the parochial definition of German citizenship as being grounded within an ethnic, rather than a geographic, identity. It also may influence the judicial appraisal of this constitutional tradition by reconciling the good features of both nationalism and liberal democracy and, thus, transform this seemingly sterile institutional mandate into a true, and benevolent, expression of the sovereign German will.

Legal Practice and Judicial Decision Making

Germany developed a pandectist civil law system that differs from the "classic" model of Roman law more closely reflected within such institutions as the *Code Napoléon*. It is rooted in the legal culture and history of Germany, thus reflecting further the influence of nationalism within its political culture. It also offers a model of legal administration that seeks efficiency and neutrality; those features have proven to be both strengths and weaknesses of the German legal system.

The German civil code initially was developed as part of the process of national unification, toward the end of the nineteenth century. Its sources included the Prussian Land Law of the eighteenth century, grounded upon the historical context of this region and its experiences, rather than the more abstract principles (in search of a universal model) that characterized Roman law. The Historical School of legal scholarship and codification, led by Friedrich Carl von Savigny, emphasized this idea of law as a cultural expression, although later developments within German law tended to become increasingly abstract in the expression of legal concepts and principles. This development gave rise to the pandectist model of a civil law system, as described within the introductory chapter of this book.

One of the consequences of this legal approach was a tendency for practitioners to employ and interpret the law in a rigidly detached and neutral manner. The

German legal system suffered from a shortage of practitioners during the period following the end of the Second World War. Legal professionals of the Nazi period generally had not been accused of active collusion with fascist authorities, but they *had* been accused of indifference to gross injustices that had been given the formal sanction of legality through the Nazi political strategy of institutional legitimation of their actions and policies. The German judges of this time, in particular, contended that they were not free to interpret the law, selectively, but must act only in a manner that applies existing laws in a dispassionate and morally detached fashion. That argument was a recourse to those fundamental proscriptions of legal positivism, as an unchallengeable "command of the sovereign," that were repudiated by the legal and political authorities of the occupying powers (including the application of certain natural law sentiments by the war crimes tribunals) after the war.

Nonetheless, a new generation of German legal professionals emerged from this experience. The traditional civil law focus upon university education and post-university testing for achieving professional accreditation, the specialization of different professional toward the various categories of legal practice, and the inquisitorial method of adjudication have been retained. The pandectist codes also are retained, although they now are articulated in a way that reflects the unique ideals, values, culture, and historical traditions of a democratic Germany.

Court System

The civil codes impose a uniform, centralized legal standard over all of Germany and its judicial system. However, the institutional structure of that judicial system is decentralized. The *länder* are responsible for administering most of the country's courts through their respective ministries of justice, even though federal law specifies the basic structure and organization of the judiciary. These courts include "regular" and "specialized" tribunals. The former group addresses general matters of civil (or private) and criminal law, while the latter group is divided into administrative, labor, fiscal, and social courts, the last category dealing with disputes involving social and welfare policy.

Regular courts exist, as courts of original jurisdiction, at the local and district levels, with approximately 550 of these courts distributed around the country. The 94 district courts also serve as the first level of appellate courts, in addition to trying particularly serious criminal and civil controversies. The specialized tribunals are organized along a similar pattern. Above the district court level exists the state appellate court, which is divided into separate panels of three to five judges that focus upon different categories of law. Beyond this level, cases can be appealed further to the federal level. The final court of appeal is the federal appellate court, which is similarly divided, according to legal categories, into over twenty specialized panels, known as "senates." Appeals may not be made beyond this level, except for constitutional challenges.

Most laws are evaluated according to the sovereign intent of the legislature, consistent with the habits of civil law systems, generally. Inconsistently with most other civil law systems, though, constitutional matters are not left exclusively to the legislative or executive authorities, for the Basic Law has adapted its judiciary to a special institutional approach to this matter. Contentions relating to the constitutionality of laws or actions may be considered at any level of the judicial system, but a special level of court has been established for the purpose of adjudicating challenges arising directly under the Basic Law, at both the state and federal levels. This federal court provides a special focus of attention within the Basic Law.

Constitutional Court

Articles 93 and 94 of the Basic Law describe and empower a judicial institution that is not usual for a civil law system. An American influence (derived from the role of that country's Supreme Court) may have contributed to this inclusion. The federal Constitutional Court exercises independent authority as a judicial body, unlike other courts that are subject to the administrative control of the government, usually in terms of the justice ministries of the various *länder*. This court has its own budget and makes all of its own administrative decisions. Furthermore, its authority is final, providing a limitation upon the delegated sovereign authority of the parliament.

Typical for a civil law system, the Constitutional Court is divided into specialized panels, or "senates." Two of these senates comprise this court: the first one adjudicates matters of rights and liberties falling under the first twenty articles of the Basic Law; the second one addresses controversies falling under the federal scheme created through the Basic Law, especially regarding the scope of federal/*länder* authority in relation to each other. Half of the sixteen judges on the court are appointed by the *Bundestag*. The other half of the court's membership is appointed by the *Bundesrat*, which further advances the principle of federalism by providing the *länder* a means of influencing this federal court's composition.

The Constitutional Court has proven to be both active and effective. Its judges seem highly cognizant of the political nature of public law, and the scholarly opinions of political scientists and other social science academicians can be influential within the process of constitutional adjudication. Many of these jurists have employed a judicial activist approach to this process, much like their American counterparts, while many critics have demanded that these jurists practice more judicial restraint, in deference to the democratic authority of the legislature.

All *länder* also have a constitutional court that addresses controversies under their respective constitutional charters, in addition to considering broader constitutional matters. These courts perform a function that complements the normal appellate system, yet is distinct from it, especially in terms of their role in interpreting the law, rather than merely explaining and applying it. The Constitutional Court also may render "abstract" rulings that do not arise from actual controversies but are referred to it concerning actual or proposed laws, much like the "reference cases" considered by the Supreme Court of Canada.

This general constitutional authority confers a sovereign role upon this part of the judiciary that resembles the continental liberal ideal of a "separation of powers," including a "judicial branch" of government. However, many observers would be tentative about making too explicit a comparison with the American system, in this respect. Nonetheless, the strong impetus to prevent any return to autocratic government and the very active desire to promote a vigorous liberal democratic society and system of government, in support of popular sovereignty, are reflected by this institution and the articles of the Basic Law that created and sustain them and their independence.

National Unification

Article 23 of the Basic Law allows other *länder* to join the Federal Republic of Germany. This article was invoked for the purpose of uniting the country with the former German Democratic Republic when its communist regime collapsed in 1990. Two treaties of unification were negotiated, signed, and ratified by the two states. This action resulted in the creation of five new *länder* from the former East German state, which were accepted by the West German parliament into its federation. The terms of unification overwhelmingly were determined by the Federal Republic of Germany in accordance with the legal norms established under its Basic Law.

The German Democratic Republic had been a communist state governed by a socialist legal system. Like other such systems, its structure was compatible with most civil law systems, while its content and the policies it supported differed significantly from most liberal democratic societies. One of the first priorities of the newly unified Germany was the additional unification of its legal system and civil code, which was affected within two years of achieving political unification—again, largely upon the basis of the preexisting West German system.

Many of the jurists of the East German legal system were regarded with deep suspicion and, even, opposition, particularly because of the role they played in upholding a system that was widely regarded as corrupt, abusive, undemocratic, and authoritarian. Many of the legal practitioners of the former German Democratic Republic have not been retained, and the ones who continue to function within the unified system have been required to adapt to it and demonstrate their professional proficiency with the legal norms and practices established under the German civil code and Basic Law. Meanwhile, the institutional court structure of West Germany has been established within these new *länder* of the former East Germany, so the legal and constitutional system is dominated by the general considerations already discussed within this chapter.

Generally, the process of incorporating the legal system of the former West Germany into the *länder* of the former East Germany has been remarkably efficient and subject to less controversy than many of the other political, economic, social, and cultural adjustments that the government and people of this unified German society continue to confront. The evaluation of those issues would warrant at least a chapter of its own, but this brief analysis of the constitutional significance of German unification will conclude with that observation. The socialist legal system of the former German Democratic Republic also would require its own chapter, which, owing to the demise of that system, no longer seems relevant to this examination of German constitutionalism. Therefore, the institutions, practices, and theories relating to the German constitutional tradition, as offered within this chapter, will be deemed to be applicable to *all* of Germany, as it emerged during the early 1990s and as it continues to function into the twenty-first century.

The Future of German Constitutionalism

The Basic Law became the constitution for all of Germany. It has not been replaced, though, by a more formally identified "constitution," largely for reasons of expediency. Unification has brought many political, social, and economic challenges. The process of adaptation of the German constitutional tradition must respond to these opportunities and challenges. It seems to have risen to meet that challenge.

The Basic Law has worked remarkably well for a constitutional institution that was suppose to be an interim legal document. It has been particularly effective in terms of restoring a liberal democratic legal and political culture to the German people and asserting a principle of constitutional sovereignty upon their government. The stability and ideals it has helped to instill not only have been beneficial to the German nation but also to the European community. Germany, throughout the twenty-first century, should enjoy a very different political legacy than it did during the previous century, and its constitutional tradition has made a lasting contribution to that progress and its future.

References

Peter C. Caldwell, *Popular Sovereignty and the Crisis of German Constitutional Law: The Theory and Practice of Weimar Constitutionalism*. Durham, NC, Duke University Press, 1997.

Anke Freckmann, *The German Legal System*. London, Sweet and Maxwell, 1999.

Klaus H. Goetz and Peter J. Cullen, eds., *Constitutional Policy in Unified Germany*. London, Frank Cass, 1995.

James E. Hergert, *Contemporary German Legal Philosophy*. Philadelphia, University of Pennsylvania Press, 1996.

H. W. Koch, *A Constitutional History of Germany in the Nineteenth and Twentieth Centuries*. New York, Longman, 1984.

Donald P. Kommers, *The Constitutional Jurisprudence of the Federal Republic of Germany*. Durham,NC, Duke University Press, 1997.

Sabine Michalowski and Lorna Woods, *German Constitutional Law: The Protection of Civil Liberties*. Brookfield, VT, Ashgate/Dartmouth, 1999.

Peter E. Quint, *The Imperfect Union: Constitutional Structures of German Unification*. Princeton, NJ, Princeton University Press, 1997.

CHAPTER 11
Mexican Constitutional Tradition

Latin American countries have struggled to maintain constitutional systems that reflect true popular sovereignty. This region offers a heritage of European and indigenous cultures that have shaped the legal and political development of all its countries. But, with that rich heritage, conflicting constitutional visions have arisen. Prior to the early twentieth century, Mexico experienced particular difficulty in this respect. Therefore, the constitutional legacy that has emerged from this country has been a testament to a legal and political persistence that has not always been entirely successful but which has, nonetheless, provided a basis for the continuing democratic evolution of this country.

The Mexican Constitution of 1917 was the product of a revolution that sought to transform this nation. It sought to end years of strife and restore the promise of democratic government that first motivated the revolutionary spirit and ended colonial domination. The greatest challenge to this constitutional legacy has been the struggle to make it achieve the promise of the fundamental values that it represents. Therefore, it is another example of a constitutional tradition that cannot be meaningfully analyzed solely through a formal-legal approach but which requires a broader method of examination.

Formal Constitutional Structure

Mexico's entrenched constitution is divided, structurally, into nine titles, which is further divided into 136 articles, plus a series of 16 "transitory" articles following the main body of the constitutional text. Title one includes four chapters that emphasize the relationship of individual persons to the constitutional system, including rights and liberties, definitions of citizenship, alien status, and a definition of individual Mexican national identity. Title two offers the general themes of this constitutional order and a geographical description of the Mexican state. Title three describes the various institutional features of the Mexican government, while title four addresses the public administration of the country, and its offices.

Title five describes the states of the federal system and their institutional parameters, while title six deals, generally, with the constitutional relationship between the government and matters of public policy, including labor policy. Titles seven and nine address various miscellaneous issues, including certain aspects of the relationship of church and state and the general principle of constitutional inviolability. Finally, title eight describes the amendment formula of this constitution that provides the basis for its entrenchment.

These articles are more lengthy and detailed than similar articles found within the entrenched constitution of Mexico's northern neighbor. However, this document does not include the overwhelming detail associated with constitutional documents of countries such as India and Nigeria, as explored within previous chapters of this book. In certain ways, it does seem to resemble the structure of the United States Constitution that partly helped to inspire it.

Principal Constitutional Themes

The Mexican constitutional tradition is notable for the way it has been used for defining and developing the sovereign relationship between the Mexican people and their government, especially in terms of fundamental economic, labor, and social policy. The government serves as a focus for a broad array of constitutionally protected social and economic services in a manner that reflects features of the broader Latin American regional political culture. It also serves as a vehicle for defining the sovereign population of the country, particularly in terms of its profound ethnic heritage. The melding of indigenous and European ancestry that provides a foundation for that heritage is promoted and protected within the Mexican constitution, while the prominence of Roman Catholicism also is constitutionally acknowledged, though in a very different way.

The revolutions that ultimately produced this constitutional tradition were prompted by profound desires to transform Mexican society in social, political, and, especially, economic terms. An ethnic and racial caste system was developed within New Spain that survived the end of colonial rule. This division was prompted by the *encomienda* economic system that not only recognized the concentration of land into the possession of an elite class of persons of direct and indirect European heritage, but it also granted them considerable legal jurisdiction over these lands. Native peoples who lived upon these lands were the subjects of this economic, political, and legal domination and exploitation and treated practically as slaves, though they were technically free. This situation was, however, only part of the socio-economic condition.

The Mexican class system was rigidly stratified. Indigenous peoples (including descendants of the sophisticated Aztec, Maya, and Toltec cultures) were the most oppressed level of this system. Persons of mixed (primarily native and European) descent, known as *mestizos*, had a socio-economic status that was only slightly elevated above native peoples, who had been decimated by disease and subjugation. Persons of African descent (slave and free) also were found among these oppressed peoples, although they were largely assimilated by the *mestizo* population by the early nineteenth century. At the apex of this system were found persons of European ancestry. This last class was divided between the ruling elite who came directly from Spain, known as the *peninsulares*, and persons of European descent but born within Mexico, known as *criollos*. Each group within this system had their own motives for seeking independence from Spain, and the revolutionary struggles were conducted by each group, often separately from, and in conflict with, each other. Mexico's constitutional tradition has sought to redress this division throughout its modern development.

The role of the Roman Catholic Church is a persistent theme of Mexican constitutionalism. The church was one of the leading landowners, both during, and after, Mexico achieved independence. An estimated one-third of Mexico's real property was controlled in this way. Furthermore, Catholic clerics have played an important role within Mexico's political and social development, including leading revolutionary figures and social reformers but, also, defenders of the elite establishment and resisters of constitutional change. The Roman Catholic Church has had, throughout Mexico's history, a constitutional status: either a positive one, as an established institution, or a negative one, as the target of deliberate secularization of the state.

The Mexican constitutional tradition is particularly conscious of its modern concept as a nation-state. Chapter one of title two of the Mexican constitution is dedicated toward the relationship of Mexican national identity with the popular sovereignty of the Mexican state. It is, interestingly, a concept that parallels the institution of Mexican citizenship, yet its separate inclusion is a testament to the underlying importance of that identity and the social and economic barriers to it that the Mexican constitution seeks to overcome.

The cultural diversity of Mexico is tied, inextricably, to this theme of national identity and citizenship addressed by title two of this constitutional document. The *mestizo* population that had been so effectively marginalized, beginning with the colonial period, has become the majority population of the country and a basis for Mexican national self-identification. These people of mixed indigenous and European ancestry find parallel populations within other immigrant societies such as the *métis* of Canada. But the rise of popular sovereignty within Mexico necessitated the elevation of the status of the *mestizos* through the elimination of traditional class distinctions. The Mexican constitutional tradition became the prime vehicle for that transformation.

These varied themes all relate to the role that this constitution performs in terms of social and economic transformation. Many constitutional traditions have addressed similar themes, but few have done it as seemingly self-consciously as within Mexico. Therefore, the interplay of the different basic beliefs and values that have shaped this constitutional development also offers a crucial insight into its legal, political, social, economic, and general institutional legacy. The revolutionary context of its creation and evolution also provides a method for gaining a truly critical understanding of its significance, especially from a comparative perspective and, also, in terms of a broad appreciation of the vast role that constitutions can fulfill, generally.

Revolutionary Constitutional Development

Different forces combined to initiate the revolutionary movement that created a modern, independent Mexico and, ultimately, its constitutional legacy. These revolutionaries included members of the clergy, oppressed native peoples and *mestizos*, frustrated *criollos*, and, even, reactionary *peninsulares*. First, they sought freedom from colonial control, including both Spanish and (during two different episodes) French domination under the Emperors Napoléon I and Napoléon III. Second, they sought liberation from ethnic and economic subjugation and inequality. Third, they sought to establish the sovereignty of a democratic polity.

Initially, a new constitutional order was sought by priests (primarily Padre Miguel Hidalgo y Costilla and, after his death, Padre José María Morelos y Pavón) who sought social justice for the oppressed members of Mexican society. Those forces that suppressed this revolt and the laws it instituted included members of the *criollos*, whose conservative leaders (most notably, General Augustín de Iturbide), themselves, sought independence from a Spain that, in 1820, was, itself, being transformed by a liberal revolution. Meanwhile, various *peninsulares* also were concerned about the consequences of being ruled by a liberal Spain, and so they reached an accord with the *criollos* to stage their own revolution and replace Spanish rule with a limited, conservative monarchy that, nonetheless, extended equal treatment and influence to both *peninsulares* and *criollos*. However, proponents of a liberal constitutional system continued to struggle for their own goals, thus perpetuating this competition between liberal and classic conservative revolutionaries and the constitutional order each side wished to institute.

The new Mexican Republic and its constitution was displaced by General Iturbide's move to make himself Emperor Augustín I of the Mexican Empire. But this reactionary response was short lived. It was replaced by a new republic, following a revolt led by General Antonio López de Santa Anna, which produced a liberal democratic constitution, under which regime Guadalupe Victoria was elected president. However, a consensus was lacking among the members of Mexican society, particularly concerning the fundamental ideological foundation for this constitutional order.

Classic conservative sentiment in favor of highly centralized government and elite democracy was led by certain members of the elite church hierarchy, *criollos*, and other wealthy landowners. Liberal sentiment in favor of a federal system, equality and democratic rights for all members of Mexican society, and economic liberation for native peoples and *mestizos* was led by more progressive leaders. Various power struggles, including assassinations of elected officials on both sides, ensued for several years, with no constitutional consensus emerging.

Meanwhile, the *encomienda* system of the colonial era persisted in altered form. Instead of an actual feudal control of peasant workers, due to their physical residence upon lands falling under the authority of wealthy landowners (including the church), these same persons were forced to serve on the land through the payment of perpetual debt, largely for work and living supplies, which cumulative debt was so overwhelming that it generally was inherited by subsequent generations. This system of debt peonage was widespread within Mexico, and it constituted a form of serfdom and instituted a new type of oppressed caste, known as the *peons*. The struggle to eliminate this peonage system would be a focal point of future Mexican constitutional development.

Antonio López de Santa Anna was elected president and advanced the conservative cause by making himself virtual dictator. Between 1833 and 1855 he dominated, intermittently, Mexican politics and helped to shape its constitutional development. The loss of Texas, in 1836, and defeat during the Mexican-American War, in 1848, provided opportunities for the restoration of more liberal regimes, and the interplay between these struggling forces would have an enduring influence upon the ultimate shaping of the Mexican constitutional tradition.

A member of the Zapotec people, Benito Juárez, emerged as the most dynamic leader of liberal constitutional reform. He instituted a new Mexican constitution, in 1857, that included provisions guaranteeing universal male suffrage and popular sovereignty, an array of civil rights and liberties, and dividing sovereign authority among various states within the country. This liberal constitutional system was opposed by conservative groups, so civil strife continued. External support for the liberals was provided by the United States, while the conservatives were assisted by Spain. Juárez extended the scope of his constitutional reforms by nationalizing the Mexican property of the Roman Catholic Church and establishing a strict separation of church and state. But his most controversial reform occurred in 1861.

President Juárez sought to advance reform policies in the areas of economic and social welfare by alleviating the national debt. Between 1858 and 1860, these efforts were opposed during a civil war between the supporters of Juárez and conservatives, backed by Spain. This War of the Reform resulted in victory for President Juárez and the constitutional vision he sought to bring to his country. But an even more formidable challenge occurred as a result of his decision to suspend interest payments of foreign loans. This action led to intervention on the part of Spain, Great Britain, and France, while the United States, engrossed in a desperate civil war, was largely helpless to oppose this armed action. Emperor Napoléon III of France had a more ambitious agenda and used this incident as an excuse for establishing colonial control over Mexico, while Great Britain and Spain withdrew their participation. A conservative constitution was established, in 1863, under the Mexican Empire of Emperor Maximilian, and the conflict of constitutional visions was renewed.

United States pressure, following the American Civil War, prompted the withdrawal of French support from this Mexican imperial government. Emperor Maximilian was deposed and executed, and President Juárez regained the political and constitutional initiative. Following his untimely death, the conservatives gained control, again, when a former opponent of Juárez, Porfirio Díaz, led a successful revolt, in 1877, suspended the constitution, and made himself dictator of Mexico. He restored, though largely informally, the constitutional position of the Roman Catholic Church. He also enforced peonage, permitted discrimination against Mexicans of aboriginal descent, and suspended many civil rights and liberties. Most significantly, he encouraged substantial foreign investment throughout Mexico, which encouraged economic development, tremendously, but which also prompted economic disparities and popular resentment.

Díaz felt sufficiently secure, after over three decades of personal rule, to restore a meaningful democratic process. His tainted victory in the Mexican presidential election of 1910 resulted in another revolt. The previously unsuccessful liberal candidate, Francisco Madero, forced Díaz to resign, became provisional president, and was formally elected in 1911. However, President Madero was not sufficiently strong to affect constitutional reform or, even, establish effective governmental control over the country. Other rebel leaders, such as Emiliano Zapata and "Pancho" Villa, refused to recognize the legitimacy of the Mexican government and persisted in armed resistance. A series of insurrections and military *coups d'etat* dominated Mexico for the next several years. Venustiano Carranza, a conservative revolutionary leader, finally established sufficient support to be elected president of Mexico, in 1917, and promulgated a new Mexican constitution that would, finally, persist, despite grave challenges to it.

This Mexico Constitution of 1917 included significant reforms. It introduced a labor code, returned communal land to native peoples, confiscated religious property and dedicated it to public use, and aggressively promoted social welfare. It also sought to weaken the abuse of executive power, partly through the imposition of limits upon the scope of that authority (including constitutional protection of rights and liberties) and through institutional safeguards, such as a provision prohibiting consecutive presidential terms of office. It was, especially in comparison to the constitutional behavior of the Díaz regime, a very progressive transformation for Mexico, even by the standards of other liberal democratic constitutional systems.

Mexican politics and government experienced periods of turbulence and instability throughout the twentieth century, including the overthrow of President Carranza after he attempted to nationalize petroleum and other natural resources, which angered foreign companies. The dominance of the Partido Revolucianaro Institucional, or PRI, often undermined democratic government, especially when charges of corruption and intimidation aroused popular resentment. However, the Mexican Constitution of 1917 persisted as the institutional source for the evolution of Mexican constitutionalism.

The revolutionary context that produced Mexico's various constitutional documents, including its currently entrenched one, has had a profound influence upon its tone, its political culture, and its implementation. Competing desires for liberty and social stability reflect the rivalry of classic conservative and liberal legal and political movements throughout Mexican history. Its constitutional significance becomes increasingly apparent in relation to other prominent themes of the Mexican constitutional tradition, including those clauses relating to labor law, property, other rights and liberties, social reform, citizenship, national identity, the federal system, and institutional features of Mexican politics and government. This revolutionary legacy is, arguably, the most profoundly influential theme of this constitutional development.

Labor Relations

One of the most notable and, perhaps, controversial features of the Mexican constitution can be found within its article 123 (which is the sole article of title six of this constitution) relating to the country's labor law. It was created as a response to centuries of discrimination and exploitation, and its aim is, in part, an attempt to secure a sense of constitutional unity among all of the Mexican people. Despite its broad social purposes, it has not been entirely successful in ensuring economic justice, especially within the areas of labor associations, including the true freedom and efficacy of labor unions.

Article 123 aims to protect, constitutionally, certain labor standards that are protected by conventional legislation within other liberal democratic societies, including the United States. Many clauses, for example, address matters such as the minimum wage, maximum hours of work per day, overtime pay, fair distribution of profits, prohibitions against child labor, and considerations for pregnant women or women with infants. It also makes provisions regarding the fair distribution of land for small landowners, especially in terms of "family patrimony" and other real property that is attached to individual persons who are not, necessarily, wealthy. Conditions of labor also are addressed, and the freedom of association in terms of labor unions (including the right to strike) is constitutionally guaranteed, rather than secured through simple legislation.

This part of the Mexican constitutional tradition is essential to its overall character. It reflects the historic importance of the economic, ethnic, and political struggles that have shaped the country's overall character. It is, arguably, the most "revolutionary" feature of this constitutional legacy, but it is not the only aspect that responds to broad socio-economic forces and the desire to enshrine these goals through constitutional mandates.

Agrarian Reform

A 1992 constitutional amendment permitted the transfer of communal land to the individual farmers who have cultivated it. Article 27, which is part of title one of the Mexican constitution (the title devoted particularly to individual rights and liberties), devotes considerable attention to this subject. This fact provides an indication of the overall significance of this provision; it reflects a broader tradition of riparian rights, in which the possession of land and water "is vested originally in the Nation" of Mexico, constituting a collective property ownership that may be converted into an individual property right only at the constitutionally sanctioned discretion of the government.

Despite modifications, the *ejidos* system of communal farm lands remains, nonetheless, constitutionally guaranteed within Mexico. This system, which was a result of general land reform in 1915, was intended to address the dominance of large landholders and the lack of distribution of real property among Mexico's population. Half of the agricultural land of Mexico has been organized into *ejidos*, providing a significant legal and economic institution that resembles principles found within socialist legal systems. The presence of these small family farms and the larger *haciendas* constitutes one of the most striking reflections of both the Mexican revolutionary spirit and the willingness to use the Mexican constitutional tradition as a vehicle for agrarian reform.

Article 27 also mandates that sovereign control of minerals and other natural resources (especially relating to energy) is delegated to the Mexican government. The transferal of real property for the purpose of individual ownership may be conferred only upon Mexican persons, either citizens or corporations. Other features within this lengthy and detailed article affect additional themes of Mexican constitutionalism, including church-state relations, the federal system, and rights and liberties. It is, arguably, the most notable facets of this constitutional tradition, providing one of its most important themes.

Church and State

The secularization of the Mexican political system has been a persistent goal of Mexican constitutional reform. The original movement for independence was led by Roman Catholic clerics, but subsequent conflicts between the church hierarchy's support for conservative regimes and anticlerical revolutionary forces resulted in a concerted effort to remove this influence from government. The Mexican Constitution of 1857 and the War of the Reform that it helped to prompt sought to impose secularization, especially through the nationalizing of the considerable property holdings of the Roman Catholic Church within Mexico.

Specific constitutional provisions enforce this very strict separation of church (including all religious denominations) and state. Elected representatives are not permitted to be religious officials, as articles 55 (relating to the Chamber of Deputies) and 82 (relating to the presidency) provide. Article 27 also includes prohibitions against the ownership of land by religious organizations. But this relationship is most comprehensively addressed under the "General Considerations"of title seven, within article 130 of the Mexican constitution. Religious officials are denied the franchise and forbidden from criticizing the government or the "fundamental laws" of the country, and violations of these restrictions may be considered by judges but may never be tried before a jury. These provisions are detailed and strict, and they reflect an often-bitter relationship between church and state and an often tumultuous relationship between the Mexican people and the Roman Catholic Church, to which denomination most of them belong.

This relationship was relaxed, somewhat, in 1991. Legal personality was restored to churches and religious education was permitted under constitutional amendments affecting articles three (providing constitutional sanctions for education) and 130. Still, despite these changes, strict secularization of the Mexican political system continues to reflect the anticlerical spirit of Mexico's revolutionary heritage and, thus, a central theme of its constitutional legacy.

Nationality and Citizenship

Title one of the Mexican Constitution of 1917 devotes considerable attention to defining Mexican national identity and citizenship. Chapter two, article 30 describes the characteristics necessary for achieving this status. It is careful to limit these requirements to the same qualities described both within political systems that base citizenship primarily upon place of birth (such as the United States) and those systems (such as Germany) that base it upon descent from other nationals. No reference to race, ethnicity, or any particular physical features is made within the Mexican constitution. Birth within Mexico's legal boundaries or having a Mexican parent both meet this standard, as does naturalization or the marriage of a woman to a Mexican national.

Article 30 is followed by two other articles of chapter two describing obligations and privileges of this national identity. They include references to military service, receiving an education, and paying taxes, in addition to priority over non-Mexicans in terms of receiving general public services and competing for public employment. They are not remarkable (except for the emphasis upon national identity) in this respect. The fact that these articles are followed by chapter three of title one (devoted to the constitutional status of foreigners) and chapter four (addressing Mexican citizenship) requires a comment, particularly since it seems to present a certain redundancy, even though the two chapters, and the conditions for losing nationality or citizenship, are not precisely similar.

Title one, chapter four, provides specific provisions relating to citizenship that seem to differ from the descriptions offered within chapter two only in terms of greater specificity. But, given the history of racial and ethnic conflict that has plagued Mexico, this separate definition of nationality, as distinct from citizenship, is highly understandable. The *mestizos* may constitute a majority of the country's population, but the traditional discrimination arising from the economic relationships among people of indigenous, European, and mixed descent has left a persistent legacy, despite such conscious attempts to overcome it, as symbolized by this part of the Mexican constitutional tradition. Therefore, the inclusive language of this constitutional designation of nationality serves a broader social, cultural, and political purpose.

Federal System

An important part of the revolutionary struggle within Mexico has involved the political and legal delegation of sovereign authority. Liberal revolutionary leaders, in particular, resisted the centralization of authority as an instrument to advance the freedom of the Mexican people, especially as a hedge against dictatorship. The Mexican Constitution of 1857 addressed that desire by including a federal system, but it lost efficacy during the extended dictatorship of Porfirio Díaz. The restoration of a federal system within the Mexican Constitution of 1917, as assured by articles 40 and 41, is a testament to its significance within the broader scheme of Mexican revolutionary sentiment and constitutional government.

Despite their importance, Mexican states are dominated, in many ways, by the central government. The express delegation of responsibility for labor laws and agrarian reform ensures the dominance of the federal government in a preponderance of public and social policy areas. Furthermore, the traditional role of the federal government in providing for the security of the country augments this strong political position. The states depend upon the express designation of their sovereign existence and powers within the federal constitution, especially through title five of that document, including the guarantees (regarding the character of those state governments) contained within article 115. This institutional character of the delegation of sovereign authority to the states provides another indication of the relatively centralized nature of Mexican federalism.

Nonetheless, both the state and federal governments remain a focal point for political, social, and economic activity. The rebellion of Mexicans of native descent in southern Mexico, called the Zapatista National Liberation Army (named in honor of the famous Mexican reformer and revolutionary leader, Emiliano Zapata), concentrated its efforts upon the state of Chiapas, with its high percentage of native peoples, even though negotiations concerning their demands (mainly greater political, economic, and social reforms) were made primarily with federal authorities. The federal system remains largely centralized, although states offer a venue for political, economic, social, and ethnic activity and identity.

Rights and Liberties

The first substantive portion of Mexico's constitutional text is devoted to the protection of fundamental rights and liberties. This protection was an essential component of the revolutionary movement that produced the current constitutional system. Title one, chapter one, of the Mexican Constitution of 1917 is the result of various influences, including the eighteenth century ideal of American civil rights and liberties and an emerging twentieth-century human rights ideal.

Many of these guarantees are directed toward the conventional subjects of civil rights and liberties. The freedom of expression, guaranteed within article seven, the prohibition against retroactive laws, found within article 14, and the due process protections, located within articles 16 through 23, are typical. But a more expansive description of rights and liberties can be found within such pronouncements as the guarantee of, and requirement to attend, public education as articulated within article two, the protection of professional pursuits as promised within article four, the prohibition against monopolies and other economically debilitating practices contained within article 28, and, of course, the previously addressed labor law protections of article 27. These rights are directed toward broader political, economic, and social purposes rather than the more parochial legal guarantees of conventional civil rights and liberties.

Political Culture

Mexico's revolutionary and constitutional history has involved conflict among different cultural and ideological forces. Native peoples, inheriting a tradition of communal life and ownership, found themselves exploited by colonial authority and by elite members of an independent Mexico. The legacies of imperial Spain and the institutional hierarchy of the Roman Catholic Church imbued this country, as they did for all of Latin America, with a classic conservative ideological influence that was particularly conspicuous among those elites of mostly European ancestry. But a liberal ideological influence also emerged, especially among *criollos*, lower-level members of the Catholic clergy, the growing population of *mestizos*, and many native peoples. These ideological influences are combined within the Mexican constitutional tradition.

The use of a constitutional system to shape a comprehensive socio-political order offers an overview of this conservative influence. Much of the constitution, itself, consciously reflects liberal democratic principles, consistent with most other Western societies. Yet the actual implementation of its provisions often has revealed a strong conservative influence. The strength of the executive authority, the historic deference to strong leaders and single-party rule, problems with the enforcement of justice, and a certain deference to traditional institutions remain practical features of this constitutional tradition. The appeal to the duties, in addition to the rights, of citizens, and an express limitation on free speech (within article seven of the Mexican constitution) that demonstrates a lack of respect for "morals," also may be expressive of this ideological influence and, perhaps, an indication of a residual influence of Catholic teaching derived from natural law.

Therefore, the Mexican constitutional tradition is a product of these ideological ideals. Native concerns also may find expression through the ultimate collective priority of agrarian resources, not unlike traditional tribal practices (which also loosely can be linked to the legacy of the ancient Aztec civilization) provide. But this liberal democratic constitutional tradition is most profoundly distinguished from the American constitutional tradition, for example, by the enduring classic conservatism that remains a cultural feature throughout Latin America. The desire to reconcile individual rights with collective needs and the attempt to provide for both constitutional freedom and political stability and security also have posed a challenge to the maintenance of a true popular sovereignty within a comprehensively Mexican context.

Executive Dominance

Mexico's constitutional system formally provides a separation of powers, distributed among executive, legislative, and judicial authorities, superficially in imitation of the American model. But the Mexican president has been dominant throughout Mexico's constitutional history, and that office has remained dominant under the Mexican Constitution of 1917. Since presidential office holders are limited to one term, other factors have emerged to reinforce the dominance of particularly strong leaders that have reinforced the central dominance of the governmental executive.

Strong leaders have been a persistent feature of Mexican history, undermining democratic reforms, providing stability in times of emergency, and either promoting or obstructing the revolutionary process. The stability that strong executive leadership provides is consistent with the pervasive influence of conservative ideological values, so it has not been as odious to much of Mexican society as it might have proven, otherwise. Nonetheless, the development of Mexico's market economy and its link to democratization have prompted attempts to weaken this executive dominance, particularly as Mexico proceeds into the twenty-first century.

The formation of the PRI as a dominant political party provided an informal reinforcement of that theme. Through the party, former presidents could maintain a strong influence, as Plutarco Calles, a former military leader, did when he helped establish the PRI, following his own term in office. This highly organized, constituent-based party served for decades as a crucial source of patronage, thus ensuring its dominance. The general strength of cabinet members (many of whom succeeded to the presidency), governmental reliance upon technical and economic elites for advice and support, and a cultural acceptance of political paternalism further enhanced this centralization of political authority within the Mexican executive, particularly throughout the twentieth century.

Court System

Title three, chapter four, of Mexico's constitution relates the institutions and power of the Mexican judiciary, which is described, formally, as a "branch of government." The formal structure of the judicial system resembles the American system, especially in terms of its division into courts of original jurisdiction (mostly at the district level) and appellate courts (both single-judge and collegiate versions), including a final court of appeal. In practice, though, significant differences can be found between the judiciaries of the two constitutional systems.

Mexico has a civil law system that can be traced back to its Spanish colonial heritage. However, in addition to conventional civil law courts, the system allows for jury courts as federal courts of first instance. The civil codes of Mexico were based upon the codes that emerged, during the late nineteenth century, in the more universal style of the *Code Napoléon*, which has been a common experience of most Latin American legal systems. Mexico has, in that sense, a fairly conventional civil law scheme, although the unified appellate structure, in imitation of the United States judiciary, is more typical of a common law system.

Challenges to judicial decisions are made through a device called an *amparo* appeal. This constitutionally protected procedure can be invoked as a conventional appeal, a writ of *habeas corpus*, an injunction, or a declaratory judgment. Mexicans can invoke it in support of claimed violations of their constitutional rights or liberties, a challenge to other allegedly unconstitutional laws, protection of agrarian reforms, and resolutions of administrative conflicts. The *amparo* appeal is described, in considerable detail, within article 107 of the Mexican constitution. Its most important role was envisioned to be a constitutional means of protecting the integrity of the federal system, although it has been subject to criticism.

Article 102 also expresses the offices and authority of the Public Ministry of the Federation. It is found within this chapter, despite the fact that it actually is controlled by the executive branch of government. This powerful public ministry has been accused of undermining the true efficacy of the judicial system, especially in comparison to the often understaffed and underfunded public defenders, who are provided by statute, rather than constitutional mandate. Furthermore, it has been cited as evidence of the persistent dominance of the Mexican presidency that undermines the full potential of this democratic constitutional system.

The apex of the system is occupied by the Supreme Court of Justice, consisting of 21 jurists, called ministers, appointed by the president and confirmed by the Senate. Only members of the Supreme Court enjoy tenure of office; lower court jurists are appointed for six-year terms, though they can have their appointments extended, indefinitely. Because of its constitutional authority, the Supreme Court of Justice is regarded as a "branch of government" in the American sense, but its true independence has been doubted by some observers, especially given the executive influence upon the system (especially through the Public Ministry of the Federation) and other noted occasions of intimidation and corruption. But this sort of problem periodically has been raised regarding the *entire* Mexican political and constitutional systems.

The Future of Mexican Constitutionalism

Mexico's constitutional development has been challenged throughout its history. Both revolutionary and counter-revolutionary forces have sought to shape Mexico's political system in different ways, reflecting different cultural and ideological influences. The result has been a Mexican constitutional tradition that offers liberal democratic institutions but often undermines them, in practice, with an overly strong executive and an overly centralized federal structure.

However, by the end of the twentieth century, signs of change within the competitive political system, greater international cooperation (both in terms of economic and security concerns), and popular demands for reform created a context for a greater effectiveness of the expression of popular sovereignty that the Mexican Constitution of 1917 was created to proclaim. Although it has been amended, frequently, throughout the twentieth century, those changes sought to make the constitutional system more stable, rather than more democratic. But a new political environment, launched at the beginning of the twenty-first century, seems to offer the possibility of a Mexican constitutional tradition that can accommodate the various forces that created it, from revolutionary radicalism to a conservative emphasis upon security to a liberal democratic promise of greater political participation.

The Mexican constitutional tradition of the twenty-first century will need to overcome the economic conditions of the nineteenth century and the corruption of the twentieth century. The formal structure and institutions already exist within it, but the implementation needs to rise to meet its promise. Plans to strengthen the legislature, the judiciary, and, possibly, the state governments could, if pursued consistently, become the dominant theme of the Mexican constitutional tradition as it continues its twenty-first century development, but only if the will exists, among all sectors of society, to accomplish that goal.

References

Francisco Avalos, *The Mexican Legal System*. Littleton, CO, F. B. Rothman, 2000.
Roderick Ai Camp, *Politics in Mexico*. New York, Oxford University Press, 1993.
Judith Gentleman, ed., *Mexican Politics in Transition*. Boulder, CO, Westview, 1987.
James E. Herget and Jorge Camil, *An Introduction to the Mexican Legal System*. Buffalo, W. S. Hein, 1978.
George D. E. Philip, *The Presidency in Mexican Politics*. Houndmills, Basingstoke, England, Macmillan, 1992.
Evelyn Stevens, *Protest and Response in Mexico*. Cambridge, MA, Massachusetts Institute of Technology Press, 1974.

CHAPTER 12

Saudi Arabian Constitutional Tradition

Saudi Arabia had, prior to 1992, an entirely unentrenched constitutional tradition. A written constitutional document, called the Basic Law of Government, was produced in that year, but the extent to which it represents a true example of entrenched constitutionalism is debatable. Sovereign authority is exercised by the Saudi king, and the country's constitution can be altered entirely at his discretion. Therefore, while a process of entrenchment is described within that constitutional document (although, in reality, requiring only the unilateral promulgation of the king), the Saudi Basic Law of Government might not appear to define the sort of real parameters by which the sovereign normally binds itself as normally anticipated from modern definitions of constitutional government according to the tenets of legal positivism. So, arguably, the Basic Law of Government does not qualify as a document representing an entrenched constitutional system. However, it could be argued that this innovation, as weak as it may be in practice, does impose a restraint upon the arbitrary actions of the sovereign, requiring a recognizable process of constitutional behavior and amendment that *does* meet these modern criteria of, at least, partial entrenchment.

One such viable constraint can be identified as the articles of faith provided by Islam, as found within the *Qu'ran* and *Sunnah*. God's authority is proclaimed, by the Basic Law of Government, as the ultimate source of legitimacy for the Saudi royal house and its political dominion. Although religious interpretation (administered through a judicial system) also is constitutionally vested within the ultimate sovereign authority of this monarch, both Islamic theology and its law remain a defining feature of Saudi constitutionalism that cannot be ignored and provide, in fact, a necessary and enduring (indeed, a defining) basis for it.

Shari'a

The legal expression of Islamic faith is found within *Shari'a*, which is roughly translated as "the clear path that must be followed." The Saudi Basic Law of

Government makes the relationship between constitutional government and Islam explicit and unmistakable. Religious, legal, and political values are merged through the principles and institutions of this broad tradition of Western religious law, creating, in a very real sense, a constitutionally sanctioned theocratic government and political system in addition to a religiously based legal system for Saudi Arabia.

Shari'a, particularly within the Sunni tradition of Islam, is intended to promote consensus of religious interpretation and its application to the legal activities of the community. This purpose is particularly pertinent to a constitutional order and the process of nation building often associated with it and the general tradition (reinforced externally through interaction with Western legal norms) of legal positivism. Variations of interpretation are avoided through this process, thus promoting unity of the religious community. That goal assumes a crucial constitutional dimension when the religious and political communities are considered to be inseparable, for the political community is expected to adapt itself to the truths of God's "eternal law."

The Islamic legal science of *fiqh* is directed toward that ultimate purpose, and it provides an interpretive basis for *Shari'a* and the legal and judicial systems of the Saudi Arabian constitutional tradition. Religious truths must be revealed, rather than developed, for they already exist within God's command, as expounded within the Qur'an and demonstrated through the *Sunnah*, consisting of the *hadith*, which are the collected statements and practices of Mohammed. Saudi law must be consistent with this revelation. The promulgation of laws and behavior occurring under the law is interpreted by the Saudi judiciary as being either *mandub* (praiseworthy) or *makruh* (blameworthy), so the law provides a context for evaluating political, as well as individual human, choices. Therefore, Saudi law offers directives (like the Western natural law tradition provides), rather than a mere system of precise prescriptions and prohibitions.

The consensus of the community is established and applied by Islamic judges, called *kādī*. It is not based upon a shared agreement of all members of that community but upon their recognized religious and legal leaders. Ultimate political authority, in this respect, also is vested within the Saudi king, reinforcing, again, the intrinsic relationship of religion, national identity, and political sovereignty. The legal consensus reached is intended to be a unanimous one, and it is achieved through a result called *ijmā*. The attainment of *ijmā* results from a process called *ijtihad*, which proceeds from one technique to another, until a unity of opinion can be agreed. However, the system secured by the Saudi monarchy actually seeks to guarantee that unanimity of opinion through its own, ultimate sovereign authority.

Unlike the application of *Shari'a* within the Nigerian constitutional tradition, the scope of Islamic law within the Saudi Arabian constitutional tradition is not isolated to family law and similar areas of civil law, nor does it apply exclusively to declared members of the Islamic faith. Therefore, all law and politics of Saudi Arabia are bound to the beliefs and practices of Islam, and the judicial system grounded upon *Shari'a* ultimately makes no distinction between sacred and secular affairs. Many Islamic countries, especially within the Middle East region, share this religious and constitutional characteristic with Saudi Arabia. However, its constitutional expression is particularly well expressed within the Saudi constitutional system.

Formal Constitutional Structure

The Saudi Arabia Basic Law of Government of 1992 consists of nine chapters, divided further into 83 articles. It does not have a separate preamble, but article one appears, substantively, to serve a similar purpose while, simultaneously, providing conventional constitutional directives. This entrenched document is not particularly long, but it is fairly comprehensive, especially considering the wide discretion that is reserved to the Saudi monarch.

Chapter one of the Basic Law of Government articulates general constitutional principles, especially in terms of its relationship to the teachings of Islam, its respect for Islamic customs, symbols, and observances, and features of national identity, including the location of the country's political capital. Chapter two describes the ultimate source of sovereign authority, retained by the king (as guided and bound by Islam), and the religious and political duty of all Saudi subjects to obey his legitimate authority. Chapter three is dedicated to the Saudi family as the social center of the national community, and it includes the duties ascribed to both sovereign and subjects in maintaining this foundation according, again, to the teachings of Islam.

Chapter four addresses more mundane constitutional concerns, particularly in terms of economic policy and institutions. The king is committed, under this chapter, to protect the economic interests and needs of his subjects, but, again, sovereign control of all economic resources also is confirmed within this chapter. The constitution provides for human rights protections within chapter five, but they also are subject to the interpretation of Islamic principles.

More important, perhaps, are the duties, also strongly influenced by religious considerations, imposed upon both subjects and sovereign, particularly in terms of social welfare of the people, educational and employment needs and responsibilities, military service and sovereign responsibility for the physical protection of the country, and the promotion of science and an Islamic vision of world peace. Responsibility for the holy sites of Islam, located within the country's borders, also is emphasized within this chapter, as is the sacred nature of the family and home. It also addresses matters of citizenship and the status of resident aliens, but the regulations governing these categories actually are delegated to the discretion of conventional statutes, as determined by the sovereign. Indeed, the entire tone of this chapter reinforces the ultimate sovereign discretion of the monarch.

Chapter six describes the governmental institutions of the state. It identifies three sources of Saudi authority, reminiscent of governmental "branches": judicial, executive, and regulatory. The judicial authority is most prominently described, particularly in terms of its relationship to the Islamic basis of Saudi Arabia's legal system and structure. This section also enumerates the institutions that assist the king in the performance of his sovereign authority. The most prominent of these institutions is the Council of Ministers, first described within article 56 of the Basic Law of Government.

However, the most notable feature of this constitutional document may be found within article 68 and the articles that immediately follow it, describing the Consultative, or *Shura*, Council. This institution was added conspicuously to the Basic Law of Government of 1992 (although it has been part of the Saudi governmental process since 1926) in response to demands for political reform within the monarchy. It will be addressed, again, within this chapter.

The regulatory authority of the state is presented, constitutionally, in more general and indirect terms by this constitutional chapter. Arguably, the most significant constitutional reference to this regulatory authority occurs within article 67 of the Saudi Arabian Constitution, which identifies the statutory source of regulatory practices, officials, and discretion, under the control of the other constitutionally sanctioned institutions of the state. In all cases, however, the ultimate sovereign authority and discretion of the monarch are explicitly reserved throughout this chapter of the Saudi Basic Law of Government.

Chapter seven of this document establishes general guidelines for conducting Saudi financial affairs and policy. It provides standards that are intended to be applicable to both public and private financial institutions, including corporations operating within the kingdom. This chapter is followed by chapter eight, which describes the "control bodies" responsible for regulating this same financial activity, again placing all economic activity of this nature under the ultimate authority of the sovereign, through the executive institutions described within chapter six of the

Basic Law of Government. These two chapters appear to be essential for establishing sovereign economic control over the country and its vast resources.

Finally, chapter nine addresses a few additional considerations, under the heading of "general provisions." The most significant part of this chapter, article 82, refers, again, to the commitment to make the secular affairs of the Saudi kingdom consistent with the tenets of Islam, unless in time of war or other declared "state of emergency." The final article of this chapter and constitutional document provides a rudimentary "amending formula." Article 83 declares that this constitutional document may be altered only in the same way in which it was promulgated, which refers to the process of royal decree, following a consultative mechanism that is described within chapter six of this same constitution.

Perhaps, the most striking structural feature of this constitutional document is the repetition of references to the retained discretionary authority of the sovereign. However, an equally compelling characteristic is the prominence of references to Islam as the ultimate source of all Saudi political and legal values. These facets of this document suggest extremely compelling themes of this country's constitutional tradition which, combined with its overall political, economic, social, and religious climate, offer an intriguing overall perspective.

Principal Constitutional Themes

The prominence of both the monarchy and Islam already have been noted in relation to the Saudi Arabian constitutional tradition. These themes have, in fact, guided Saudi constitutionalism since the beginning of the modern kingdom, and they continue to serve as its foundation. Additional constitutional themes are, indeed, related to, or derived from, them. Yet they are important in themselves and merit further evaluation.

Important political institutions distinguish the Saudi constitutional tradition. The most prominent of these institutions is the Consultative, or *Shura*, Council. This body first was established in 1926, and its status is consistent with the general tenor of a political system grounded upon Islamic law, especially in terms of its role in promoting the development of a consensus of opinion. It retains traditional respect, so it maintains a highly visible presence within the governmental process. A more explicitly religious institution that plays a prominent political role is the Council of Senior Scholars, or Senior *Ulema* Body, as introduced within article 45 of the Basic Law. Its role is central to the determination of Islamic law and practice, including its requirements relating to politics and government, which is the self-proclaimed central premise of constitutional law within the Saudi kingdom. Finally, the ongoing role of the Council of Ministers (as articulated within article 56 of the Basic Law) is essential for the constitutional development of public policy, particularly in terms of assisting the king in retaining and expressing his dominant sovereign authority.

These institutions, in addition to the judiciary established under *Shari'a*, reinforce the fundamental themes of Islam and monarchy. They also provide, through their actual functioning, insight into the arguably restrained constitutional nature of the Basic Law of Government and the system it perpetuates. In that way, they are indicative of the claim that could be made regarding the enduring unentrenched quality of Saudi Arabian constitutionalism, especially in terms of its ultimate deference to a construct of legal and political absolutism that appears to be a defining feature of this system and many other, similar, political and legal systems throughout the Arab world and the Middle Eastern region.

Islam and Saudi Constitutionalism

The military and political victory of the Saudi family, by the beginning of the twentieth century, also represented a religious victory for the *Wahhabi* school of Islamic theological thought. That particular school emphasizes the dominant role of the *sheik*, or paternal leader of a people, including a king who rules over the broader Arab community. The king's authority extends, according to the *Wahhabi* teachings, over all matters, both secular and religious. He is commander over, and responsible for the spiritual and physical welfare of, all Moslems within his realm; therefore, any dissent from his religious rulings and interpretations, unless they are unambiguously blasphemous, is regarded as sedition.

This theological interpretation of the authority of the king often is extended, in reference to the Saudi monarch, even beyond those territories that fall under his direct control. The fact that the sacred cities of Medina and, especially, Mecca (and their holy sites which are centrally important to Islam) fall under Saudi control, the Saudi monarch frequently implies both a religious and political authority that extends to neighboring Islamic states and Moslems, generally. Certain royal actions and statements made in connection with the promulgation of this Saudi Basic Law of Government strongly suggested that it was intended to be a model for all Islamic states, especially in its refusal to embrace democratic principles of free elections and internationally sanctioned guarantees of due process and other specific civil rights and liberties. This emphasis upon the absolute discretion of the king in all matters, both secular and sacred, and over all his subjects and, perhaps, beyond is one of the most important contributions of the *Wahhabi* theological school to the development of Saudi constitutionalism.

The most dominant denomination of Islam among Saudi Arabians (including the royal family and other political, economic, social, and religious elites) is the Sunni branch. Interpretive authority is derived, under this branch, from both the *Qu'ran* (the word of God as transmitted to Mohammed through the Archangel Gabriel) and the *Sunnah* (consisting of the collected traditions of the actions and statements of Mohammed, known as the *hadith*), as emphasized within article one of the Basic Law of Government, which declares "God's Book and the *Sunnah* of his Prophet, God's prayers and peace be upon him, are its constitution." Therefore, the interpretive scope of Islam, in this respect, can be relatively broad.

One principle of *Shari'a* under Sunni Islam that has particular constitutional significance is the desire for consensus in achieving legal rulings and applications. This process traditionally is achieved through a science of Islamic law, known as the *fiqh*, which is directed toward a *revelation* of legal truths, rather than their conscious development, especially as established historically through various doctors of Islamic theology. This pattern is well established within Saudi Arabia, with a body of legal scholars of *Shari'a*, traditionally known as the *fukahā*, directing this interpretive process, especially through the Council of Senior Scholars. The consensus of the community (obtained through the consultative process of *ijmā*) is established through them and applied by Islamic judges, or *kādī*, who are appointed by, and subject to the ultimate sovereign authority of, the Saudi king.

Thus the achieved consensus is one that is subject to the ultimate approval of the monarch. It also is achieved by clerics, scholars, and other religious leaders who are subject to royal control. This fact often has undermined popular confidence in the unity of theological opinion, based upon a true consensus (rather than singularly imposed decree) that is supposed to be the religious goal of *Shari'a*. Given the inextricable relationship between Islamic religious interpretation and Saudi constitutional and political power and institutions, this difficulty is profound and, potentially, one that could undermine the legitimacy and stability of current Saudi Arabian constitutionalism.

Monarchy

The Saudi royal family has achieved a level of absolute sovereign control that has become increasingly rare. This same model of government can be found within certain other Islamic countries of the region but not always in this sort of self-perpetuating form. The most conspicuous comparative examples of a similar monarchical rule might include the historical examples of China under the Ch'ing dynasty or France during the Bourbon dynasty. The supremacy of the Saudi king is the most prominent obstacle to the recognition of the Basic Law of Government as a true constitutional document in the twenty-first century sense of the term.

A superficial reading of the Basic Law of Government creates an immediate impression of limitations imposed upon the powers of the king. However, a more careful examination of that document reveals that the monarch's sovereign authority remains, directly or indirectly, entirely within his prerogative. In fact, the Basic Law of Government and all of its supporting statutes were promulgated upon the sole authority of royal orders. Although a process of consultation and advice, especially regarding the Council of Ministers, is implied through that process, none of these constitutional enactments received the actual approval of any political or religious body except the king. Indeed, any future constitutional change also will take place, according to article 83 of the Basic Law of Government, in the same manner, thus ensuring the continued monopolization of the Saudi Arabian constitutional tradition by the monarch.

An evaluation of the other constitutionally sanctioned political and religious institutions of Saudi Arabia confirm that royal dominance. Article 44 of the Basic Law of Government insinuates the existence of distinct "branches" of government, supposedly accompanied by the concept of "checks and balances" that is such a prominent feature of American constitutionalism and its emphasis upon limited government. However, that article also states that the king is the "point of reference" for the authority of each of these "branches." That fact is reinforced by the stipulations, for each of them, of the king's authority of appointment and dismissal. That authority is specified within the Basic Law's article 53 (although it also makes reference to the advisory role of the Higher Council of Justice for making judicial appointments), regarding the Saudi judiciary, article 56, regarding the Council of Ministers (of which body the king also remains head, assuming, therefore, the dual role of head of state and prime minister), and article 58, regarding a wide variety of lower-ranking ministers and administrative officials.

The Basic Law of Government makes reference to supplementary statutes that reinforce this royal supremacy, despite the implication of restraint by relevant political institutions. This arrangement is particularly evident in terms of the Consultative (or *Shura*) Council, which was regarded by many observers as the most significant Saudi Arabian constitutional reform introduced by the Basic Law of Government of 1992. The only substantive reference to the Consultative Council within that document occurs within article 68, which merely defers matters of its composition and authority to subsequent statutory instruments. The most important source has been the *Shura* Council Establishment Act of 1992, which quickly followed the promulgation of the Basic Law of Government. Although it appears that this statute, and the references made within the Basic Law of Government, make this council a pivotal and indispensable part of constitutional government, the king's authority to appoint and dismiss its members, and the fact that its powers are limited to an advisory capacity, may belie its true efficacy.

A "supremacy clause" can be discerned for this constitutional document within articles six and seven. The first of these articles emphasizes the absolute duty of the subjects of the kingdom to pay allegiance to, and obey, the monarch, under all circumstances. Article seven identifies the ultimate source of all authority within Saudi Arabia within the *Qur'an*, *Sunnah*, and the general guidance of Islam. However, the fact that the king remains the final interpretive religious source, in addition to being the political sovereign, actually makes article seven a constitutional instrument for reinforcing the royal supremacy.

The centrality of the king to the Saudi constitutional process also results in considerable constitutional attention being imposed upon the broader role of the royal family and, especially, the succession to the throne. The tradition of succession among the members of the family of King Abdel-Aziz (founder of the third dynasty, established in 1902) favored the oldest son, followed by his next oldest brother, rather than the elder son's own sons. Article five of the Basic Law of Government now seems to specify, however, that the king should choose from among the next generation and that he has wide discretion to make a choice upon the one who appears to be, in the king's judgment, the "most upright." The crown prince is provided a constitutional role, at the explicit discretion of the reigning monarch, both in terms of succession, additional prerogatives, ministerial responsibilities, and the role of serving as regent for the king when he travels abroad, especially as specified within articles 65 and 66 of the Basic Law of Government. Again, these provisions are subject to explicit royal approval, and all power delegated to the crown prince must be the result of a royal decree.

Other members of the royal family play a pervasive role within Saudi constitutional government. The Council of Ministers tends to be dominated by close relatives of the king, especially the most important positions, such as Foreign Minister, Defense Minister, and Deputy Prime Minister, with the king usually retaining the position of president of the Council and, thus, prime minister for himself. The Basic Law of Government was drafted by an *ad hoc* committee led by the Minister of the Interior, Prince Nayef, the brother of the reigning King Fahd. This fact underscores the deeply personal nature of Saudi government.

The king may veto any decision of the Council of Ministers, although that outcome seldom occurs. The king also retains other powers that are separate from his position as president of the Council and prime minister. The king can issue two types of statutes: a royal decree, or *marsoom*, is issued upon the sanction of the Council of Ministers; a royal order, or *amr*, is issued by the king, unilaterally. The choice of statutory instrument generally is dictated by considerations of expediency or a desire to generate political support and a sense of greater legitimacy.

One exception to this apparently unassailable dominance is the requirement of article 70 of the Basic Law of Government for the ratification of treaties to be affected through *marsoom*, thus apparently requiring approval from the Council of Ministers. But even these sorts of restrictions appear to be subject to a certain degree of royal discretion. Political choices remain, almost unhindered, with the king's discretion, reinforcing the extremely centralized nature of Saudi government and its constitutional structure. Article 58 of the Basic Law ensures the king unilateral authority in appointing the most senior members of government, so the possibility of opposition from within the government seems unlikely in any event.

It is difficult to overstate the dominance of the king as sovereign within this constitutional system. It is that very dominance and centralization of authority that challenge the very notion of a Saudi constitutional tradition in the modern sense and the legitimacy of the Basic Law of Government as a true constitutional instrument. However, institutions *do* exist that fulfill, at least nominally, a constitutional role (particularly in an essential advisory capacity), and they should not be ignored, simply because the position of the monarch appears to be so firmly shielded from conventional political and legal challenge.

Council of Ministers

The role of the Council of Ministers long preceded its establishment within the Saudi Basic Law of Government of 1992. The king has relied upon similar consultative bodies throughout the modern history of Saudi Arabia. The presence and role of the Council of Ministers was established formally through a royal decree, the Law of the Council of Ministers of 1958. This statute has been amended several times (including the Council of Ministers Act of 1993, in response to the Basic Law of Government), but the essential nature and function of this council remain, essentially, consistent. The most important adjustment to the council occurred through a 1964 amendment to the 1958 law which made the king, simultaneously, president of this council and, subsequently, prime minister. But even that change merely confirmed the basic role and prominence of the Council of Ministers within the Saudi constitutional tradition.

Despite the changes introduced by the Basic Law of Government of 1992, the Council of Ministers remains the institutional core of the Saudi constitutional system. Its political authority is nearly absolute, subject only to the final discretion of the king. It considers, develops, and approves matters of policy addressing all facets of government, especially financial (largely in terms of taxation and the drafting and approval of the state budget), military, educational, and foreign affairs issues. It also is delegated overall responsibility for supervising the implementation of all state policies and the general conduct of all government ministries.

But despite its *de jure* quasi-legislative appearance, the Council of Ministers serves as a *de facto* instrument for extending the personal rule of the monarch. Nonetheless, its advisory role can be extremely important, for its members possess administrative responsibility for the most crucial areas of government activity. They are the primary experts in their respective roles and policy areas, and the king frequently depends upon this expertise, much like the English and British monarchs relied upon their privy councils for advice, prior to the ascendency of parliamentary government within the British constitutional tradition.

Nominally, policies are developed and implemented, and laws are promulgated, with the "consent" of the Council of Ministers; more substantively, constitutional government is conducted through its "advice." The king ultimately may reject that advice and bypass the solicitation of consent, but he remains, as a practical matter, dependent upon it (especially for information and guidance), thus confirming the central importance of the Council of Ministers, even while using it as an instrument for maintaining his own centralized, sovereign authority. It is not, however, the only government institution that performs this function.

Shura Council

The most important apparent reform introduced by the Basic Law of Government of 1992 was the commitment to a Consultative Council, also known as the *Shura* Council (from the Arabic word for "consultation"), as an essential feature of Saudi Arabian constitutionalism. Yet the *Shura* Council is not an innovation; a formal council of the same name has existed, as already noted, within Saudi government since 1926. Nonetheless, its *de jure* prominence has been elevated within the Saudi constitutional system, although its *de facto* operation may offer little in the form of limitations, or any other substantive effect, upon royal sovereignty and the centralization of political authority within Saudi Arabia.

Most of the references to the *Shura* Council within the Basic Law of Government of 1992 indicate (particularly within article 68) that its substantial authority and composition would be derived from subsequent statutes. The two most significant statutes that followed the promulgation of this constitutional document have been the *Shura* Council Establishment Act of 1992, which confirms its constitutional role and responsibilities, and the *Shura* Council Act of 1993, which outlines the composition, procedural rules, and committees of this body. However, the activities of the *Shura* Council remain, essentially, similar to its position since 1926, although demands for political reform that motivated the adoption of the Basic Law of Government also made this institution increasingly conspicuous, if not, necessarily, more effective.

The concept of consensus is significant within the Islamic (especially Sunni) tradition. However, from a political and constitutional perspective, it is not entirely clear whether the *Shura* Council accomplishes the substance, or merely the appearance, of consensus within the Saudi Arabian constitutional system. The king is under no obligation to follow any advice, or be bound by any of the decisions, of this council. Furthermore, opinions of the *Shura* Council must be submitted to the Council of Ministers. If the two councils concur, the decision is submitted to the king for his confirmation. If they do not concur, the king makes his own determination. Again, this royal discretion is, ultimately, absolute.

Prior to the promulgation of the *Shura* Council Act of 1993, its predecessor served an oversight role. It was first created as a political concession to various political and religious elites and other parties in response to the controversy of the Saudi annexation of Mecca and other holy sites of Islam, in 1926. It was intended as a means of providing supervision for the royal Saudi family in its expanded religious and political capacity, especially given concerns among many Moslems regarding the implications of the *Wahhabi* school of theology that dominated the legal system of this regime.

Until 1953, the *Shura* Council served as the primary consultative body for the development of statutes and other legal instruments. Although its powers ultimately were only advisory, ministers were required to appear before it when summoned, and treaties, budgets, and other policies were required to be submitted to it before they could be put into effect. But the enactment of the Council of Ministers Act of 1953 transferred much of that oversight authority to the ministerial body, and statutes promulgated in support of the Basic Law of Government have not altered that arrangement.

The 60 members of the *Shura* Council serve four-year terms. They are appointed by the king and may be replaced by him, especially, but not exclusively, for failure to attend meetings of the council or general malfeasance. This council may propose legislation, and it may request the attendance of ministers before it, but it has no authority to enforce these activities. Still, the fact that its place has been confirmed within the Saudi Arabian constitutional scheme may be significant. Informal pressure to gain the approval of this council may prove crucial to the continued political legitimacy of the government.

The British example of unentrenched constitutional development, especially prior to the union of England and Scotland, may be instructive. The very real limitations of various English institutions of the sixteenth and seventeenth centuries upon the monarchy, despite the ultimate sovereign authority retained by those monarchs, was based upon changing features of political culture, political expectations, and economic activity. These institutions, such as the privy council, the courts, and parliament, served, by their very existence, as sources for limiting, though gradually, the *de facto* authority of the sovereign. Perhaps, the constitutional guarantee of the existence and role of the *Shura* Council, though effectively restricted, may achieve, eventually (though very gradually), the same result. Other constitutionally sanctioned institutions of Saudi Arabia also conceivably might advance this end, incrementally, thus overcoming the ambiguity between the entrenched and unentrenched natures of Saudi constitutionalism.

Judicial System

The legal system of Saudi Arabia is based upon *Shari'a* and the general interpretations of Islam. The judiciary of this country exists in support of that law. It receives considerable attention within the Basic Law of Government, indicating its political and cultural importance. But the judicial system is subject to the provisions of separate statutes and, more generally, to interpretations derived generally from *Shari'a*. Article 45 of the Basic Law of Government identifies the Senior *Ulema* Body (or Council of Senior Scholars) as the highest judicial body for Saudi Arabia. Its members are chosen by the king, who maintains final interpretive authority over its decisions as stressed within article 48 of the Basic Law of Government and as further implied by article 55 and its reference to the king's sovereign supremacy. The Senior *Ulema* Body may render legal rulings over controversies submitted to it, and it also reserves the authority to interpret policies, statutes, and other political and constitutional matters.

However, some Islamic scholars have argued that these rulings cannot be used as substitutes for trials and other formal judicial proceedings, before judges, in either criminal or civil matters. Nonetheless, the Senior *Ulema* Body often has been employed for that purpose. It has been so authorized by the king, despite the provision of article 46 of the Basic Law of Government, guaranteeing the independence of the judiciary, and the guarantee of a right to litigation for all Saudi subjects, provided within article 47 of the Basic Law of Government.

A Higher Council of Justice is established by article 51 of the Basic Law of Government at the apex of the Saudi judicial system. Article 53 further establishes the institutional supremacy of the Tribunal of Complaints, while article 49 reinforces the judicial role of independent tribunals and the rights of Saudi subjects to refer all legal disputes to them. But no constitutional final court of appeal exists; these matters are addressed by the Senior *Ulema* Body. Still, in practice, a high degree of autonomy has been observed concerning the operation of the Saudi judicial system, confirming its persistent and practical significance within the overall Saudi constitutional tradition.

Rights and Duties

Despite the presence of a chapter of the Basic Law of Government devoted to the subject of rights and duties, these constitutional guarantees remain vaguely expressed, subject to a wide discretion of religious interpretation, and severely limited by the prerogatives of the sovereign. The most definitive of these guarantees actually seem to be derived from those articles, beyond chapter five of the Basic Law of Government, that are devoted to access to the judiciary and, by implication, a rudimentary concept of due process and the rule of law. Another interesting feature of this chapter is its description of the duties of the sovereign, in addition to general references to human and civil rights and liberties of individual subjects of the kingdom. These articles both express, and place limits upon, those rights, according to the discretion of the sovereign. The difference between this relationship and a similar relationship expressed within most Western constitutional traditions is based upon the degree of discretion assumed by the Saudi sovereign.

Certain notable rights and liberties are absent from the Basic Law of Government, including freedom of speech, freedom of assembly, and religious expression. Individual property rights *are* mentioned, within article 17. They also are not expressly guaranteed but, rather, may be exercised only in a manner consistent with the interests of the state. The Basic Law of Government *does* refer to the general subject of personal expression, within article 39, but in terms of the limits imposed upon its exercise, the decorum expected of people and organizations who exercise it, and the prohibition against any speech that might "foster sedition or division or harm the state's security and its public relations or detract from man's dignity and rights." This tone dominates this chapter of the Basic Law of Government, strongly suggesting a limited commitment to a conventional understanding of rights and liberties protections.

Human rights are subject to a very general protection within Saudi Arabia, according to article 26 of the Basic Law of Government, which simply states that any protection of unspecified human rights by the Saudi government will be subject to the interpretations provided through *Shari'a*. Meanwhile, the state undertakes, within this document, the constitutional obligation to provide work, public welfare, environmental safeguards, protection and maintenance of holy sites, scientific development, education, and military protection, among the other sovereign powers conventionally associated with the modern state. Article 37 addresses limited privacy rights, particularly in reference to the "sanctity of the home" and interests of the Saudi family. But similar provisions regarding other individual rights and liberties refer to subsequent statutory expressions of these considerations, such as the general commitment to a rule of law in matters of arrest (subject to the overriding consideration of providing security for the Saudi state and its people) found within article 36 of the Basic Law of Government.

This chapter of the Basic Law of Government may have been included primarily as a response to critics of the Saudi regime. Article 23, which is the first article of this chapter, emphasizes the more important consideration of the central place of Islam, the obligation of the state to protect and advance it, and its responsibility to compel its subjects to "do right and shun evil." This emphasis is consistent with the overall character of Saudi constitutionalism and the relationship between sovereign and subject that it advances.

Unitary System

Another important feature of Saudi constitutional reform has been the reorganization of provincial and local governments. This issue is not addressed directly by the Basic Law of Government, but subsequent statutes promulgated directly after its enactment include the Regional Authorities Establishment Act of 1992, indicating its constitutional significance. These reforms support the general trend toward centralization of sovereign authority within Saudi Arabia. This structural trend may provide an even more daunting obstacle to constitutional reform within this country than other provisions, although it complements other general themes that already have been described.

Previous statutes concerning provincial and local governments had permitted a degree of electoral experimentation. The Law of Administrative Councils of 1940 provided, for example, for the popular election of representatives to provincial administrative councils. Although it was replaced by the Law of Provinces of 1963, eliminating these elections, the regional administrative system continued to be relatively responsive to certain local demands and concerns. However, the constitutional provisions introduced in 1992 and 1993, within this area, have reinforced the king's direct authority over all provincial officials.

Likewise, the Law of Municipalities of 1939 and the Law of Municipal Elections of 1942 provided for a degree of popular control over local government councils. However, beginning in the early 1960s, the Saudi government began a trend toward eliminating this sort of local control and strengthening the authority of the Ministry of Municipal and Rural Affairs. The constitutional reforms following the adoption of the Basic Law of Government of 1992 have reinforced that trend, which targets the elimination of democratic challenges to royal authority, the suppression of regional opposition to the central government, and the increased overall centralization of the constitutional system throughout Saudi Arabia. All regional and local officials now are firmly and directly accountable to the king, the Council of Ministers, and the respective ministers and senior administrators. The legal and judicial systems similarly are centralized.

Political Culture

Islamic theology, especially as interpreted through the *Wahhabi* school of thought, remains the dominant influence upon the operation of the Saudi Arabian constitutional tradition. Its assumptions and values focus upon the primacy of a single God and a single community of the faithful, bound by individual profession of belief, communal worship, charity, commitment to the family unit, obedience to rightful authority, and morally upright behavior, including abstinence, restraint, amity, and peaceful fellowship. Nonetheless, the spread of the faith and its defense against all enemies also have been features of the Islamic tradition. Most significantly, modern liberal distinctions between secular and sacred matters (an idea that became largely accepted within Christianity) are not generally acknowledged within most societies dominated by Islam, including Saudi Arabia.

The specific implications of Islamic thought and belief for the Saudi Arabian constitutional tradition have been addressed elsewhere within this chapter. That influence cannot be underestimated. However, variations of interpretation within Islam also have a profound effect upon the country's continued social, political, and legal development. The precise expression of Islam provided by the Saudi judicial system and constitutional institutions is not embraced by all Saudi Arabian people, especially adherents of this religious tradition who embrace a more fundamental interpretation of its tenets. Therefore, this factor needs to be acknowledged when gauging this aspect of the political culture of Saudi Arabian constitutionalism.

A secular observation of this society and government might draw philosophical parallels between it and the classic conservative ideological tradition of Western political thought. The perception of the polity as a corporate body, the patriarchal expressions of royal rule, the stress upon order, stability, and submission, all reflect an ideological perspective that is reminiscent of early modern European states and even important aspects of certain contemporary Latin American societies. The notion that, within this political community (bound, as it is, by paternal concern and control), a wide discretion of activity is both allowed and encouraged (especially within the economic sphere) is a feature that is consistent with overall assumptions of classic conservative thought as providing the stable basis for the growth and prosperity of all subjects.

The Saudi Arabian constitutional tradition offers many examples of this attitude, which may reflect an ongoing cross-cultural influence that finds its origins within the competition and interaction that has occurred between the European and Arab worlds since the time of the Crusades. That exposure often resulted in a profound philosophical exchange, as observed through the reintroduction of ancient Greek thought to Europe through the preservation and development of this thought by Arab philosophers and the cultivation of a system of logic among Arab thinkers that gradually would be adapted by late medieval and early modern European scholars to their respective legal and political traditions. Likewise, European ideas (including modern ideological influences) were not unknown to Arab scholars and other elites. Therefore, it might well be appropriate to describe Saudi constitutional development in terms of classic conservative principles, even though it makes reference to an ideological system of largely European origin.

The Saudi royal family emerged as the dominant political force of this region as a result of its successful struggle with its rivals. Other families and tribal groups (derived from the historic Bedouin origins of this part of the world) had vied for dominance for centuries, establishing a pattern of loyalty and leadership that has left a strong cultural legacy upon Saudi Arabia and its legal and constitutional norms. The tribal origins of this competition may be responsible for yet another cultural influence upon the modern country and its constitutional development. In particular, broad attitudes toward the role of political leadership, the control and distribution of resources and other forms of "property," and the use of family relationships as essential components of social, economic, and political organization suggest this enduring influence.

Resources are controlled, for example, by the king for the benefit of all the people of the realm, in the same manner as the head of a tribe or kinship group. In fact, this pattern of loyalty and mutual support continues to be practiced at the kinship and family levels, throughout Saudi Arabia. So, the constitutional provisions regarding the king's discretion concerning the control of finances and the distributions of the benefits of the country's natural resources fall into a legal pattern that is very consistent with broad norms of tribal law and organization.

The rejection of liberal democratic values and institutions has been a notable source of commentary concerning Saudi Arabian society, its political system, and its constitutional tradition. King Fahd made the point emphatically clear during the period leading to constitutional reform and the promulgation of the Saudi Basic Law of Government of 1992. He has argued that the process of electoral competition, diversity of religious belief, tolerance of disparate political opinions, and policies based upon the will of a mere majority or, even, plurality of the eligible population is too inconsistent with the protection and promotion of Islam and the cultural heritage of Saudi Arabia to serve as an acceptable source of Saudi constitutional values.[1]

Many critics of the Saudi regime within the country have agitated for democratic reforms. External pressures for democratic and liberal (especially concerning economic matters) innovations in Saudi government also have prompted moves toward constitutional reform within the country, especially during the period of the Persian Gulf War, when international attention was focused upon the Middle East region, including Saudi Arabia. References to selective civil rights and liberties within the Saudi Basic Law of Government of 1992 reflect those liberal democratic pressures, although that inclusion has not, necessarily, indicated a true ideological shift within the political and legal systems of the country. Therefore, those cultural values most supportive of political absolutism continue

---

1. Interview of King Fahd ibn Abdel-Aziz, *al-Siyassah* [Kuwait], March 28, 1992.

to dominate the Saudi Arabian constitutional tradition despite strong efforts to provoke change.

The Future of Saudi Arabian Constitutionalism

Despite the presence of a quasi-entrenched constitutional document and other gestures in the direction of constitutional reform, the current Saudi Arabian constitutional tradition appears to have become even more centralized and absolutist than its previous expressions. The system has proven resistant to internal and external pressures in favor of more substantive reform, particularly in terms of the integral relationship between politics and religion that most conspicuously distinguishes it. Nonetheless, those pressures have not disappeared, despite the persistent strength of the regime and its current constitutional order.

A potential danger associated with this resistance to constitutional change may be an eventual popular rejection of the entire system and its replacement with a radical alternative. The analogy of an object that will not bend being vulnerable, eventually, to breaking may be applicable to this example of Saudi constitutionalism. Therefore, it is likely that the Saudi Arabian constitutional tradition will be subject to some sort of change, but the nature and degree of that change will depend upon the future, if any, of the constitutional reforms initiated through the adoption of the Saudi Arabian Basic Law of Government of 1992.

References

Jerichow Anders, *The Saudi File: People, Power, Politics.* New York, St. Martin's, 1998.
Ahmed Hassan Dahlan, ed., *Politics, Administration, and Development in Saudi Arabia.* Jeddah, Saudi Arabia, Dar al-Shorouq, 1990.
Christine Moss Helms, *The Cohesion of Saudi Arabia: Evolution of a Political Identity.* Baltimore, Johns Hopkins University Press, 1981.
Summer Scott Huyette, *Political Adaptation in Saudi Arabia: A Study of the Council of Ministers.* Boulder, CO, Westview, 1985.
Alison Lerrick and Q. J. Mian, *Saudi Business and Labor Law: Its Interpretation and Application.* London, Graham and Trotman, 1982.
Frank E. Vogel, *Islamic Law and Legal System: Studies of Saudi Arabia.* Boston, Brill, 2000.

CHAPTER 13

Constitutionalism, Sovereignty, and Human Freedom

The Constitutional Ideal

Constitutional law has been one of the great accomplishments of the modern age. It has provided both a sense of stability and a focus for identity, and both of these features have contributed to the socio-political and legal environment needed to achieve the positive human endeavors of the contemporary world. Constitutions are no mere technical process, for they have become the very embodiment of that spirit that seeks to transcend the limits that have defined, within the human condition, the realm of the possible.

Constitutions should not merely be the will of the sovereign; they should reflect and promote those qualities that represent the best features, highest ideals, and most lofty aspirations of that sovereign—particularly when it is the comprehensive expression of a sovereign people. The constitutions of the twenty-first century are a resource of an emerging post-modern world. They also may be the vehicle for defining the international order of this world. The crucial role of the study and understanding of the world's coexisting and competing constitutional traditions will be overlooked only at the risk of undermining their positive potential for the global community.

Future Themes of Constitutional Law

Constitutions confer an image of legitimacy upon a regime, regardless of the actual sovereign authority a regime truly represents. They are a reflection of, and a source for expressing, the nation. Despite the often homogenizing effects of a global market system, constitutions help to promote a sense of sovereign control, legal distinction, social cohesion, and political identity that people often desire in response to the international marketplace.

One of the most important features of the twenty-first century constitution is its entrenchment. Amending formulas serve not only to elevate the status of constitutional law but to reaffirm the belief in a truly popular sovereignty, as opposed to the sovereignty of a particularly dominant political group, an electoral plurality, or, even, the "will of the majority."

The entrenchment process is not, of course, a guarantee of the indication of the "command" of a truly popular sovereign. The process can be manipulated through coercion, deceit, or apathy. A population that refuses to participate in a plebiscite called for the purpose of enacting a substantial constitutional change can be cited by unscrupulous authorities as a source of "tacit" sovereign support. Furthermore, amending formulas that depend exclusively upon the activities of a representative body potentially weaken further this concept of popular sovereignty, especially when the electoral and legislative systems are corrupt or merely flawed.

This theme has become particularly important since the end of the Cold War and the proclaimed "victory of democracy." But the true test of the increased proliferation of democratic societies will be the success of their respective constitutional reforms that are intended to serve as an expression of this emerging democratic sovereign. Even the presence of free and fair elections fails to provide an absolute assurance of the successful transformation of an electoral result into an actual imposition of a particular sovereign intent.

Part of that problem is a persistent one found within any democratic system. The practical limits of "direct democracy" (as practiced among the limited number of citizens of the ancient Athenian city-state or the modest scale of the contemporary New England town meeting) necessitate the less ideal variation of "representative democracy." Voters may insist that their elected representatives should reflect their collective commands as accurately as possible, but such replication of this will cannot occur in relation to the immense amount and complexity of legislation and policies that the modern state addresses. Therefore, the elected representatives substitute, often by necessity, and sometimes by design, their own judgment and inclinations for the diverse desires and interests of the voters. The result is a transferal of sovereign authority rather than its converted expression.

The same conditions occur within the process of constitutional entrenchment and amendment. The distinction between the mass of people who, under a democratic order, theoretically constitute the ultimate source of sovereign authority and those political elites who have been delegated the responsibility for translating that will into action can be difficult to discern. More importantly, those same political elites can be susceptible to a process of substituting not only their own judgment but their own interests for the popular will, particularly since they often do not share social, economic, and cultural perspectives and objectives with the mass members of their society. The result can be a corruption of the ideal constitutional process within a democratic society, especially in terms of maintaining a true sense of sovereign identity.

Therefore, the relationship between constitutional law and democracy is stressful. Sovereign authority vested within a monarch is much easier to reflect through constitutional government (even when that authority is delegated) than the indirect expression of popular sovereignty. That problem is exacerbated within the context of the relationships that occur among sovereign states, for constitutions also identify the legitimate source of international diplomacy for each state. It also is manifested through the concern among members of a democratic polity that their loss of control over this sovereign identity presents a danger for each one of them and not merely the sovereign whole.

The Expansion of Constitutional Rights and Liberties

The vast majority of twenty-first century constitutional traditions include a significant reference to, and protection of, rights and liberties. Part of the impetus for this trend has been derived from the brutal experiences of the Second World War, but part of it also is the result of a much longer historic development that can be traced to the relationship between the basic concept of property rights and the expansion of the market economy from its late medieval European origins through the proliferation of industrial and post-industrial economic systems. It also offers an indication of the persistent spirit of humanism as it, too, has expanded throughout the modern world.

The institutions of rights and liberties also serve, though, as a means for addressing the perceived inadequacies of maintaining true popular sovereignty or of mollifying populations that live under non-democratic constitutional orders. They are intended to enhance autonomy; this increase in autonomy often serves to offset a perceived decrease in popular sovereign control over government and non-governmental sources of power, including economic sources. The empowerment of the individual person within a society enhances that person's ability to compete, survive, and prosper within the "marketplace," while the empowerment of the individual human enhances that human being's capacity for control over their own destiny. Rights and liberties, both civil and human, have become the most effective institutional means of promoting that goal.

It is not surprising, therefore, that entrenched rights and liberties seemingly have become an indispensable feature of the contemporary constitutional tradition, globally. This desire has been expressed even within the unentrenched British constitutional system. British society occasionally has debated the idea of adopting an American-style "Bill of Rights." Although this entrenched document never actually has been adopted, the mere consideration of it offers an indication of the sustained popularity of the political culture of rights and liberties, even within a society as devoted to its unentrenched constitutional tradition and principle of parliamentary supremacy as Great Britain.[1] This attraction has been even stronger in other parts of the world, and newly sovereign countries, in particular, have responded to this expectation by making entrenched rights and liberties a mandatory part of their respective constitutional systems.

Constitutional Law and International Law

The significance of constitutionalism has been magnified by the increasing interdependence and interaction of the world community. Economic consolidation (including the rise of the multinational corporation) may be the most consequential feature of this "shrinking world," but legal integration provides its most visible manifestation. International law is the context of this process; constitutional law is its political subtext.

Treaties are the statutes of international law, and sovereign states are its subjects. These "subjects" are presented to the world through their constitutional law. Individual people and groups have gained some status within international law, since the end of the Second World War, but they have not achieved the efficacy that a state can provide, and a state needs its constitution for the purpose of showing the world its legal "personality." Therefore, constitutional law and the institutions it creates remain essential to the world, and not just to each separate society.

Indeed, international covenants have assumed a form that emulates the structure, if not the specific content, of modern constitutionalism. The General Agreement on Tariffs and Trade [GATT], for example, seeks to establish an overriding economic system for the global community, based upon fundamental ideological values that describe the marketplace upon a transnational basis. It is not, of course, an international constitution, but the relationship between the GATT and the world community has assumed some of those properties, and many

---

1. Interest in entrenched constitutional protection for civil rights and liberties within Great Britain is addressed in G. W. Jones, "The British Bill of Rights," 43 *Parliamentary Affairs*, no. 1 (1990), 27.

people, throughout the world, respond to it in a similar way. A better example of this influence can be found within the conventions of the European Union, which have created a confederal system transcending conventional international organizations and based upon the model that constitutions provide.

Other attempts at international unity, usually beginning with economic cooperation (including the North American Free Trade Accord), attempt to merge diverse legal cultures to serve a transnational purpose. Constitutions serve as a model for transforming simple treaties into enduring institutions. They also provide a means for asserting the claim that this sort of law delegates sovereign authority, rather than displacing it, and should, therefore, protect individual people, rather than merely imposing an overarching structure upon them.

The Future of Constitutionalism

Constitutions can serve as a model for the world only when differences are appreciated. Comparative politics is geared toward the attainment of that profound appreciation, and comparative constitutional law is an essential starting point for that process. Every other political consideration is derived from, and merges back toward, that constitutional genesis.

As new states emerge, they will seek expression through constitutional institutions. As established states voluntarily relinquish aspects of their sovereignty for purposes of economic consolidation, the lessons of constitutional law, and the ability to approach that most fundamental of legal categories from a comparative perspective, will become an essential feature of political science and its field of public law. Therefore, comparative constitutional law is as valuable to all citizens of the world as it is to the social scientist and the legal practitioner.

References

Aristotle, *Basic Works*, Richard McKeon, ed. New York, Modern Library, 2001.
Gabriel A. Almond and Sydney Verba, *The Civic Culture Revisited*. Newbury Park, CA, Sage, 1989.
Kirstin Hastrup, ed., *Legal Cultures and Human Rights: The Challenge of Diversity*. Boston, Kluwer, 2001.
Antero Jyränki, *National Constitutions in the Era of Integration*. The Hague, Kluwer, 1999.
Giovanni Sartori, *The Theory of Democracy Revisited*. Chatham, NJ, Chatham House, 1987.
Mortimer Sellers, ed., *The New World Order: Sovereignty, Human Rights, and the Self-Determination of Peoples*. Oxford, Berg, 1996.

Bibliography

Bamgbose J. Adele, *Fundamentals of Nigerian Politics*. Lagos, 1998.
Gabriel A. Almond and Sydney Verba, *The Civic Culture Revisited*. Newbury Park,CA, Sage, 1989.
Jerichow Anders, *The Saudi File: People, Power, Politics*. New York, St. Martin's, 1998.
Aristotle, *Basic Works*, Richard McKeon, ed. New York, Modern Library, 2001.
Charles Auerbach, *The Talmud: A Gateway to the Common Law*. Cleveland, Western Reserve University Press, 1952.
Granville Austin, *The Indian Constitution: Cornerstone of a Nation*. Oxford, Oxford University Press, 1965.
John Austin, *Lectures on Jurisprudence*, Robert Campbell, ed. London, John Murray, 1885.
Francisco Avalos, *The Mexican Legal System*. Littleton, CO, F. B. Rothman, 2000.
Epiphany Azinge, *Law-Making Under Military Regimes: The Nigerian Experience*. Benin City, Oliz, 1994.
Walter Bagehot, *The English Constitution*. Boston, Little, Brown, 1873.
Bernard Bailyn, *The Ideological Origins of the American Revolution*. Cambridge, MA, Belknap, 1967.
John Hamilton Baker, *The Common Law Tradition: Lawyers, Books, and the Law*. London, Hambledon Press, 2000.
Louis Baudouin, *Le Droit civil de la province de Québec*. Montréal, Wilson et Lafleur, 1953.
David M. Beatty, *Constitutional Law in Theory and Practice*. Toronto, University of Toronto Press, 1995.
John Bell, *French Constitutional Law*. Oxford, Clarendon, 1992.
Jeremy Bentham, *The Works of Jeremy Bentham*, John Bowring, ed. Edinburgh, William Tait, 1843.
Sir Isaiah Berlin, *Four Essays on Liberty*. Oxford, Oxford University Press, 1986.
Henri Brun and Guy Tremblay, *Droit constitutionel*. Cowansville, QC, Blais, 1982.
Peter C. Caldwell, *Popular Sovereignty and the Crisis of German Constitutional Law: The Theory and Practice of Weimar Constitutionalism*. Durham, NC, Duke University Press, 1997.
John Eaton Calthorpe Blofeld, *Taoism: The Road to Immortality*. Boston, Shambhala, 2000.
Roderick Ai Camp, *Politics in Mexico*. New York, Oxford University Press, 1993.
Sir George Bowyer, *Introduction to the Study and Use of the Civil Law*. London, Stevens, 1874.
Alan C. Cairns, *Charter versus Federalism: The Dilemmas of Constitutional Reform*. Montréal and Kingston, ON, McGill-Queen's University Press, 1992.
James A. Coriden, *An Introduction to Canon Law*. New York, Paulist, 2000.
Christian Dadomo and Susan Farran, *The French Legal System*. London, Sweet and Maxwell, 1996.
Ahmed Hassan Dahlan, ed., *Politics, Administration, and Development in Saudi Arabia*. Jeddah, Saudi Arabia, Dar al-Shorouq, 1990.

Rodolphe A. J. De Seife, *The Shari'a: An Introduction to the Law of Islam*. San Francisco, Austin and Winfield, 1994.
A. V. Dicey, *Introduction to the Study of the Law of the Constitution*. London, Macmillan, 1967.
Jack Donnelly, *The Concept of Human Rights*. London, Routledge, 1989.
Guillaume Drago, *Contentieux constitutionnel français*. Paris, Presses Universitaires de France, 1998.
Billy Dudley, *Introduction to Nigerian Politics and Government*. London, Macmillan, 2000.
Jerry Dupont, *The Common Law Abroad: Constitutional and Legal Legacy of the British Empire*. Littleton, CO, Rothman, 2001.
Ronald Dworkin, *Taking Rights Seriously*. Cambridge, MA, Harvard University Press, 1978.
Daniel J. Elazar, *The American Constitutional Tradition*. Lincoln, University of Nebraska Press, 1988.
Daniel J. Elazar, *Exploring Federalism*. London, University of Alabama Press, 1987.
Daniel Engster, *Divine Sovereignty: The Origins of Modern State Power*. DeKalb, IL, Northern Illinois University Press, 2001.
Pierre Esplugas, *Le Conseil constitutionnel et service public*. Paris, L. G. D. J., 1994.
Feng Li, *Constitutional Law in China*. Hong Kong, Sweet and Maxwell, 2000.
John Finnis, *Natural Law and Natural Rights*. Oxford, Clarendon Press, 1980.
George P. Fletcher, *Rethinking Criminal Law*. Oxford, Oxford University Press, 2000.
Michael Foley, *The Politics of the British Constitution*. Manchester, Manchester University Press, 1999.
Ralph H. Folsom, John H. Minan, Lee Ann Otto, *Law and Politics in the People's Republic of China in a Nutshell*. St. Paul, West, 1992.
Anke Freckmann, *The German Legal System*. London, Sweet and Maxwell, 1999.
Judith Gentleman, ed., *Mexican Politics in Transition*. Boulder, CO, Westview, 1987.
Max Gluckman, *Politics, Law, and Ritual in Tribal Society*. Oxford, Blackwell, 1965.
Klaus H. Goetz and Peter J. Cullen, eds., *Constitutional Policy in Unified Germany*. London, Frank Cass, 1995.
William D. Graf, *The Nigerian State*. London, James Currey, 1988.
John Owen Haley, *The Spirit of Japanese Law*. Athens, University of Georgia Press, 1998.
H. L. A. Hart, *Punishment and Responsibility: Essays in the Philosophy of Law*. Oxford, Clarendon, 1995.
Kirstin Hastrup, ed., *Legal Cultures and Human Rights: The Challenge of Diversity*. Boston, Kluwer, 2001.
David Andrew Heard, *Canadian Constitutional Conventions: The Marriage of Law and Politics*. Toronto, Oxford University Press, 1991.
Christine Moss Helms, *The Cohesion of Saudi Arabia: Evolution of a Political Identity*. Baltimore, Johns Hopkins University Press, 1981.
Peter Hennessy, *The Hidden Wiring: Unearthing the British Constitution*. London, Gollancz, 1995.
James E. Herget and Jorge Camil, *An Introduction to the Mexican Legal System*. Buffalo, W. S. Hein, 1978.
James E. Hergert, *Contemporary German Legal Philosophy*. Philadelphia, University of Pennsylvania Press, 1996.

Robert A. Hillman, *The Richness of Contract Law: An Analysis and Critique of Contemporary Theories of Contract Law.* Dordrecht, The Netherlands, Kluwer Academic, 1998.
Hiroshi Oda, *Japanese Law.* New York, Oxford University Press, 1999.
Paul Q. Hirst, *On Law and Ideology.* Atlantic Highlands, NJ, Humanities, 1979.
Glenn D. Hook and Gavan McCormick, *Japan's Contested Constitution: Documents and Analysis.* New York, Routledge, 2001.
Peter W. Hogg, *Constitutional Law of Canada.* Toronto, Carswell, 1997.
Hsin-chung Yao, *An Introduction to Confucianism.* Cambridge, Cambridge University Press, 2000.
Summer Scott Huyette, *Political Adaptation in Saudi Arabia: A Study of the Council of Ministers.* Boulder, CO, Westview, 1985.
Jianfu Chen, *Chinese Law: Toward an Understanding of Chinese Law, Its Nature and Development.* The Hague, Kluwer Law International, 1999.
Antero Jyränki, *National Constitutions in the Era of Integration.* The Hague, Kluwer, 1999.
Ronald C. Keith and Zhiqiu Lin, *Law and Justice in China's New Marketplace.* New York, Palgrave, 2001.
H. W. Koch, *A Constitutional History of Germany in the Nineteenth and Twentieth Centuries.* New York, Longman, 1984.
Koichiro Fujikura, ed., *Japanese Law and Legal Theory.* New York, New York University Press, 1996.
Donald P. Kommers, *The Constitutional Jurisprudence of the Federal Republic of Germany.* Durham, NC, Duke University Press, 1997.
Pradeep Kumar, *Studies in Indian Federalism.* New Delhi, Deep and Deep, 1988.
Kyoko Inoue, *MacArthur's Japanese Constitution: A Linguistic and Cultural Study of Its Making.* Chicago, University of Chicago Press, 1991.
Alison Lerrick and Q. J. Mian, *Saudi Business and Labor Law: Its Interpretation and Application.* London, Graham and Trotman, 1982.
Frederick K. Lister, *The European Union, the United Nations, and the Revival of Confederal Governance.* Westport, CT, Greenwood, 1996.
Denis Lloyd [Lord Lloyd of Hampstead], *The Idea of Law.* London, Penguin, 1987.
Percy R. Luney, Jr. and Kazuyuki Takahashi, eds., *Japanese Constitutional Law.* Tokyo, University of Tokyo Press, 1993.
Donald S. Lutz, *The Origins of American Constitutionalism.* Baton Rouge, Louisiana State University Press, 1988.
C. B. Macpherson, *The Life and Times of Liberal Democracy.* Oxford, Oxford University Press, 1989.
Michael Mandel, *The Charter of Rights and the Legalization of Politics in Canada.* Toronto, Thompson, 1994.
Christopher P. Manfredi, *Judicial Power and the Charter: Canada and the Paradox of Liberal Constitutionalism.* Norman, University of Oklahoma Press, 1993.
Susan Marks, *The Riddle of All Constitutions: International Law, Democracy, and the Critique of Ideology.* Oxford, Oxford University Press, 2000.
Geoffrey Marshall, *Constitutional Conventions.* Oxford, Clarendon Press, 1984.
James McClellan, *Liberty, Order, and Justice: An Introduction to the Constitutional Principles of American Government.* Indianapolis, Liberty Fund, 2000.

Brian E. McKnight, ed., *Law and the State in Traditional East Asian Law*. Honolulu, University of Hawaii Press, 1987.
Sabine Michalowski and Lorna Woods, *German Constitutional Law: The Protection of Civil Liberties*. Brookfield, VT, Ashgate/Dartmouth, 1999.
Susan Millns and Noel Whitty, eds., *Feminist Perspectives on Public Law*. London, Cavendish, 1999.
Surya Narayan Misra, Subas Chandras Hazary, and Amareswar Mishra, eds., *Constitution and Constitutionalism in India*. New Delhi, APH Publications, 1999.
J. K. Mittal, *Indian Legal and Constitutional History*. Allahabad, Allahabad Law Agency, 1990.
Marcel Morabito and Daniel Bourmaud, *L'Histoire constitutionnel et politique de la France, 1789-1958*. Paris, Montchrestien, 1991.
Bradford W. Morse, ed., *Aboriginal Peoples and the Law*. Ottawa, Carleton University Press, 1989.
F. L. Morton and Rainer Knopff, *The Charter Revolution and the Court Party*. Peterborough, ON, Broadview, 2000.
Stephen R. Munzer, *A Theory of Property*. New York, Cambridge University Press, 1990.
John K. Nelson, *Enduring Identities: The Guise of Shinto in Contemporary Japan*. Honolulu, University of Hawaii Press, 2000.
Benjamin Obi Nwabueze, *Nigeria's Presidential Constitution*. New York, Longman, 1985.
David M. O'Brien, *Constitutional Law and Politics*. New York, W. W. Norton, 2000.
Evgenii Bronislavovich Pashukanis, *Law and Marxism: A General Theory*, Barbara Einhorn, trans., Chris Arthur, ed. London, Pluto, 1989.
George D. E. Philip, *The Presidency in Mexican Politics*. Houndmills, Basingstoke, England, Macmillan, 1992.
Owen Hood Phillips and Paul Jackson, *O. Hood Phillips' Constitutional and Administrative Law*. London, Sweet and Maxwell, 1987.
Peter E. Quint, *The Imperfect Union: Constitutional Structures of German Unification*. Princeton, NJ, Princeton University Press, 1997.
G. R. S. Rao, *Constitution of India: Vision, Reality, and Reform*. Hyderabad, Center for Public Policy and Social Development, 1998.
John Rawls, *A Theory of Justice*. Cambridge, MA, Belknap, 1971.
Heinrich Rommen, *The Natural Law: A Study in Legal and Social History and Philosophy*, Thomas R. Hanley, trans. St. Louis, Herder, 1959.
Giovanni Sartori, *The Theory of Democracy Revisited*. Chatham, NJ, Chatham House, 1987.
Mortimer Sellers, ed., *The New World Order: Sovereignty, Human Rights, and the Self-Determination of Peoples*. Oxford, Berg, 1996.
Marshall S. Shapo, *Basic Principles of Tort Law*. St. Paul, West, 1999.
Charles H. Sheldon, *Essentials of the American Constitution: The Supreme Court and Fundamental Law*. Boulder, CO, Westview, 2001.
V. N. Shukla, *V. N. Shukla's Constitution of India*. Lucknow, Eastern Book, 1990.
John Bryan Starr, *Understanding China: A Guide to China's Economy, History, and Political Structure*. New York, Hill and Wang, 1997.
Peter Stein, *Roman Law in European History*. Cambridge, Cambridge University Press, 1999.
Anne Stevens, *The Government and Politics of France*. New York, St. Martin's, 1996.

Evelyn Stevens, *Protest and Response in Mexico*. Cambridge, MA, Massachusetts Institute of Technology Press, 1974.
William Stubbs, *The Constitutional History of England*. Oxford, Clarendon, 1880.
G. Alan Tarr, *Constitutional Politics in the States*. Westport, CT, Greenwood, 1996.
Laurence Tribe, *American Constitutional Law*. Mineola, NY, Foundation, 2000.
Colin C. Turpin, *British Government and the Constitution: Texts, Cases, and Materials*. London, Butterworths, 1995.
Sir Egbert Udo Udomo, *History and the Law of the Constitution of Nigeria*. Lagos, Malthouse, 1994.
Frank E. Vogel, *Islamic Law and Legal System: Studies of Saudi Arabia*. Boston, Brill, 2000.
Max Weber, *The Religion of India: The Sociology of Hinduism and Buddhism*, Hans H. Gerth and Don Martindale, trans. and ed. New Delhi, Munshiram Manoharlal, 1992.
Lloyd L. Weinreb, *Natural Law and Justice*. Cambridge, MA, Harvard University Press, 1987.
Brian S. J. Weng, ed., *Studies on the Constitutional Law of the People's Republic of China*. New York, M. E. Sharpe, 1983.
Gordon Wood, *Creation of the American Republic*. Chapel Hill, University of North Carolina Press, 1969.
D. C. M. Yardley, *Introduction to British Constitutional Law*. London, Butterworths, 1990.
Konrad Zweigert and Hein Kötz, *An Introduction to Comparative Law*, Toney Weir, trans. Amsterdam, North Holland, 1977.

Index

A

Abdel-Aziz, king of Saudi Arabia, 201
Abuja, 144
Administrative Councils Law of 1940, 208
administrative law, 44
Africa, 133-135, 138, 140, 142
    traditional values, 142-143
Alberta, 88, 89
Algeria, 150-151
American Revolution, 34, 41, 95
amparo appeal, 189
Animism, 136-137
Arab philosophy, 208-210
Aristotle, 2, 21
Articles of Confederation, 34
Athenian Constitution, 2, 214
Athens, ancient, 214
Augustín I, Emperor of Mexico, 178, 179
Aum Shinrikyo, 129
Austria, 132
authoritarian government, 164, 173, 180, 181, 193, 197-202, 209, 210, 215
autonomy, 2, 3, 12, 40, 43, 128
Aztec people, 177, 187

B

Bangladesh, 103
barristers, 59
Bedouin people, 209-210
Biafra, 137, 141
Bible, 21, 198
Blackstone, Sir William, 61
Bourbon dynasty, 149, 194
British Constitution, 47-63, 122, 134, 143, 215-216
    Act of Settlement of 1701, 52, 59
    Act of Union of 1707, 52
    and convention, 51-53
    and *habeas corpus*, 51
    Bill of Rights of 1689, 52
    Magna Carta, 51
    Parliament Act of 1911, 52
    Parliament Act of 1949, 52
    Parliament Act of 2000, 52
    parliamentary system, 49, 50, 53-56, 59, 215
    political offices, 50, 53, 204
    Reform Bill of 1830, 52
    Reform Bill of 1867, 52
    Reform Bill of 1883, 52
    Statute of Westminster of 1931, 86
    unitary system, 57
British Empire, 16, 37, 83-84, 86, 87, 99, 101, 104, 108, 112, 114, 133, 135-136, 139, 142
Bryce, Lord James, 61
Buddhism, 127
Burke, Edmund, 58

C

Calles, Plutarco, 188
Canada, 83-99
    bilingualism, 85, 91-93, 95
    constitutional structure, 84-85
    constitutional themes, 85
    federal system, 86-89, 92, 138
    legal system, 96-97
    métis, 178
    multiculturalism, 85, 91, 95, 178
    nationalism, 98, 105
    parliamentary system, 86
    political culture, 94-96

Supreme Court, 84, 87, 89, 96, 97, 99, 172
Canadian Constitution, 83-99
   and convention, 90
   Charter of Rights and Freedoms, 84-86, 90, 91, 93-97, 99
   Constitution Act of 1867, 84-88
   Constitution Act of 1867, section 91, 89
   Constitution Act of 1867, section 92, 87-88
   Constitution Act of 1867, section 92A, 88
   Constitution Act of 1867, section 93, 88
   Constitution Act of 1886, 84
   Constitution Act of 1982, 84, 86, 89, 91-93, 98
   notwithstanding clause, 94-95, 97, 99
   patriation, 88, 91, 97
canon law, 21
Carranza, Venustiano, 181
caste system, 105, 110
Chiapas, 186
China, imperial, 65, 67, 124, 199
China, People's Republic of, 65-80
   Communist Party, 66-71, 73, 76
   constitutional structure, 67
   constitutional themes, 69
   court system, 77-79
   legal system, 77-78
   People's Assembly, 68, 69
   political culture, 75-76
   Standing Committee of the People's Congress, 78-79
   Supreme People's Court, 79-81
   unitary system, 72-73
China, Republic of, 65, 70
Chinese Civil War, 70
Chinese Constitution, 65-80
   and economic policy, 70-72
   article 67, 78
   chapter four, 69
   chapter one, 67

   chapter three, 68
   chapter two, 67, 68, 75
   of 1949, 70, 71
   of 1953, 71
   of 1975, 71
   of 1979, 71
   of 1982, 71
   preamble, 67
Chinese Revolution, 65
Ch'ing dynasty, 200
Christianity, 137, 209
   Anglican, 21, 137
   Methodist, 137
   Orthodox, 21
   Roman Catholic, 21, 137, 176-177, 184, 183-184, 187
citizenship, 163-164, 167, 184-185
civil law systems, 18-21, 66, 67, 77, 96, 120, 121, 124-127, 130-133, 154-155, 157, 167-169, 176, 185, 186, 188-189
   and courts, 19, 20, 79, 130-132, 157-158, 171
Code Napoléon, 19, 21 66, 99, 122, 150, 155, 169, 189
Coke, Lord Edward, 61
Cold War, 214
colonialism, 134, 136, 136, 145, 150, 151, 178, 186, 188
commercial law, 25, 26, 153, 163
common law systems, 16-18, 51, 61, 95, 112, 143, 189
   and courts, 17, 59, 61, 112-113
comparative political science, 1, 217
confederal systems, 23, 24, 37
Confederate States of America, 37
Confucianism, 6, 7, 70, 75, 77, 124, 127, 129
Confucius, 6
Congress Party, 110
conservatism, 14-15, 57, 58, 63, 154, 178-181, 187, 190, 209
constitutions, 1-29, 213-221
   and nation-states, 2, 18, 148, 166, 168-169, 177, 194, 195

and rules, 4
and sovereignty, 2
civil, 29
entrenched, 33, 34, 193
partially entrenched, 83, 85, 98, 215
unentrenched, 47, 48, 51-55, 57, 61, 98, 193, 205
contract law, 26, 27
corporatism, 128
Corpus Juris Civile, 18
Corsica, 153
Council of First Nations, 95
Council of Ministers Act of 1953, 205
Council of Ministers Act of 1993, 201
Council of Ministers Law of 1958, 202, 203
criminal law, 24, 25, 62, 87, 150, 167
Crusades, 209
Cultural Revolution, 71
customary law, 23, 143-144

D

de Gaulle, Charles, 150, 151
democracy, 12, 53, 56, 58, 85, 95, 96, 112, 119, 120, 133, 138, 139, 149, 150, 152, 155, 170, 172, 178, 188, 208, 210, 211, 213-217
dharma, 8, 9
Díaz, Porfirio, 180, 181, 185
Dicey, A.V, 61

E

Eastern law, 4, 6-9, 69, 70, 74-77, 111, 117, 119, 120, 123-125, 127, 128, 130
economic development, 109-110, 133, 141, 167, 178, 180-182, 186, 195, 210
Edo people, 137
England, 16, 17, 47, 49, 51, 52, 56, 59, 203, 205
court system, 62, 63

English Civil War, 58
equity, 56, 60
European Union, 55, 174, 217
extraterritoriality, 120

F

fa, 7
fascism, 161, 168-170
Fahd, king of Saudi Arabia, 202, 210
family law, 62, 195, 207
federal systems, 23, 24, 37, 39, 85, 138, 166-168
feminism, 15-16
   liberal, 15, 16
   radical, 15, 16
feudalism, 10, 11, 49, 57, 119, 120, 215
fiqh, 22, 194, 199
France, 19, 85, 99, 120, 135, 147-157, 178, 180, 200
   and diversity, 153
   civil code, 147, 154, 155
   condominium government, 151, 152
   Constitutional Council, 148, 152, 154-156
   constitutional cycles, 149-150, 154
   constitutional structure, 147, 161
   constitutional themes, 148-149
   Consulate, 150
   cour de cassation, 157
   court system, 148, 156-157
   Directory, 150
   Economic and Social Council, 148
   fifth republic, 147, 148, 150, 151, 157
   first empire, 149
   fourth republic, 147, 150, 151
   legal system, 149, 154-155
   National Assembly, 148, 151, 152, 154, 155
   nationalism, 153, 154
   parliament, 147, 148, 151, 152, 154, 155
   party politics, 151

political culture, 153-154
political offices, 147, 151
premier, 148, 151, 155
presidency, 151
president, 151, 152, 154, 155
quasi-presidential system, 148, 150-152
second empire, 149
second republic, 150
Senate, 151, 155
third republic, 150
unitary system, 153
Vichy government, 149, 151
French and Indian Wars, 91
French Constitution, 139, 147-157
  administrative law, 153
  Declaration of the Rights of Man and Citizen, 93, 147, 152-154, 156, 157
  decrees, 155
  historical development, 149, 150, 154
  ordinary laws, 155
  organic laws, 155
  preamble, 147
  regulations, 155
  republican cycle, 151
  title five, 147
  title four, 147
  title one, 147
  title three, 147
  title two, 147
French Revolution, 58
fukahā, 199
Fulani people, 134, 137, 139

G

Gabriel, Archangel, 199
Gandhi, Indira, 109
Gang of Four, 71, 80
geist, 168, 169
General Agreement on Tariffs and Trade, 216
German Constitution, 124, 159-172

and citizenship, 160, 163, 164
and renunciation of war, 161
and rights and liberties, 169
right to resist, 165
section eight, 160, 165-167
section five, 160
section four, 160
section nine, 160, 167
section one, 160-162
section seven, 160, 169
section six, 160, 161
section three, 160
section two, 160, 165, 170, 171
German Empire, 166
Germany, Democratic Republic of, 159, 172, 173
  civil code, 173
  court system, 173
  legal system, 173
  unification, 161
Germany, Federal Republic of, 19, 119, 120, 124, 159-172, 184
  and rights and liberties, 162-164
  civil code, 167-169
  Constitutional Court, 169-170
  constitutional structure, 159-160
  constitutional themes, 161-162
  court system, 168-172
  federal government, 160, 162, 164-166, 169-172
  legal system, 167-169, 171
  nationalism, 170-172
  parliament, 166-168, 177
  political culture, 166-167
  political offices, 161-162
  unification, 159, 161, 170-171
Germany, Nazi, 161, 162, 164, 166, 168, 170
  civil code, 168
  court system, 168
  legal system, 168
Germany, Weimar Republic, 164, 166
giri, 6, 7, 68, 75, 76, 123, 128, 129
global markets, 213, 215, 217
Glorious Revolution, 52

God, 21-22, 193, 194, 209
Great Britain 47-63, 119, 180
    constitutional structure, 48-49, 161
    constitutional themes, 51
    court system, 59-62
    House of Lords, 17, 62-63
    legal system, 60-61, 205
    parliament, 49, 216
    parliamentary system, 58, 60, 84
    party politics, 50
    political culture, 57-59, 63
    unitary system, 56
Great Leap Forward, 71
Greek philosophy, 4, 209

H

habeas corpus, 51, 189
hadith, 22, 194, 199
Han Fei-tzû, 7
Hausa people, 134, 137, 139
Hegel, Georg Wilhelm Friedrich, 13, 168
Henry II, king of England, 16
Hidalgo y Costilla, Miguel, 178
Hinduism, 8, 9, 105-106, 111-114
    and caste system, 9
Hitler, Adolf, 163, 164
Hobbes, Thomas, 58
Holy Roman Empire, 164
humanism, 215

I

Ibibio people, 137
Ibo people, 137, 139
ideology, 2, 12, 15, 16
    and law, 9, 10
Ijaw people, 137
India, 101-115, 176
    and diversity, 103-107, 110, 113, 114
    and language, 102, 103, 105, 106
    and national unity, 104, 113, 114
    and regionalism, 104
    communalism, 111
    constitutional structure, 101-103
    constitutional themes, 103-104
    court system, 104, 106, 112-113
    federal system, 102-107
    legal system, 112-113
    local government, 107- 108
    panchayata raj, 108
    parliament, 102-103
    party politics, 109
    political culture, 110-111
    Supreme Court, 103, 109, 112-113
Indian Constitution, 101-115
    and political offices, 102, 103
    concurrent powers, 107
    emergency powers, 109-109, 111
    part eighteen, 102, 108-110
    part four, 101-103, 112, 113
    part one, 101
    part seventeen, 102, 104
    part twenty-two, 102, 103, 111, 112
    state list, 107
    union list, 107
Inns of Court, 17
international law, 5, 216-217
    and diplomacy, 215
    and treaties, 216, 217
International War Crimes Tribunal, 5
Islam, 105, 106, 112, 134, 137, 143, 144, 193-199 ,201, 203, 204, 207, 209-211
    Sunni, 22, 136, 194, 199, 204
    Wahhabi theological tradition, 198, 199, 204, 208, 209
Iturbide, General Augustín de, 178

J

Jammu, 104
jang I-tien, 76, 79
Japan, 117-131
    and corporatist model, 128
    and legal concept of benefactor, 126, 127, 129

and legal concept of shame, 125-126
and legal relevance of custom, 126-127
civil code, 120, 125, 126-127
constitutional structure, 117
constitutional themes, 118
court system, 129-130
Diet, 118, 121
emperor, 117, 119-121, 127, 128
legal system, 124, 126, 130
local government, 124
Meiji period, 118-120, 124, 128
parliamentary government, 118, 119, 121
political culture, 125, 127
political offices, 118, 119
political parties, 118
shogun period, 119
Supreme Court, 129
unitary system, 124, 130
Japanese Constitution, 117-131
chapter eight, 124
chapter eleven, 117
chapter nine, 117
chapter one, 117, 120, 121
chapter six, 129
chapter ten, 117
chapter three, 122, 123
chapter two, 117, 119, 121, 122
jen, 6, 7, 75, 76
Jewish people, 165
Jesuits, 6
jokoku appeal, 130
jori, 125, 126
Juárez, Benito, 179, 180
Judaism, 21, 165
Judicial Committee of the Privy Council, 98
Justinian the Great, Byzantine emperor, 18

K

kādī, 22, 194, 199

Kanem-Bornu Empire, 134
Kanuri people, 137
Kashmir, 104, 106
Kesavananda Bharati vs. State of Kerala, 114
koso appeal, 130

L

labor law, 181, 182, 185, 186
Lagos, 135
Lao Tzu, 7
Latin America, 175, 176, 187, 189, 209
law, 2-4, 29
and nation-states, 18, 148, 166, 168-169, 177
and objectivity, 3
as a source of empowerment, 3
as protection, 3
private, 12, 25, 26, 57, 62
public, 3, 4, 12, 25, 26, 216
Legalism, 7, 76
Lenin, V.I., 14
li, 6, 7, 75
liberal democracy, 12, 13, 25, 27, 45, 57, 58, 87, 111, 112, 117, 118, 127, 128, 142-143, 152, 162, 163, 168 183 183,185, 186,191,194, 212, 214-215, 220-221
communitarian, 12, 97-98, 153-154, 166-167
libertarian, 12, 40-42, 96, 154, 166-167
republican, 12, 39-42, 150, 154
liberalism, 11, 12, 27, 68, 145, 152, 153, 179-181, 185, 187, 209-211, 216-217
local government, 214
Locke, John, 36, 40, 43
Louis XIV, king of France, 149

M

MacArthur, Douglas A., 118, 120
Madero, Francisco, 181

Mao Zedong, 71, 74
Marbury vs. Madison, 1804, 43
Marshall, John, 43
Marx, Karl, 13
Marxism, 13, 14, 65-66, 70, 77
　Maoist, 67, 73-74, 76
　Marxist-Leninist, 65, 67, 73
Maximilian, emperor of Mexico, 180
Mayan people, 177
Mecca, 198, 204
Medina, 198
Meech Lake Accord, 89
Mencius, 7
Mexican Constitution, 175-190
　and church-state relations, 176
　and citizenship, 175, 177
　and national identity, 175, 177
　revolutionary origins, 175, 177-182, 184, 185, 189, 190
　separation of powers, 188
　title eight, 176
　title five, 176, 185, 186
　title four, 175, 184
　title nine, 176
　title one, 175, 182-186
　title seven, 176, 189
　title six, 176, 182
　title three, 175, 188
　title two, 175, 177
Mexican Empire, 179
Mexican Republic, 179
Mexican-American War, 179
Mexico, 175-190
　agrarian reform, 182, 183
　and church-state relations, 177-180, 183, 184
　and citizenship, 181, 184, 185
　and diversity, 176, 177, 180, 181, 184-186
　and military rule, 181
　and national identity, 181, 184, 185
　civil code, 188, 189
　constitutional structure, 175-176
　constitutional themes, 176-178
　court system, 188-189
　criollos, 177-189
　ejidos system, 183
　encomienda system, 176, 179
　executive dominance, 187-190
　federal system, 180-181, 183, 185, 186
　legal system, 188-189
　legislature, 187-189
　mestizos, 177-179, 185
　party politics, 181, 188
　peninsulares, 177-179
　peonage system, 179, 180
　political culture, 186-187
　political offices, 184, 187, 189
　political patronage, 188, 189
　presidency, 187-189
　Public Ministry of the Federation, 189
　revolutionary history, 177-182, 189, 190
　Supreme Court of Justice, 189
Middle East, 195, 198, 209, 211
military government, 137, 141, 143-146, 145, 180
mixed law system, 57, 59, 97, 99
Mohammed, 22, 199
monarchy, 49, 50, 53, 58, 85, 117, 119-121, 127, 128, 147, 149, 152, 178, 193-195, 197-203, 209, 210, 215
Montesquieu, Charles de Secondat, Baron de, 36, 42, 43
Morelos y Pavón, José Mariá, 178
Municipal Elections Law of 1942, 208
Municipalities Law of 1939, 208
Mutsuhito, emperor of Japan, 119

N

Napoléon I, emperor of France, 153, 178
Napoléon III, emperor of France, 178, 180
National Energy Policy, 89
natural law, 4-6, 125, 194

Nayef, crown prince of Saudi Arabia, 202
Nazism, 5, 163-164, 165-166
New Brunswick, 84, 91, 92
New France, 91, 95
New Spain, 176
Nigeria, 133-145, 176
 and *coups d'etat*, 141, 195
 and diversity, 133-137, 139, 144, 145
 and military rule, 133, 137, 139-142, 145
 and patronage, 139-142
 and state of emergency, 134
 constitutional structure, 133-134
 constitutional themes, 134-135
 Court of Appeal, 143
 court system, 143
 customary courts, 144, 145
 electoral system, 136
 federal system, 138-139, 145
 legal system, 143, 144
 National Assembly, 138
 National Election Commission, 140
 parliament, 138
 political culture, 142-143
 political offices, 139, 140
 presidency, 139, 140, 145
 separation of powers, 139
 shari'a courts, 144, 145
 Supreme Court, 143
 vice-presidency, 140
Nigerian Constitution, 133-145
 chapter eight, 130
 chapter five, 134, 138
 chapter four, 136, 137
 chapter one, 134, 138
 chapter seven, 134, 143, 144
 chapter six, 134, 136
 chapter two, 136
 Court of Appeal, 144
 federal system, 144
 Supreme Court, 144
Nixon, Richard, 45
North American FreeTrade Accord, 217

Northern Ireland, 47, 56
 court system, 62
Nova Scotia, 84, 91
Nunavut, 93
Nupe people, 137
Nuremburg Trials, 5

O

Official Languages Act, 92
oligarchy, 149, 150
Ontario, 84, 89
Orléan dynasty, 150

P

Pakistan, 103, 104, 105, 106
pandectist models, 19, 21, 68, 125, 126, 169-170
parliamentary systems, 49, 50, 54, 55, 58, 117-118, 151
 Westminster model, 50, 54-56, 85, 86, 99, 103, 104, 119, 134, 216
Partido Revolucianaro Institucional, 181, 188
penal law, 25, 26
Persian Gulf War, 124, 211
Portugal, 135
positive law, 5, 6, 56, 63
 and command theory, 5, 214
post-modernism, 213
property, 11-13, 23, 26, 27, 66, 68, 119, 162, 178, 181, 183, 210
Provinces Law of 1963, 208
Prussia, 169
Prussian land law, 169

Q

Quebec, 84, 88-93, 98-99
 clause, 95
 court system, 97, 99
 legal system, 97, 99
 nationalism, 95, 96, 99

Quebec Constitution, 98-99
    Charter of Human Rights, 99
    Charter of the French Language, 99
    civil code, 99
Qur'an, 22, 193, 199, 201

R

Regional Authorities Establishment Act of 1992, 208
rights and liberties, 27, 28, 40, 94, 93, 119, 122, 124, 136, 147, 152, 156, 166, 169, 181, 182, 184, 187, 215-216
    and duties, 68, 123, 128, 165, 184, 195
    and privacy, 40
    civil, 28, 29, 68, 87-88, 122, 152, 160, 162, 163, 180, 186, 199, 206, 207, 215
    collective, 95
    dispositive, 68
    consensual, 28
    human, 28, 29, 122-123, 162, 164-166, 186, 195, 206-207, 215
    inalienable, 28, 41-45
    preemptory, 68
Roman Empire, 10, 18, 125
Roman law, 18, 21, 66, 169
    and nation-states, 18
Romany people, 165
Rousseau, Jean-Jacques, 98, 154
rule of law, 5, 51, 55, 56, 60, 61, 69, 85

S

Santa Anna, Antonio Lopéz de, 179
Saudi Arabia, 193-211
    constitutional structure, 195-197
    constitutional themes, 197-198
    Council of Ministers, 196, 198, 200-204, 208
    court system, 200, 205, 206, 208
    Higher Council of Justice, 200, 206
    king, 194, 195, 197, 199-201, 203, 205, 210
    legal system, 194-199, 205, 206, 208
    local government, 208
    political culture, 208-212
    political offices, 196, 200-202, 208
    provincial administrative councils, 208
    royal family, 198-202, 204, 210
    Senior *Ulema* Body, 197-199, 206
    Shura Council, 196-198, 200, 201, 203-205
    unitary system, 207-208
Saudi Arabian Constitution, 193-211
    amr, 202
    and regulatory authority, 196
    chapter five, 195, 199, 204, 206-207
    chapter four, 195, 199, 206
    chapter nine, 197, 200
    chapter one, 195
    chapter seven, 196
    chapter six, 196, 197, 200-202, 204-206
    chapter three, 195
    chapter two, 195, 201
    marsoom, 202
Savigny, Friedrich Carl von, 169
Scotland, 47, 49, 51, 52, 56, 99, 205
    court system, 62, 63
    legal system, 57, 59, 193-195, 198, 199, 203, 207
shari'a, 22, 111, 137, 144
    ijmā, 194
    ijtihad, 194
    makruh, 194
    mandub, 194
sheik, 198
Shinto, 127, 128
Shura Council Act of 1993, 204
Shura Council Establishment Act of 1992, 201, 204
Sikhism, 104, 105, 111
Slavic peoples, 163
social contract, 154

socialism, 57, 67, 71, 73
socialist law systems, 16, 65-67, 69, 75-78, 173
solicitors, 59
sovereignty, 2, 23, 35, 37, 39, 51, 54-56, 69-70, 83, 85, 87, 90, 96, 105, 110, 117, 121, 122, 134, 135, 137-139, 145, 147-149, 151, 153, 157, 160-162, 164-167, 170, 174, 176-178, 181, 185, 186, 193, 196, 199, 201 202, 207, 208, 213-217
Soviet Union, 13, 76, 161
Spain, 177, 168, 180, 186, 168
stare decisis, 16, 21, 97, 129
Sunnah, 22, 193, 199, 201

T

Talmud, 21, 22
Taoism, 7, 8, 78, 118, 127-128
Texas, Republic of, 179
theocracy, 193, 194, 198, 199, 211
Tiv people, 137
Tokyo, 129
Toltec people, 177
Torah, 21
tort law, 125
tribal law, 10, 22, 23, 142-143, 210
Trudeau, Pierre Elliot, 90, 91

U

Uniform Code of Military Justice, 45
unitary systems, 23, 24, 56, 57, 72-73, 124, 153, 164, 173, 207-208
United Kingdom (see Great Britain)
United Nations, 163
United States, 16, 33-45, 83, 85, 117, 118, 120, 121, 128, 155, 180, 182, 184, 186, 189
  and diversity, 41
  Civil War, 37, 45
  Congress, 35, 36, 41

  constitutional structure, 34-35, 161
  constitutional themes, 35
  court system, 36, 40-45, 104, 172
  federal system, 37, 39, 167
  political culture, 39-40
  Senate, 103
  separation of powers, 35, 37, 40-42, 139, 155, 200
  Supreme Court, 36, 41-45, 98
United States Constitution, 33-45, 110, 118, 120, 176, 187
  article four, 39
  article one, 38
  Bill of Rights, 40, 43, 91, 93, 96, 122, 152, 165, 215
  constitutional adjudication, 42-44
  Declaration of Independence, 34, 40
  eighth amendment, 44
  fifth amendment, 44
  fifthteenth amendment, 38, 39
  first amendment, 43
  fourteenth amendment, 38, 43, 165
  fourth amendment, 44
  ninth amendment, 44
  sixteenth amendment, 38
  tenth amendment, 37
  thirteenth amendment, 38
  twelfth amendment, 39
  twenty-second amendment, 39
University of Bologna, 18

V

Victoria, Guadalupe, 179
Villa, Pancho, 181

W

Wales, 47, 49, 51, 56
  court system, 62
War of the Reform, 188, 183
Western law, 4-6, 10, 21, 22, 117, 118,

120, 124, 125, 127, 128, 145, 194, 209
World War I, 135, 166
World War II, 53, 54, 117, 118, 120, 125, 131, 134, 139, 153, 159, 165, 166, 170, 174, 219

Y

Yoruba people, 137, 139

Z

Zapata, Emiliano, 181, 186
Zapatista National Liberation Army, 186
Zapotec people, 179

TEACHING TEXTS IN LAW AND POLITICS

David Schultz, *General Editor*

The new series Teaching Texts in Law and Politics is devoted to textbooks that explore the multidimensional and multidisciplinary areas of law and politics. Special emphasis will be given to textbooks written for the undergraduate classroom. Subject matters to be addressed in this series include, but will not be limited to: constitutional law; civil rights and liberties issues; law, race, gender, and gender orientation studies; law and ethics; women and the law; judicial behavior and decision-making; legal theory; comparative legal systems; criminal justice; courts and the political process; and other topics on the law and the political process that would be of interest to undergraduate curriculum and education. Submission of single-author and collaborative studies, as well as collections of essays are invited.

Authors wishing to have works considered for this series should contact:
>Peter Lang Publishing
>Acquisitions Department
>275 Seventh Avenue, 28th floor
>New York, New York 10001

To order other books in this series, please contact our Customer Service Department at:
>800-770-LANG (within the U.S.)
>(212) 647-7706 (outside the U.S.)
>(212) 647-7707 FAX

or browse online by series at:
>WWW.PETERLANGUSA.COM